The Global Politics of Pesticides

The Global Politics of Pesticides

Forging Consensus from Conflicting Interests

Peter Hough

Earthscan Publications Ltd, London

First published in the UK in 1998 by
Earthscan Publications Ltd

A catalogue record for this book is available from the British Library

ISBN: 1 85383 546 3 paperback
       1 85383 545 5 hardback

Typesetting by JS Typesetting, Wellingborough, Northants.
Printed and bound by Biddles Ltd, Guildford and King's Lynn
Cover design by John Burke
Cover photo © Panos Pictures/David Dahmén

For a full list of publications please contact:

Earthscan Publications Ltd
120 Pentonville Road
London, N1 9JN, UK
Tel: +44 (0)171 278 0433
Fax: +44 (0)171 278 1142
Email: earthinfo@earthscan.co.uk
http://www.earthscan.co.uk

Earthscan is an editorially independent subsidiary of Kogan Page Limited
and publishes in association with WWF-UK and the International Institute
for Environment and Development

This book is printed on elemental chlorine free paper

Contents

Figures and Tables .... *vii*
Acronyms and Abbreviations .... *viii*
Glossary of terms .... *xi*
Acknowledgements .... *xiii*

1 **Introduction** **1**
   A Brief History of Pest Control 3
   What's Your Poison? A Brief Guide to Pesticides 4
   Pesticides and Politics 5
   The Norms of Pesticide Politics 9

2 **Reaping the Rewards – The Use of Pesticides for**
   Increasing Crop Yields...................... **17**
   The Drive to Increase Food Yields.................. 17
   The Politics of Using Pesticides to Increase
      Crop Yields.................................... 21
   Conclusion 24

3 **Fighting Plague and Pestilence – The Role of**
   Pesticides in Controlling Pest Transmitted
   Diseases 26
   Introduction 26
   The Politics of Using Pesticides in Public Health
      Programmes 31
   Conclusion 35

4 **The Killing Fields – The Issue of Human Poisoning**
   by Pesticides **37**
   The Extent of the Problem 37
   Types of Poisoning 39
   The Politics of Preventing Human Poisoning by
      Pesticides 52
   Conclusion – A Regime?........................... 65

5   **When a Weapon Misses the Target – The Issue of
     Environmental Pollution by Pesticides** 67
     Introduction 67
     Forms of Pesticide Pollution 67
     The Politics of Environmental Pollution by Pesticides .. 76
     Conclusions 86

6   **The Secret Ingredient – The Issue of Food
     Contamination by Pesticides**.................... 88
     Introduction 88
     The Extent of the Problem 88
     The Politics of Pesticide Residues 93
     Conclusion 106

7   **Peddling Poisons – The International Trade in
     Pesticides** 109
     The Problem Defined 109
     Regulating the International Trade in Pesticides 111
     Conclusions 121

8   **Steering a Middle Course: Avoiding the Overuse
     of Pesticides – The Concept of Integrated Pest
     Management.**............................... 124
     Introduction 124
     The Alternatives to Chemical Pesticides 127
     The Politics of Avoiding Pesticide Overuse 135
     Conclusions 141

9   **From Value Systems to Regulatory Systems:
     Reflections on the Seven Issues of Pesticide
     Politics** 143
     Pesticide Norms and the Global Agenda 143
     Explanatory Factors for Regime Creation 151
     Conclusions 169

*Appendix: The FAO International Code of Conduct on the
          Distribution and Use of Pesticides* *173*
References and Notes *199*
Index *216*

Figures and Tables

FIGURES

2.1   World production of formulated pesticides 20
2.2   EU production of active pesticide ingredients 20
2.3   The organizational structure of GCPF 23
5.1   Regional regimes which regulate pesticide pollution.... 80
6.1   Organizational structure of the Codex Alimentarius
      Commission and subsidiary bodies 98
6.2   Codex Alimentarius decision-making for the
      establishment of Maximum Residue Limits 100
8.1   Relationship between the norm of avoiding
      pesticide overuse and the other norms and values
      within pesticide politics 124

TABLES

2.1   Pesticide use and yields of major crops in certain
      countries and areas 18
4.1   WHO classification of pesticides according to
      degree of hazard to human beings.................. 56
4.2   Advertising infringements of FAO Code in Ecuador
      (1987) 64
7.1   Pesticides subject to the PIC procedure in 1998....... 118
9.1   Estimated costs of US pesticide use 150
9.2   Summary table of the seven norms of pesticide
      politics and their derivative issue-systems 170

Acronyms and Abbreviations

AAAS	American Association for the Advancement of Science
ABM	anti-ballistic missile
ADI	acceptable daily intake
BAA	British Agrochemicals Association
BHC	benzene hexachloride
CAC	Codex Alimentarius Commission
CCPR	Codex Committee on Pesticide Residues
CFC	Chloro-fluoro-carbon
CHEMRAWN	Chemical Research Applied to World Needs
CoP	Conference of the Parties
CRC	Chemical Review Committee
DDT	dichlorodiphenyltrichloroethane
DGD	decision guidance document
Dioxin TCDD	2,3,7,8-tetrachlorodibenzo-p-dioxin
DNA	designated national authority
EC	European Community
EHC	Environmental Health Criteria
ELC	Environmental Liaison Centre
EPA	Environmental Protection Agency (USA)
EU	European Union
FAO	Food and Agriculture Organization
FAO Code	The FAO Code of Conduct on the Distribution and Use of Pesticides
FEPCA	Federal Environmental Pesticide Control Act
FIFRA	Federal Insecticide, Fungicide and Rodenticide Act
FoE	Friends of the Earth
GAP	good agricultural practice
GATT	General Agreement on Tariffs and Trade
GCPF	Global Crop Protection Federation
GEMS	Global Environmental Monitoring System (WHO)

GIFAP	Groupement International des Associations Nationales de Fabricants de Produits Agrochimiques
GMO	Genetically Modified Organism
HAC	Herbicide Assessment Commission
HEOD	1,2,3,4,10,10-hexachloro-6,7-epoxy-1,4,4a,5,6, 7,8,8a-octahydro-1,4,5,8-dimethamonaphthalene
IARC	International Agency for Research on Cancer
IATA	International Air Transport Association
ICSU	International Council of Scientific Unions
IFCS	Intergovernmental Forum on Chemical Safety
IITA	International Institute of Tropical Agriculture
IJC	International Joint Commission
ILO	International Labour Organization (UN)
INC	Intergovernmental Negotiating Committee
INFOTERRA	International Retrieval System for Sources of Environmental Information
IO	international organization
IOCU	International Organization of Consumer Unions
IPC	integrated pest control
IPCS	International Programme on Chemical Safety
IPM	integrated pest management
IRPTC	International Register of Potentially Toxic Chemicals
IUCN	The World Conservation Union (formerly the International Union for Conservation of Nature and Natural Resources)
IUPAC	International Union of Pure and Applied Chemistry
JMPR	Joint FAO/WHO Meeting on Pesticide Residues
KRAPP	Indonesian Network Against the Misuse of Pesticides
LD50	dose required to kill 50 per cent of test animals
MAC	maximum admissable concentration
MAFF	Ministry of Agriculture, Fisheries and Food
MAP	Mediterranean Action Plan
MIC	methyl isocyanate
MRL	maximum residue limit
NATO	North Atlantic Treaty Organization
NFU	National Farmers Union
NGO	non-governmental organization

NOEL	no-observed-effect level
NRDC	National Resources Defense Council
NRPTC	National Register of Potentially Toxic Chemicals
OECD	Organisation for Economic Cooperation and Development
OP	organophosphate
OSPARCOM	Oslo and Paris Commission
PAN	Pesticide Action Network
PEGS	Pesticide Exposure Group of Sufferers
PCP	pentachlorophenol
PIC	prior informed consent
PLUARG	Pollution from Land Use Activities Reference Group
POP	persistent organic pollutants
REIO	Regional Economic Integration Organization
RSPB	Royal Society for the Protection of Birds
SEATO	South East Asia Treaty Organization
STCA	sodium trichloroacetate
TBTO	tributylin oxide
UNCED	United Nations Conference on Environment and Development
UNEP	United Nations Environment Programme
UNITAR	UN Institute for Training and Research
USAID	United States Agency for International Development
WALHI	Indonesian Environmental Forum
WHO	World Health Organization
WHOPES	WHO Pesticide Evaluation Scheme
WTO	World Trade Organization
WWF	World Wide Fund For Nature

Glossary of Terms

active ingredient the component(s) of a pesticide which is toxic to the pest

arsenical compound containing arsenic

carbamates insecticides made from an ester of carbamic acid. They have anti-chlorinesterase properties, ie they destroy an enzyme essential to a pest's nervous system

carcinogenic causes cancer

defoliant pesticide that causes leaves to fall from a tree or plant

enzyme a biological chemical that serves to accelerate specific bodily functions

entomology the study of insects

epidemiology the study of patterns of disease amongst people

formulated products the final product of a pesticide, ie the active ingredient mixed with other chemical components

fumigant pesticide applied in the form of a fume

fungicide pesticide that is used against fungi and moulds

hepatoxic toxic to the liver

herbicide pesticide that is used against plants

larvicide pesticide that kills larvae

lipophilic dissolves more readily in fat than water

mutagenic	causes genetic changes which may affect the next generation
nematode	small, unsegmented worm
organochlorines	pesticides containing chlorine atoms (also known as 'chlorinated hydrocarbons')
organophosphates	pesticides containing phosphorus
persistent	slow to break down
pyrethroid	pesticide derived from the pyrethrum plant
rodenticide	pesticide used against rodents
systemic pesticide	pesticide that can enter a plant and move within it. Eg a systemic fungicide can kill fungi on a part of a plant away from the point of application
teratogenic	causes birth defects

Acknowledgements

A number of people helped make this book possible. The book originates from a PhD thesis at City University, the researching of which was funded by the Scientific and Engineering Research Council (SERC). Early drafts of this work were discussed with colleagues at City University, in particular with Peter Willetts, who was an encouraging and patient PhD supervisor. Mandy Bentham, David Humphreys, Lewis Clifton, Mira Filipovic and Chris Parks also discussed my work and gave advice as part of the Trans-governmental Relations Research Group. In addition, an early version of this script was read by Lawrie Reavill and John Vogler, who offered many useful opinions for which I am grateful.

Thanks should also be extended to the staff of the United Nations Information Centre Library in London for making their facilities available to me and to the Pesticides Trust for providing me with much useful information. In addition, Lisa Hough deserves thanks for assisting my research by collating press clippings and for being generally supportive of me.

A number of other people deserve recognition for helping me in various ways over the last eight years as this book has evolved. My mother and father have been a constant source of support, as has my sister Angela. Jan Wilton and Andy Morrison, also, have been invaluable in offering technical help at various times. Finally, I must offer my gratitude to Rowan Davies and the staff at Earthscan for believing in this project and allowing a long held ambition to be an author to become a reality.

1 Introduction

The use of pesticides in their various forms, in agriculture, public health programmes and everyday domestic life has become the subject of much debate in the domestic and international arenas in recent years. For the first two decades after the discovery of chemical pesticides in 1939, their use provoked little controversy. The success of DDT (dichlorodiphenyltrichloroethane) in helping control malaria and other pest-transmitted diseases, and the effectiveness of various insecticides and herbicides in reducing crop losses, gave pesticides the aura of another technological breakthrough destined to improve human standards of living forever.

The publication in 1962 of the ground-breaking *Silent Spring* by Rachel Carson, however, highlighted side-effects associated with pesticides and for the first time their use and production became a matter of contention.[1] Carson focused mainly on the capacity of pesticides to pollute the environment and wildlife, helping establish this as an international issue. The impact of pesticides on human health was also considered by Carson, but this did not become an area of great contention until nearly a decade later when the horrific effects of defoliants sprayed by American troops in the Vietnam War became known.

Throughout the 1970s and 1980s pesticide use and production increased but at the same time became more and more contentious, leading to the emergence of other issues on the domestic and international political agendas. Concern over the potential dangers inherent in the capacity of pesticide residues to remain in foodstuffs long after application heralded the phenomenon of organic farming and much consumer group activity. As a corollary of this issue of food contamination and those of environmental pollution and human safety, efforts to apply pesticides more cautiously and to develop non-chemical alternatives in pest control led to the popularization of the concept of integrated pest management (IPM) and the genesis of another political issue concerning pesticides. In addition, the coming to light of pesticide poisonings in developing countries allied to concern in developed countries over contaminated food imports from the South led to the formation of an issue concerning the trade in pesticides.

Pressure groups have helped ensure the maintenance of these issues on the international agenda, prompting individual government responses and the establishment of international guidelines by organizations within the United Nations (UN) system. The 1984 disaster at Bhopal, India, when a leak of chemicals intended for pesticide use killed thousands living near the production plant, stimulated public awareness of the hazardous nature of these chemicals. This served to strengthen the position of the pressure groups vis-à-vis the agrochemical industry in negotiating the means of regulating the various pesticide issues on an international level.

This book analyses the various political questions that surround the use and production of pesticide chemicals. The method of analysis employed orders these policy questions into distinct issues, where it can be seen that groups of questions are related, in terms of representing matters of contention centred on a particular norm of behaviour.

It emerges from this exercise that seven norms of behaviour can be identified as determining the behaviour of actors within the whole set of pesticides policy questions. Consequently, seven issue systems, each comprising a set of actors for whom a norm is salient, can be isolated.

Each of the seven issue systems is examined in turn, highlighting the nature of the policy questions and the political behaviour of the salient actors. Of these seven issue systems, the first two are based on the prescriptive norms that uphold the use and production of pesticides. These norms are relatively uncontentious in themselves and achieve most significance as the counterbalances to the five proscriptive norms. Hence, most of the political activity related to pesticides emerges in the issues covered by Chapters 4 to 9, where actors are forced to choose between competing norms to guide their behaviour.

Central to this political activity is the development of international regimes. These are subsets within an issue system, responsible for decision making and the implementation of rules in line with the norm from which the issue is derived. Two such international regimes are found to be in existence within the pesticides policy area, regulating the issues of pesticide trade and the contamination of food by pesticides. The five other issue systems can be seen as essentially unregulated. A number of theories concerning the causal factors in the formation of regimes are then outlined and their applicability to the presence or absence of regimes in the seven issues of pesticides politics is considered.

The general conclusion and underlying premise of this book is that the formation of international regimes is facilitated by many factors and not solely by the desire of actors to maximize their interests viewed in terms of power and short-term calculations of the utility of an act. Rather, it is posited that values are a significant force in the emergence of global norms. Hence it transpires that the behaviour of actors in the global system, as in pesticides politics, should not be understood simply in terms of a traditional rational actor model according to which actors (usually assumed to be states) are motivated by the need to maximize their power in relation to other actors (states).

A BRIEF HISTORY OF PEST CONTROL

Pest control is as old as agriculture. Once humans had taken on the task of rearing plants and animals for their own needs, rather than relying on the random successes of hunting and gathering, any natural competitor for their food became a pest. Measures to protect crops from such pests naturally followed, starting simply with manual weeding and the picking off of harmful insects. Through time, societies developed more systematic practices such as destroying crop residues after harvesting and rotating crop fields to remove pest habitats and thus inhibit their proliferation. Such practices continued for centuries with little refinement, bar the employment of some particularly eccentric tactics to augment them. The Romans used magic rituals to protect vines from moth attack, including the practice of wiping the pruning knife on beaver skin prior to use. In medieval France it was a common occurrence for the Church to excommunicate caterpillars, or for grasshoppers to be tried in court for the crime of attacking crops.[2]

The use of chemicals as an aid to pest control did not take off until the late nineteenth century, although some use was made of sulphur as a domestic insecticide prior to this. Homer refers to this practice, seemingly proving the superiority of the Greeks over their rival ancient civilization in this area of scientific advance.

The effects of Colorado beetles on potato crops and gypsy moths on trees in the US prompted the entomologist Charles Riley to pioneer the use of the arsenical compounds Paris Green (an acetoarsenite of copper originally used as a paint pigment) and London Purple (an arsenical dye residue) as insecticide sprays. The most extensive use of Paris Green in the immediate years after its development in 1867 was actually as a deterrent to human pests. Roadside vines were sprayed to prevent pilfering by passers-by, and a number of children were killed in this way.[3] No records exist as to the quality of the wine produced from such vineyards!

The next major development in pest control history occurred with the creation of synthetic organic pesticides during the Second World War. The insecticidal properties of dichlorodiphenyltrichloroethane (DDT) were discovered by Dr Paul Muller of Switzerland in 1939 and it was quickly patented. A whole series of other chlorinated hydrocarbons were soon found to have similar properties, leading to the marketing of benzene hexachloride (BHC), aldrin, dieldrin and others. A second branch of new synthetic pesticides, the organo-phosphorous compounds, came as a side-effect of wartime research into toxic gases by the German scientist Dr Gerhard Schrader. After the war Schrader put his research before the Allied states and revealed the potential insecticidal application of the compounds. Parathion was the first major pesticide of this form to be marketed, and others soon followed.

What's Your Poison? – A Brief Guide to Pesticides

The term pesticide refers to any substance used in the control of pests as defined by humans. Such pests include: insects (hence the term insecticide), weeds (herbicides) and fungi (fungicides). Pesticides may also be used to control pests in ways which fall short of killing them. The term also incorporates defoliants used to strip trees and plants of their leaves, plant growth regulators, and various substances which deter insects from certain locations (for example mosquito repellants) or attract them away from crops (for example the use of pheromones, sex hormones).

Not covered by the term pesticide are fertilizers or veterinary drugs though the three are often subsumed under the generic term agrochemicals. The term also does not encompass medicines taken by humans to counteract diseases caused directly by organisms, such as antibiotics or anti-fungal chemicals.

Pesticides may also be subdivided according to their chemical make-up. Four principal categories can be identified:

1 **natural** (botanical) – substances extracted directly from plants such as nicotine and pyrethrium;
2 **biological** – the use of micro-organisms in pest control – for example, the use of the bacteria *bacillus thuringiensis*;
3 **inorganic** – substances derived from minerals such as sulphur and arsenic; and
4 **synthetic** (organic) – the dominant form of pesticides comprising chemical substances manufactured from combinations of carbon, hydrogen and oxygen with other elements. Synthetic pesticides can be sub-divided thus:
   - organochlorines (eg DDT);
   - organophosphates (eg parathion);
   - phenoxyacetic acids (eg 2,4,5-T);
   - carbamates (eg aldicarb); and
   - synthetic pyrethroids.

The most common names of pesticides are usually distinct from their technical chemical names. The herbicide paraquat, for example, is the popular term for the chemical 1,1'-dimethyl-4,4-bipyridinium ion. Pesticides also acquire trade names. Paraquat is marketed under a variety of names such as 'Pathclear' and 'Gramoxone'.

PESTICIDES AND POLITICS

The development and subsequent proliferation of chemical pesticides since the 1940s has had a profound social impact in a number of ways. The use of pesticides has undoubtedly helped increase crop yields in recent decades, which has been invaluable in an age of unprecedented population growth. These chemicals have also assisted in the struggle against diseases spread by insects, particularly in curbing the considerable death toll attributable to malaria.

On the other hand, however, pesticides have also affected society in negative ways. Field workers spraying the chemicals have suffered poisoning, sometimes to fatal extents; food has been contaminated with occasionally lethal consequences; and the environment has been polluted, to the detriment of many living things within it.

These impacts on human society ensure that the whole question of pesticide production and usage enters the realm of politics. Once a phenomenon is seen to affect society in some way, it naturally follows that opinions are formed on the desirability or undesirability of such change. These opinions may derive from established values or norms which the phenomenon has challenged, or else from new norms of behaviour that emerge as a result of the new circumstances brought on by the phenomenon. The initial development of chemical pesticides in the 1940s was borne of the desire to increase food yields and control the spread of pest-carried diseases, two well-established norms. Chemical crop protection thrived as a means of satisfying these norms until the 1960s, when public realization of a new set of circumstances prompted new norms to be formed countering the previously unchallenged practice. The emergence of evidence that pesticides were not a panacea for crop protection and that many pests could develop resistance to the chemicals, was accompanied by the publication in 1962 of Rachel Carson's *Silent Spring*, which heralded a wave of opinion concerned by evidence of environmental pollution caused by pesticide use. It was at around this time that pesticides became a political matter.

Politics as defined by Easton represents the 'authoritative allocation of values'.[4] Reynolds expands on this, stating that for an act to be deemed political it should incorporate the following elements:

> . . . *the fact of control or government or authority, the propriety or otherwise of that control, its purposes or functions, and the forms and methods by which it is exercised or competed for.*[5]

While precise definitions used by theorists may vary in this way, the common theme of them is the idea that a political act must incorporate an authoritative dimension. Pesticide production and usage was not a political question prior to the 1960s, essentially because it was not controversial. The values at stake did not have to be authoritatively allocated because most people accepted them, and very few found them to be in conflict with other norms. Bosso, writing about the development of pesticides in American politics, has described this situation as 'clientele politics':

> *The pesticide issue was not salient to any but those benefiting from pesticides, and the scope of the debate was severely limited by those most intimately involved.*[6]

With the advent of the new information surrounding pesticide use, however, opinions needed to be formed in the light of different, and somewhat contradictory, norms. Pesticides continued to command great support for their contribution to improving crop harvests and fighting diseases like malaria, but this support now had to be justified and reason used to convince others that these benefits outweighed the costs. At the same time, environmentalists and sceptics had to set out their stall by trying to mobilize opinion behind the new values they were expounding. In this way, an area of political contention was founded, which has continued and evolved to take on its present form.

Identifying what it is that determines the behaviour of actors in the international system must, of course, be a fundamental goal of international relations theory. Even the traditionalists, the realists, in time have come to accept that this task must incorporate some consideration of international influences, alongside the old idea of the rationally acting state, continually striving to maximize its power in relation to other states. The orthodox realist position was epitomized by Morgenthau:

> *The nation state is to a higher degree than ever before the predominant source of the individual's moral and legal valuations and the ultimate point of reference for his secular loyalties. Consequently, its power among the other nations and the preservation of its sovereignty are the individual's foremost political concerns in international affairs.*[7]

The undeniable growth of interdependence in the world in the last half century has caused a rethink of this position. International organizations today provide a rich source of moral and legal guidelines to which individuals adhere, as is evidenced by the now commonplace resort by individuals to the European Court of Human Rights, in opposition to their own state. In addition to this, pressure groups, aided by advances in communications technology, have mobilized public opinion across boundaries for international issues such as environmental conservation and pollution, and even for issues solely within the jurisdiction of other states, as with the global anti-apartheid movement.

International relations theorists responded to these developments by adopting new conceptual tools to bring the phenomenon of interdependence within their framework of analysis. Neo-realists were principally responsible for introducing the concept of an international regime, as a means of revamping the power politics philosophy of Morgenthau, which was in danger of appearing out-moded. A regime, it is argued, is a multinational agreement on an area of contention which can have an independent impact on world politics. Such regimes however are still understood to rise and fall in line with the powers of the state actors comprising them. The Bretton Woods exchange rate system, for example, an international monetary agreement which fixed international currencies to gold and the US dollar, collapsed at a time when US power was waning. In this way, realism could be modified to account for international phenomena whilst retaining its basic axioms of inter-state relations that are governed by power.

A second concept used to refine international relations theory in the face of interdependence comes from focusing primarily on the interactions between actors, be they states or otherwise, rather than the units themselves. Pluralist writers such as Rosenau, Mansbach and Vasquez have adopted a methodology which tries to comprehend world politics by considering the behaviour of actors in relation to specific issues. According to this approach, issue systems, consisting of all actors for whom a particular set of related policy questions is salient, can be abstracted from the international system as a whole. Political behaviour then is able to be explained in relation to these subsystems, rather than simply in accordance with the international system as an entirety.

The pluralists have, in general, not attempted to synthesize this usage of issue systems with the predominantly neo-realist construction of the international regime. The two terms clearly must possess some common ground, however, as any regime must have an issue that it aims to regulate, whilst an issue system can presumably exist at different levels of complexity, the more complex of which take on greater significance in world politics. This study attempts to reconcile the two concepts by understanding them as different levels of international behaviour modification. The behaviour of international actors can be patterned to different extents, and it seems profitable to recognize this.

Distinguishing between issue systems and regimes as international phenomena necessitates a narrower understanding of an issue than is often conceptualized. Rather than considering an issue to be a broad set of related policy questions, such as environmental pollution, which incorporates a range of distinctive questions linked by the value that environmental pollution should be avoided, or pesticides, which encompasses a number of different values linked by a common subject, this study views issues as areas of contention around particular norms. Hence many commonly perceived issues must be reconceptualized as amalgamations of issues derived from a common general value or within a similar context of politics. Thus it emerges that the international politics of pesticides is not an issue in itself, but rather a grouping of different issues which can be shown to involve different actors, and modify the behaviour of those actors in different ways. The issues are linked by the fact that they concern a common subject – pesticides. Similarly, environmental pollution can be seen as an amalgamation of issues based on particular norms derived from the common value of avoiding pollution, such as that of avoiding environmental pollution by pesticides.

The first task of this book, it follows, is to isolate the norms that are influential in determining the behaviour of the actors involved in international pesticide politics. After adopting a suitable definition of a norm, a concept more frequently used in sociology and anthropology, we will see that there are seven (at least) that play a part in this political arena. Each of these norms forms the basis of an issue system, consisting of the actors to whom the norm is salient. The seven identified norms of pesticide politics will be considered in turn as separate chapters and the make-up of each issue system compared and contrasted in the conclusion. The principal interest in this exercise is to consider how levels of adherence to each of the norms vary and offer explanations for this variance. Where a relatively high level of adherence to a norm exists, this may be reflected in the existence of a regime, a subset of actors within the issue system responsible for authoritatively allocating a value by implementing rules reflecting the norm upon which the issue system is based.

Of the seven issues considered, it is shown that only two have consistently seen the norm implemented with regards to all actors within the system. In both of these issues a definitive international regime can be seen at work, successfully implementing international policy on the matter at hand. The fact that actors in the other five issue systems do not adhere consistently to the norm can be attributed either to the lack of any regime regulating the issue, or to the failure of an existing regime to implement policy that corresponds to the norm.

THE NORMS OF PESTICIDE POLITICS

It is clear that the politics of pesticides involves a number of different norms, each of which is sought to be legitimized in society by the actors upholding them. A method of analysing an area of political contention, such as that concerning pesticide use and production, is to break it down into issue systems, which are areas of contention derived from a particular norm. Rosenau, for example, considers an issue system to be in operation wherever it can be seen that actors 'engage in distinctive behaviour designed to mobilize support for the attainment of their particular values.'[8] Norms are the informal rules that emerge from this contention to guide the actors to whom they are salient. As the political arena of pesticides contains a number of different norms, it can be seen that it should not be understood as a single issue in itself, but rather as an amalgamation of issues, involving different actors and modifying the behaviour of such actors in different ways.

The first step towards analysing the issues of pesticide politics, and any regulatory structures that derive from them, is thus to isolate the norms which guide the behaviour of the actors concerned. A sociological definition of norms is provided by Robin Williams:

> *Norms . . . are rules of conduct; they specify what should and should not be done by various kinds of social actors in various kinds of situations.*[9]

Although primarily intended for the study of individuals in community settings, this definition is flexible enough to be used with respect to the international political behaviour of organizations and governments.

The fact that pesticide politics operate around a number of norms has already been referred to. It is possible to find at least seven such norms in contention in the international discourse on pesticide matters.

1 We should strive to attain optimal food yields.
2 Disease and damage due to pests should be limited.
3 The misuse of pesticides leading to human poisoning should be prevented.
4 The international trade in pesticides should be regulated.
5 Pesticides should not be overused.
6 Environmental pollution by pesticides should be limited.
7 The contamination of food by pesticides should be limited.

Norms and Values

These norms, as rules of conduct for the actors in pesticide politics, are derivative of more general values and principles which govern the behaviour of individuals and groups in many walks of domestic and international life. This distinction between specific norms and more abstract values is eloquently expressed by Kratochvil:

Values are not only more general than rules, or norms, but they influence decisions on the basis of largely cathectic considerations. As opposed to rules which prescribe specific actions, values inform the attitudes of actors. Rather than addressing the rational calculating abilities of decision makers, values serve to strengthen the will and the emotional attachment to social objects or states of affairs.[10]

Norms and their derivative issue systems emerge from this contention between actors aiming to attain certain values.

Making this connection between specific norms and more general values requires a consideration of international norms as something more than observable patterns of behaviour, arrived at through a rational maximization of interest. Thus, the age-old philosophical debate, as to whether people's actions are guided purely by self-interest or whether morality or 'divine love' play a part, resurfaces in the inter-paradigm debate in international relations theory. Hobbes' pessimistic view of a society in which all actions are guided by fear and avoidance of 'social bad'[11] corresponds to the realist's model of rationally acting states aiming to maximize their power to maintain order in an anarchical world. Durkheim's vision of a moral code made up of norms as 'social facts', constraining individual choices,[12] finds favour in pluralist international relations theory with its stress on interdependence and the development of international systems (phenomena which necessarily imply that international behavioural forces exist).

Opinion in both philosophy and international relations is divided on whether such rules of conduct are derived from the interests of the actors, or have independent influence and constrain such interests. The former opinion is expounded by Hume, who considers norms to be 'artificial virtues'[13] in that they are conventions of behaviour arrived at when actors' interests are furthered by cooperation. Many of the conventions that make up international law seem to bear this out. The customary rules that bays or continental shelves should belong to the adjacent state developed because of the salience of the idea to maritime states. Similarly, Smart refers to norms as 'mere rules of thumb'[14] used by rational actors (act-utilitarians) as rough guides to behaviour based on past experience. Realist thinkers in international relations have adopted this approach to hypothesize about the behaviour of international actors. Rosencrance made this explicit in stating 'history is a laboratory in which our generalizations about international politics can be tested'.[15] Theories such as the balance of power system emerge from this approach to explain and predict the behaviour of international actors.

Opponents of this school of act-utilitarianism/realism do not believe that actors only follow rules of conduct when it furthers their interests to do so. Kratochvil criticizes the methodology of observing past behaviour to demonstrate norms, pointing out that this is not a value free exercise.

> *Because rule-following is part of moral assessments, the question of whether a norm predicted the actual outcome accurately telescopes several important concerns that ought to be distinguished into one factual observation.*[16]

Kratochvil also points out that norms are not invalidated if they sometimes fail to determine an actor's behaviour, as is the case with the development of international law. Furthermore, non-observance of a norm can even serve to strengthen its influence, if the actor concerned seeks to excuse or explain its behaviour. Governments frequently justify arms trade links with countries with poor human rights records as morally problematic but necessary for the national interest, demonstrating that a value had entered the calculation, even though it had been overridden.

Kratochvil proceeds to argue that values play a part in norm compliance, pointing out the fact that people will often follow legal norms because of the value that one should observe the law, rather than merely through fear of sanctions. Values thus are seen as distorting the rational calculations of an act-utilitarian.

> *Rather than addressing the rational calculating abilities of decision makers, values serve to strengthen the will and the emotional attachment to social objects, or states of affairs'.*[17]

It is the presence of values in a society that gives norms the status of a phenomenon and not merely an epiphenomenon.

Thus it transpires that the seven norms outlined above can be seen as specific forms of more general codes of conduct by which human relations are guided. Norm 1 on optimizing yields is related to the general practical fact that any society needs to produce sufficient food to supply the needs of its constituents. Norm 2 on preventing disease is derived from the moral principle that human suffering should be alleviated where possible. All human societies accept this principle to some extent, as is evidenced by the universality of practising medicine and healing. Norm 3 on preventing poisoning can also be seen to derive from this ethic. Norm 4 on the trade in pesticides is a specific version of the general principle that inter-state trading in any hazardous commodity needs to be subject to some control. The issues of trading arms and industrial waste are thus related to the corresponding practice with pesticides, in the sense that they all share a common principle. Norm 5 on the overuse of pesticides is unique to pesticide politics but ultimately can be seen as a corollary of all the other norms and values of pesticide politics, as the idea of avoiding the overuse of pesticides is to respect the need for optimizing food yields and curbing disease whilst avoiding general pollution and poisoning. Norm 6 on pollution is the specific interpretation of the value that any environmental pollution is undesirable, and should be limited. Norm 7 on food contamination relates to the general norm that food should be kept as free as possible from impurities, which again ultimately exists as a product of the ethic of alleviating human suffering.

Norms 1 and 2 can also be categorized as prescriptive in that they represent the bases for an actor positively choosing to produce and/ or use pesticides. The value of making money could, of course, be added to this list. The rest of the seven norms are proscriptive as they represent the factors explaining why an actor should not take a particular course of action relating to pesticide trade, use, or production.

The Rationality of Norm Compliance

A clear demonstration of how norms can emerge comes from considering the theories of public goods and the 'prisoners' dilemma'. A public good is something which, if available to one actor, is correspondingly also available to others free of cost. Examples include fish and ozone, in that they have both suffered depletion to the detriment of all, because environmental quality and food supplies are treated as a free good by actors. The rational act in terms of a straight cost-benefit analysis would be for all actors to continue discharging chlorofluorocarbons (CFCs) and destroy the ozone layer, and with it themselves. Similarly, the prisoners' dilemma illustrates how actors can come to cooperate and act contrary to the maximization of act utility for purely self-serving reasons. According to the game, two prisoners held for the same crime in different cells are aware that giving evidence could get them cleared and result in the other prisoner being prosecuted. However, if both were to blame the other then neither would get off. So in reality, therefore, it is in both their interests to stay silent and accept the light sentence that this entails. To do this requires trust in the other prisoner to do likewise. Keohane coined the term 'myopic self-interest'[18] to distinguish between such a narrow, short-term view of the rational act and what he describes as 'bounded rationality'[19] by which behaviour can be better understood.

The irrationality of acts of myopic self-interest demonstrates that the truly rational act is often to follow a norm generated by a common interest. Sartorius upholds this in formulating a theory by which conduct can be explained by reference to shared systems of social morality, in which actors accept that they cannot directly appeal to utility.

> *Considerations of utility lead to the participation of each in the creation and support of a system of norms which bar direct appeals to utility and which are backed by sanctions which each has a role in applying.*[20]

This mirrors the concept of an issue system in international relations theory, without abandoning the traditional idea of the rational actor.

From Norms to Regimes

Sartorius goes on to describe how actors can come to calculate that the rational act is not a direct appeal to utility (in other words outline the solutions to the prisoners dilemma). The first method he describes is for an individual or group of individuals unilaterally to contribute to the cost of providing a public good, in the expectation that others will follow the example and so make the initially irrational act rational. This seems to correspond to Keohane's belief in the importance of 'entrepreneurial actors'[21] in regime formation, particularly in the sphere of environmental politics. The voluntary, unilateral cutting of CFC emissions by certain states in recent years provides an illustration of this idea. The second of Sartorius' solutions is for individuals to form organizations which redefine their interests in favour of providing public goods. As the cost of establishing such organizations may make the act irrational, however, Sartorius envisages a third scenario. In the situation he describes there are 'specific social norms backed by social sanctions which are neither legal nor quasi-legal' (organizational rules).[22] This appears to parallel the pluralist interpretation of regimes in international relations.

Regimes may, however, develop from issues which have no apparent rational interests at stake for actors, even in a long-term or indirect sense. The sort of international altruism apparent in the establishment of conservation or human rights regimes goes beyond entrepreneurial actions. The regime currently in operation in Arctic regions concerning the conservation of polar bears cannot be understood as serving the interests of any of the signatory governments, which include the US and Russia who committed themselves to its rules amidst the tensions of the Cold War.[23] Similarly, the regime centred on the European Convention on Human Rights appears to constrain the signatory governments to a general social good without apparently serving the interests of a single entrepreneurial government. Indeed this regime's effectiveness centres on its ability to persuade governments against taking certain steps in their own national interest by threatening them with the loss of face and damage to their reputation by being seen to contravene internationally accepted standards of morality.

Although the seven norms of conduct identified as guiding behaviour within the pesticides policy system are related and often derivative of the same basic moral value, each can be shown to produce a distinctive issue system, featuring its own particular form of political processes and regulatory structures. One principal way in which the issues within the pesticides policy system vary is in the existence or absence of a regime. The classic definition of a regime in international relations literature is provided by Krasner as: 'sets of implicit or explicit principles, norms, rules around which expectations converge in a given area of international relations'.[24]

An issue system can exist independently of the interests of principal international actors, and a regime will develop from this when its values and norms are tacitly legitimized by actors in so far as they come to expect an authoritative allocation of those norms and values to occur. This process, we will see, is often facilitated by an 'epistemic community'; a transnational set of actors within the issue system who derive influence from their expertise on that issue.

For each of the following seven chapters I first attempt to demonstrate the existence of an international norm, by looking at how actor behaviour relates to the particular prescription or proscription. If the same actors contended the seven norms in the same way, international pesticide politics could be dealt with as single issue but, as will become evident, this is not the case. The following chapters will highlight the fact that levels of adherence to each of the norms varies considerably, which is to some extent reflected in the existence or absence of regimes, assuming responsibility for implementing rules based on the norm to the salient actors. The distinctive effects that pesticides have on the world socially and ecologically are mirrored by distinctive patterns of political responses, requiring an analysis of this subject to take on a correspondingly fragmented approach.

2
Reaping the Rewards – The Use of Pesticides for Increasing Crop Yields

THE DRIVE TO INCREASE FOOD YIELDS

The original reason for the development and use of pesticide chemicals was to reduce crop losses to insects, fungi, and weeds, and so ensure better yields. The fact that crop yields need to be increased is accepted by all in the face of an ever increasing world population, and as such this constitutes a norm. Pesticides represent one potential means of satisfying this norm, through the process sometimes referred to as 'agromedicine'.

> *Agromedicine is the integrated interdisciplinary application of the skills and knowledge of agriculture, applied chemistry and medicine to the promotion of an adequate and wholesome food supply for the welfare of man.*[1]

Pesticides are also employed in the protection of non-food crops, such as cotton.

The barrier that pests, in their various guises, pose to satisfying the norm of obtaining optimal crop yields is considerable. Pimentel, in a paper for the 1983 CHEMRAWN (Chemical Research Applied to World Needs) II Conference, demonstrated that 35 per cent of the world's food crops prior to harvesting, and between 10 and 20 per cent afterwards, are destroyed annually by a combination of insects, plant pathogens, weeds, micro-organisms, rodents, and birds. In the US, Pimentel estimates that 37 per cent of all crops are lost each year, despite the use of pesticides and other forms of crop protection. Of this total, 13 per cent are believed to be lost to insects, 12 per cent to weeds, and 12 per cent to plant pathogens.[2] His conclusion is that: 'Clearly the continued use of both non-chemical and chemical pesticides is essential to food and fibre production in the world'.[3]

It is, of course, in the overpopulated developing countries that the norm of obtaining optimal crop yields is most pertinent, the same arena in which the prohibitive norms concerning pesticide use are most pertinent. The moral dilemma facing the actors concerned with pesticide politics is the stark fact that while imposing strict restrictions on pesticide use and imports in developing countries would reduce accidental deaths and environmental pollution, it would also be likely to reduce the amount of food on the plates of already undernourished peoples. This continues to be the spur for the maintenance of pesticide use amidst the international voices calling for restraint in the name of human safety, environmental protection, and food purity. The compromise practice of adopting integrated pest management, balancing the norms of optimizing crop yields and minimizing pesticide use, is a complex procedure making up a separate issue which is looked at in Chapter 8.

Chemical pesticides have undoubtedly made food and fibre production more efficient. It is estimated that while the average farmer in the US produced enough food for himself and nine others in the 1940s, this had increased to include himself and 31 others by the 1970s.[4] This statistic is not wholly attributable to the introduction of pesticides in agriculture. The mechanization of farming, the introduction of high yielding crop species and advances in the use of chemical fertilizers have also played their part, but other data do bear out the fact that pesticides have helped improve crop yields (Table 2.1).

Table 2.1, although based upon highly aggregated data, does show a clear correlation between the input of pesticides and the subsequent yield in crops, but the relationship between the two

Table 2.1 *Pesticide use and yields of major crops in certain countries and areas*[5]

Country/area	Pesticide use (kg/ha)	Rank	Crop yield (tonne/ha)	Rank
Japan	10.8	1	5.5	1
Europe	1.9	2	3.4	2
US	1.5	3	2.6	3
Latin America	0.22	4	2.0	4
Oceania	0.20	5	1.6	5
Africa	0.13	6	1.2	6

variables is not straightforward and needs to be qualified. Yields do not rise in strict proportion to the amounts of pesticide used. Japan may average yields that are four and a half times the size of those in Africa, but they use 85 times as much pesticide. It appears that, ultimately, more pesticide does not equate to more food or fibre. A number of cases show evidence of this.

In India, where cotton growers used three million kilograms of DDT in 1970 to produce just over five million bales of fibre, DDT use had doubled but cotton yields remained the same six years later.[6]

A more extreme example comes from Nicaragua, where cotton yields 'fell by a total of 30 per cent from 1965 to 1969', despite increased insecticide applications.[7] Partial explanations for such cases and this general trend include: the raising of cosmetic standards demanded of fruit and vegetables by retailers, the unintentional destruction of natural pest predators, the use of high yielding but more vulnerable crop species, and the move away from crop rotation to monoculture.[8] The chief cause of continued crop losses in the face of pesticide use, however, is pest resistance, which develops in the face of continued exposure to chemicals. In the Nicaraguan case the explanation offered for the drop in cotton yields was an increase from five to nine in the number of species of resistant cotton pests that were 'economically important' in the previous ten years.[9] The problems posed by pest resistance and resurgence, examined in Chapter 8, are such that even the agrochemical industry has come to question the future of purely chemical crop protection and to explore alternative options. However, despite the growth in non-chemical integrated pest control techniques, pesticide sales continue to grow and they are still widely considered as an essential means of satisfying the norm of optimizing crop yields.

Figure 2.1 shows how the level of world pesticides production increased continually from the 1940s, when they were first introduced into agricultural and public health use, until the mid-1980s. The histogram uses figures for the volume of produced pesticides, rather than their sales value. These figures are not frequently quoted (hence the unusual layout of the time axis), but give a more accurate reflection of production as sales figures are obviously distorted by the rate of inflation and corporate pricing policy.

Comparable world production figures after 1985 are hard to come by, but accurate figures for EU production suggest a slight tailing off in the 1990s after the mid-1980s peak.

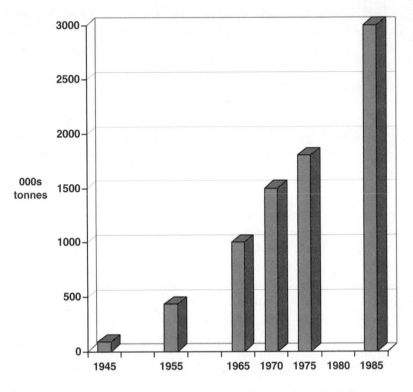

Figure 2.1 *World production of formulated pesticides*[10]

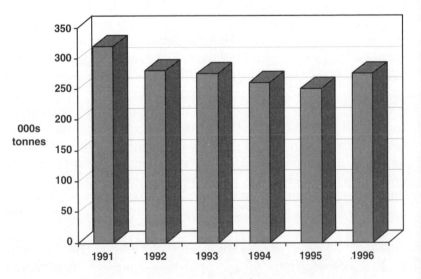

Figure 2.2 *EU Production of active pesticide ingredients*[11]

The Politics of Using Pesticides to Increase Crop Yields

The need to ensure food security in the face of the famines that continue to afflict many developing countries is clear. Continued population growth looks likely to place ever greater demands on the world's food and fibre supplies and one solution to this is to strive to increase crop yields. Pesticides, even when allowing for the problems of pest resistance, have provided a means of achieving this. However the evidence that emerges throughout this book is that the achievements of pesticide chemicals in this regard have not been without some costs. Human poisoning, environmental degradation, and food contamination have all been side-effects of the production, distribution and use of pesticides on food crops in the latter part of this century. Pesticide use on fibre crops, of course, does not invoke any food contamination problems, but is still controversial in terms of environmental pollution and worker safety. These problems have given rise to the development of the prohibitive norms of conduct concerning pesticides, which are considered in later chapters. The political choices facing the actors within the pesticides policy area thus have tended to amount to a prioritizing of goals – choosing between the norms prescribing pesticide use and those that proscribe it in some way.

Naturally, the chief advocates of pesticides as a tool for boosting crop yields are the representatives of the chemical industry. Two organizations involved in this political process of advocacy are the International Union of Pure and Applied Chemistry (IUPAC) and the Global Crop Protection Federation (GCPF).

The International Union of Pure and Applied Chemistry (IUPAC)

Founded in 1919, IUPAC is 'an international, non-governmental organization dedicated to the advancement and application of chemical science and technology',[12] and includes crop protection chemicals amongst its range of interests. It is a member of the prestigious International Council of Scientific Unions (ICSU), a body serving to coordinate international scientific research. IUPAC is an association of over 40 national professional chemists bodies, with 12 other subordinate members known as observer countries. It hosts a General Assembly every two years at which future research projects and Conferences are discussed. 1500 scientists work for IUPAC on a voluntary basis, staffing 32 commissions representing different branches of chemical research. In addition, some 8000 scientists from over 80 countries are affiliated to IUPAC as individuals, enabling them to cooperate in the work of IUPAC commissions. Some of these affiliate members from developing countries are sponsored by IUPAC grants.

A number of international conferences are sponsored by IUPAC, of which the best known are the CHEMRAWN (Chemical Research Applied to World Needs) series. The second of the CHEMRAWN conferences, held in Manilla in 1982, was a forum for IUPAC's work on crop protection chemicals. Entitled *Chemistry and World Food Supplies: The New Frontiers*, the conference was attended by a number of leading pesticide scientists, many of whom presented papers, and was co-hosted by the International Rice Research Institute.[13]

The World Health Organization (WHO) and the Food and Agriculture Organization (FAO) of the United Nations regularly obtain technical advice from IUPAC on pesticide and other chemical matters and the organization has enjoyed 'specialized consultative' status with the FAO since 1955. Under this arrangement, representatives of the FAO Director-General attend all IUPAC meetings, whilst IUPAC is able to send representatives to FAO Conference and council sessions. Thus, IUPAC carries a significant level of respect as a source of authoritative knowledge on the issue of increasing crop yields through pesticide use. Hence, IUPAC is part of an epistemic community within the issue system. It also contributes to the epistemic communities of other pesticide issues through its all round chemical expertise. IUPAC's role in relation to pesticides is not solely one of advocacy. Its knowledge in regards to chemical toxicity gives it an input into the issues of environmental pollution, human poisoning and food contamination. For example, IUPAC regularly provides technical assistance to the International Programme on Chemical Safety (IPCS), the focus of the United Nations' activities concerning the issue of human poisoning by pesticides and other chemicals (see Chapter 4).

The Global Crop Protection Federation (GCPF)

The GCPF is the international representative of agrochemical companies and the most important organization involved in the promotion of pesticides for improving crop yields. The Federation is the successor to GIFAP (Groupement International des Associ- ations de Fabricants de Produits Agrochimiques) which was formed in 1967 as a network of national agrochemical associations. The national associations of the world's five main pesticide producing and exporting states (US, Japan, Germany, UK, and Switzerland) are full members, and in all over 1000 companies and 90 per cent of the world's pesticide producers are represented.

GCPF has an annual General Assembly made up of representatives from each of the national member associations and from this elects an Executive Network, including a President and Vice-President, from which its policy positions are formulated. A secretariat is based in Brussels and finance comes from member subscriptions.

GCPF work is carried out in a series of groups as depicted in Figure 2.3. National crop protection associations, such as the British Agrochemical Association, are coordinated into regional groupings. Industrial experts are organized into functional networks dealing with either technical or politico-legal matters or into Resistance Action Committees which provide information to pesticide users. The implementation of Executive Network policy is carried out by five International Project Teams, each of which is headed by a chairman.

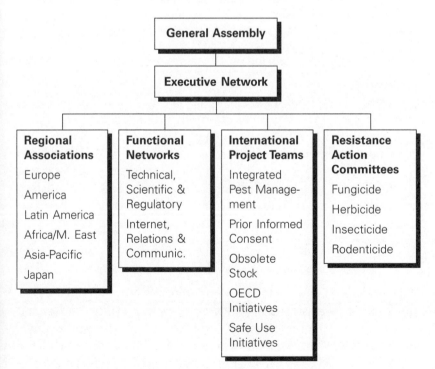

Figure 2.3 *The Organizational Structure of GCPF*

The GCPF is involved in all pesticide issues as the voice of the industry, including regulation setting and research into integrated pest management (IPM), but obviously its chief concern is promoting the positive angle on crop protection and resisting what it feels are excessive regulatory constraints from being placed on the industry by the FAO, European Union, or individual governments. The achievements attained through pesticide use are proudly articulated by the GCPF.

> *In recent years, modern intensive agriculture using manmade CPPs (Crop Protection Products), has achieved the following for mankind:*
>
> ■ *Doubled the production of world food calories since 1960.*
> ■ *Tripled the output of resource intensive foods such as cooking oil, meat and fruit and vegetables.*
> ■ *Increased per capita food supplies in developing countries by 25 per cent . . .*[14]

GIFAP acquired liaison status with the FAO in 1967 and the GCPF upgraded this to special consultative status in 1997. The relationship between the two institutions has always been strong, reaching a high point in the early 1970s, when the Industry Cooperation Programme was set up as a joint bureau organizing seminars in developing countries outlining the importance of chemical technology in furthering development. This programme was short-lived owing to pressure put on the FAO from various non-governmental organizations (NGOs), but the FAO has continued to be criticized for being over receptive to the interests of industrial lobbies.[15] The GCPF has representatives present at most FAO and WHO Expert Committee meetings dealing with pesticides and has observer status on the FAO/WHO Food Standards Programme and its regulatory organ, the Codex Alimentarius Commission.

CONCLUSION

The work of IUPAC, and more importantly GIFAP/GCPF, within the issue of increasing crop yields by pesticides can be understood as amounting to an epistemic community which serves to counter the knowledge based systems promoting a retreat from pesticide usage. The effect of this situation where separate epistemic communities are competing for the high ground in providing knowledge to concerned actors has been to confuse technical areas – a recurrent theme in pesticide politics. List and Rittberger have referred to this as 'scientific politicking',[16] considering it a factor in the failure of regime creation in environmental issues. It seems reasonable to argue that the work of the GCPF in promoting the positive aspects of chemical protection given scant coverage elsewhere, and in countering claims made in opposition to pesticides, has been influential in inhibiting regime development within the issues of human poisoning by pesticides, pesticide pollution and the introduction of IPM.

The issue of obtaining optimal crop yields through pesticides is itself not regulated in any way, as it represents an area of agreement over a prescriptive norm. Regimes usually only serve to prohibit certain practices, and are rarely a feature of issue systems which derive from a norm providing the basis for doing something. Regimes that serve to promote a common good do exist. The World Trade Organization (WTO), for example, basically regulates the issue of promoting free trade in the world economy. However, free trade is a common good that requires promotion because it does not exist, in the fullest sense, in the world economy. Rules and decision making procedures are needed to prevent actors from inhibiting free trade, but they are not needed to induce actors into using pesticides to improve their crop yields. Rules and decision making procedures are required, however, to prohibit or put restrictions upon actors using, producing, or trading pesticides in any way. Activist political actors within issue systems based on prescriptive norms thus will tend to serve a role of advocacy, promoting that norm with the intention of persuading other actors of its saliency to them, in the hope that it will be placed higher on their political agenda of preferences than competing proscriptive norms.

Thus it can be seen that the political role of the actors, within the issue of increasing yields by pesticide use, basically amounts to promoting that norm to a higher position on the agenda of the actors within pesticides politics than is held by the proscriptive norms. This competition for a prime location on the political agenda forms the basis for much of the international politics of pesticides.

3

Fighting Plague and Pestilence – The Role of Pesticides in Controlling Pest Transmitted Diseases

INTRODUCTION

A second prescriptive norm upholding the use of pesticides derives from the value that human suffering should be minimized wherever possible. Human suffering from pest-carried diseases has been, and continues to be, considerable, and the key means of alleviating this suffering has been through the chemical control of the pests. Whilst noting the negative impact that pesticide toxins have had on human health, McEwen and Stephenson conclude that 'their role in improving world health is one of the outstanding chapters of preventive medicine'.[1] A number of fatal diseases have been brought under at least partial control with the aid of chemicals used to eradicate the insect, or other organism, responsible for transmitting them to man.

Malaria

This devastating disease, transmitted by mosquitoes of the *Anopholes* genus, has probably been responsible for more human deaths than any other. Even though instances of it declined this century, it was still claiming around 2.5 million deaths a year in the early 1950s.[2] In response, in 1955 the WHO launched a global eradication programme, the largest of its kind in public health history. The use of DDT around human dwellings in the late 1950s and 1960s rapidly killed all mosquitoes that came into contact with it, and virtually eliminated the disease in all areas in which it was used. An illustration of DDT's success in eliminating malaria comes from comparing the numbers of infections before and after its extensive use in Sardinia, Italy. There were 78,000 cases of malaria on the island in 1942 prior to the use of DDT, compared with only nine in 1951, after several years of treatment with the insecticide.[3]

This success story was echoed throughout the world, although ultimately pesticides have proven not to be the panacea that the WHO and others had anticipated. Mosquito resistance to DDT and other insecticides arose in response to their extensive usage in public health programmes, and also indirectly from their use in agriculture. Resistance to DDT was first recorded in 1946,[4] only seven years after its discovery, and the number of resistant species has risen continually since then.

Added to the problem of resistance were the well documented side-effects of DDT, namely its persistence in the atmosphere, wildlife and human body fat. As a result, DDT use in malaria control has diminished over the years and it is now banned or severely restricted in over 30 countries. The WHO formally abandoned its global eradication programme in 1975 which had been based largely on DDT applications, and the disease has since been partially controlled by a variety of techniques. DDT treatments have continued in a lesser role, other insecticides have been employed, and non-chemical control methods based on destroying mosquito habitats utilized. In general, the value of avoiding human suffering has come to be less clearly satisfiable through the use of pesticides in public heath campaigns, allowing the proscriptive norms associated with pesticide use to become more salient.

Replacement insecticides have not matched the success of DDT in its early years, and malaria has resurged in Africa, South East Asia and South America. In Sri Lanka, where DDT had reduced the annual number of malaria outbreaks to 17 by 1963, its withdrawal prompted a resurgence of the disease to greater levels than ever, reaching an estimated two million cases in 1970.[5] By the 1990s malaria was claiming around 1.5 million lives a year worldwide,[6] with the disease gaining resistance to drugs such as chloroquine and mefloquine, in addition to the *Anopholes* mosquito's resistance to DDT and other insecticides.

A 1992 Malaria Summit in Amsterdam, organized by the WHO and bringing together health ministers from 95 countries, con-centrated on fighting the deepening malaria problem by earlier diagnosis and treatment of the disease. The use of insecticides, and even non-chemical pest control methods such as introducing natural predators to the mosquitoes, or draining the swamplands to destroy their habitats, appear to be near abandonment. Most noticeable was the modest overall aim of the Global Malaria Control Strategy adopted at the summit and reaffirmed in 1995. Global eradication is long gone as an aspiration; the declared goal by the 1990s is 'that by the year 2000 malaria mortality has been reduced by at least 20 per cent compared to 1995 in at least 75 per cent of affected countries'.[7] In this particular battle it would seem that the insect is close to victory and that man is ready to settle for a damage limitation strategy.

Schistosomiasis

After malaria, schistosomiasis is widely believed to be the most significant parasitic disease of humans, affecting between 200 and 250 million people a year in tropical regions.[8] It is caused by flatworms and transmitted to man via aquatic snail larvae in freshwater habitats. Molluscicides are frequently applied to such habitats, particularly niclosamide and copper sulphate. In addition, biological control methods have been adopted, such as introducing fish predators to the snails and releasing benign snails which can compete with the pest snails for food.

Onchocerciasis

This disease, sometimes referred to as river blindness, is caused by nematode worms and transmitted by the *Simulium* black fly. It is endemic in West Africa, where in 1976 the WHO coordinated an international campaign to eradicate it in the Volta Basin region. The disease has not been eradicated, but it has been partially controlled through the use of larvicides such as temophos, and more recently by biological control methods including the use of *Bacillus thuringiensis* bacteria. A global strategy for onchocerciasis control was declared in a resolution of the 47th World Health Assembly in 1994. The strategy upheld the continued use of larvicides but in con-junction with the early administering of a successful drug, *ivermectin*, to limit transmission of the disease.[9]

Filariasis

Like onchocerciasis, this disease is caused by nematode worms, and in 1992 was estimated to have infected some 78 million people worldwide.[10] Filariasis can be passed on to man either by *Simulium* black flies or mosquitoes and can lead to elephantiasis. Diethyl-carbamazine applications have often been used for controlling the carrying genus of mosquitoes, but current research centres on the use of the biopesticide *Bacillus sphaericus* to eradicate the parasitic worms.

Dengue

Dengue fever and the related dengue haemorrhagic fever are also mosquito-borne diseases. DDT applications around human dwellings and the destruction of mosquito habitats are techniques which have been employed to control the disease.

Trypanosomiasis

Also known as sleeping sickness, trypanosomiasis has long been endemic to tropical parts of Africa and is caused by a protozoan parasite transmitted to man or cattle by tsetse fly bites. The disease continues to infect sporadically, but has been kept at low levels partly through the use of endosulfan sprays and the removal of vegetation forming the flies' habitats by herbicides. The use of dieldrin to try to eradicate the flies has diminished, owing to resistance and revelations of its effects on human health. As a result, the use of traps incorporating other insecticides has become an increasingly popular method of control.[11]

Leishmaniasis

Around two million infections a year caused by the Leishman protozoa can occur in man through transmission by sandflies. Infections come in a variety of forms and can occur through sandfly bites, or indirectly via dogs and rodents. Sandflies can be repelled indoors with conventional sprays, whilst wider control with larvicides and the destruction of breeding grounds have also been employed. Since 1990 the WHO Expert Committee on Leishmaniasis have been implementing a global strategy maintaining insecticide use but curbing household sprayings in favour of more subtle applications such as impregnating bednets with the chemicals. To a large extent control of the disease can be achieved by improving sanitary standards and employing preventative measures such as the blood testing of local dogs and this is a strong theme of the strategy.[12]

Lice-borne Typhus

Typhus of the form transmitted by body lice is generally avoided by observing basic sanitary standards and as such has disappeared apart from some areas of North East Africa and the Middle East. Pesticides have proved effective for louse control on occasions, however, as evidenced by the use of DDT powder by Allied troops in Naples during the 1943 invasion of Italy.

Plague

Although this historically destructive disease, which is transmitted by oriental rat fleas, has not reached epidemic levels since the 1920s, it is still known to reoccur periodically in South East Asia. It has been restricted to low levels, however, and its spread has been halted through the use of rodenticides and insecticides on board ships and at their ports.

Other Uses of Pesticides in Public Health

Other vector-borne diseases which have prompted the use of pesticides for their control include: Japanese encephalitis, an inflammation of the brain transmitted by mosquitoes, and Chaga's disease (American trypanosomiaisis) caused by Cone-nose bugs.

In addition to the control of such diseases, pesticides have also contributed to improving general aspects of modern domestic life. Bactericides keep homes cleaner, particularly in the kitchen, whilst insecticides reduce the possibility of infection via house flies and cockroaches. Pesticides also contribute to the control of what is termed 'biodeterioration', a collective term for a variety of harmful effects caused by pests to human artefacts. Examples of this include the gnawing of electric cables by rodents, the clogging of ship engines by seaweed, and the presence of fungi in textiles or paintings.

Problems Associated with Pesticides Used in Public Health Programmes

The side-effects of DDT use are well documented. The stability of the chemical was part of its original attraction, but ultimately it has proved to be its Achilles' heel. The persistence of DDT in the atmosphere and in animal tissue has created sufficient alarm in the last 30 years for it to be gradually phased out of use in many public health programmes. Though the impact of DDT on human health remains subject to dispute, its effects on wildlife have been significant (see Chapter 5). In addition, resistance to DDT has reached such levels that its use in some spheres of public health is now impractical even before environmental costs are considered. In many instances, resistance to DDT or other insecticides such as dieldrin or malathion has resulted from the overuse of these chemicals agriculturally, making the problem even more difficult to contain.

Aside from the use of DDT, the use of pesticides in areas of public health has been widely accepted as necessary and generally less controversial than their use in agriculture. David Bull of Oxfam maintains this in his book, *A Growing Problem*. 'There is no question of advocating the complete withdrawal of pesticides from public health use.'[13]

Bull does, however, qualify the acceptance of using pesticides in this way in the light of the associated problems of human poisoning, environmental pollution and pest resistance. His conclusion is that a policy of combining non-chemical control with pesticide use, known as 'integrated vector control', should be adopted in public health programmes.[14] This principle of keeping pesticide use at a necessary minimum mirrors the theory of integrated pest management in agriculture, which has already been touched upon and constitutes another issue of pesticide politics, considered in Chapter 8. The case of malaria, however, in which we have seen that the *Anopholes* mosquitoes appear to be beyond any form of chemical control, represents a further erosion of the once near universal acceptance of pesticide use in public health operations.

THE POLITICS OF USING PESTICIDES IN PUBLIC HEALTH PROGRAMMES

We have seen that the norm stating that the damage and disease caused to man by other pest organisms should be restricted is very widely accepted in human society and has provided a powerful prescriptive force for the use of pesticides in this context. Acceptance of the importance of pesticides in attempting to satisfy this norm has, in general, been wider than for their role in increasing crop yields, the other norm underpinning pesticide use and production. The stark reality of mass human suffering and death in the face of diseases such as malaria, has provided political actors with a less problematic choice between the prescriptive and proscriptive norms of pesticide use than the one they encounter when making decisions on whether or not they should be used for increasing crop yields.

This fact is evidenced by government decisions given under the 'prior informed consent' rule, whereby they are required to indicate whether they wish to permit the future import of particular pesticides (see Chapter 7 for a full elaboration). A number of governments have given consent to the future importing of aldrin, dieldrin and DDT, but for public health operations only. The governments of Ethiopia, Malaysia, Sudan, Tanzania and Zimbabwe have prohibited the use of the three insecticides for agricultural use, but have reserved the right to import them for assisting in any present or future campaigns to control pest-transmitted tropical diseases.[15]

In addition to this, the examples of successful integrated pest management schemes utilizing fewer chemicals (see Chapter 8) have tended to weaken the validity of the basic principle that pesticides increase crop yields. This is a situation that, until recently, had not been arrived at for the use of pesticides in public health programmes. Bull referred to the need for the employment of non-chemical controls to be increased in public health,[16] but, until recently, no commentator or actor of note had ever advocated the wholesale phasing out of chemical methods of pest control in health programmes, as they had for the purpose of optimizing crop yields.

Recently, however, the principle that pesticides help prevent the transmission of vector-borne diseases has come to be seen as questionable, chiefly in the light of extensive insect resistance. Thus, the issue system has begun to be subject to far more contention amongst its constituent actors than has ever been the case before. In general, however, the global politics of pesticide use in public health programmes is dominated by the non-controversial decision making of an epistemic community centred on various WHO expert groups.

WHO Expert Committee on Vector Biology and Control

The principal global actor within the issue system of vector-borne disease control is the WHO Expert Committee on Vector Biology and Control. This is basically an academic gathering which serves as a focal point for the epistemic community working on this issue. The committee usually meets once a year in Geneva, and produces technical advice papers on particular areas of vector biology, which are then made available through the WHO Technical Report Series.

The committee came into being when it replaced the WHO Expert Committee on Insecticides (founded in 1949) in 1976. It regularly includes leading academics in the field of pesticides, such as Dr Copplestone and Professor Jeyaratnam, and also invites relevant representatives from the United Nations Environment

Programme (UNEP), FAO, the International Labour Organization (ILO) and GCPF, along with three or four secretariat officials.

The members of this and all other WHO expert committees are drawn from a panel of experts set up by the Director-General (head of the secretariat) after consulting the national delegates. The panel in this case is the Division of Vector Biology and Control which also provides the personnel for a number of the other expert committees dealing with the control of individual diseases. The Director-General is not involved in the actual selection of experts for a committee, but he/she encourages the committee to involve as wide a range of nationalities as is possible.

The technical reports which derive from the meetings are intended to contain independent opinions, and conclude with lists of recommendations for general governmental actions and for WHO action. The 1990 meeting, for example, responded to requests from WHO member state delegates for information concerning the domestic use of pesticides. The committee drew up a list of recommendations for ensuring the safety of domestic pesticides, which it proposed the WHO should incorporate into the pesticide evaluation scheme (WHOPES). It also called upon the WHO to make the provisions known to the FAO when preparing guidelines for national registration schemes.[17] The committee has continually maintained the importance of pesticides in meeting their aims.

> *The Expert Committee on Vector Biology and Control has always realized that the achievement of its principal objective – the control of vector-borne diseases – depends to a large extent on the use of pesticides.*[18]

The problem of insect resistance to many pesticides used in public health operations did, however, in the 1980s lead to the expert committee discussing aspects of integrated vector control and promoting the use of some biological control methods. A 1982 meeting of the expert committee began reviewing the question of the biological control of vectors,[19] and at the 1985 meeting[20] it for the first time considered the safety aspects of introducing the genetically manipulated organisms (GMOs) *Bacillus thuringiensis* and *Bacillus sphaericus* into operational use. The use of other GMOs for biological vector control has been researched but, as yet, only the aforementioned two bacteria strains have been adopted for WHO backed programmes. Despite advances in research into the use of GMOs, the expert committee maintains that pesticides remain the principal weapon in the fight against insect transmitted diseases:

'Chemical pesticides will continue to play a dominant role in disease vector control in the foreseeable future.'[21]

Other WHO Expert Committees

Other forums for research and debate within the WHO structure have had an input into the issue system of the chemical control of vector-borne diseases. An expert committee exists for most of the diseases reviewed earlier in this section, and the use of insecticides obviously features prominently on their agendas when discussing recommendations to make to governments and WHO public health programmes. There are WHO expert committees on: malaria, schistosomiasis, filariasis, onchocerciasis, trypanosomiasis, and leishmaniasis, which serve to collate recent advances in understanding and controlling the diseases.

The recommendations of such committees become WHO policy if approved by the World Health Assembly, the annual gathering of all member state delegations. The implementation of policy is carried out by the Executive Board, a 31-person body of experts (not delegates) elected by the Health Assembly. The Director-General (who is appointed by the Health Assembly on the nomination of the Executive Board) is required to be present at all Executive Board meetings to report how far the recommendations of the various expert committees have been acted upon.[22]

WHOPES

The WHO Pesticide Evaluation Scheme provides an international system for testing and evaluating pesticides intended for public health use. WHOPES in 1982 took over this role from the WHO Pesticide Evaluation Programme, which had screened over 2000 chemicals since its inception in 1960.[23] The scheme consists of a network of laboratories in WHO collaborating centres, universities, and industrial premises throughout the world, which test various formulations that are then passed on for further assessment by WHO staff in field studies, carried out in conjunction with national authorities. Finally, specifications for chemicals which have gone through the evaluation scheme are produced to accompany the pesticides when sold, and are published in a periodically updated manual. [24]

Other Organizations Involved in the Politics of Pesticide Use in Public Health Programmes

Whereas the expertise of the WHO in public health matters is generally accepted by international organizations, other global actors also play a part in the issue-system. The funding of WHO directed programmes, for instance, can come from diverse sources. The Onchocerciasis Control Programme, for example, is sponsored by the FAO, United Nations Development Programme and the World Bank, in addition to the WHO. The WHO staff on this programme, including entomologists and epidemiologists, are recognized as having the chief executive responsibility in overseeing operations, but the World Bank manages the finances and directs the distribution of resources to areas affected by the disease.[25]

In addition, the WHO has increasingly drawn on the expertise of scientific groups specializing in bio-pesticides, strains of bacteria able to eliminate disease-carrying pests, as part of their control programmes. The French Scientific Research Institute for Development and Cooperation has worked under the WHO's Tropical Disease Research Programme in the use of *Bacillus sphaericus* in eradicating mosquitoes carrying filariasis in Cameroon.[26]

CONCLUSION

An epistemic consensus on the importance of utilizing chemical methods of pest control in the fight against pest-transmitted diseases has for many years allowed WHO bodies to recommend and sponsor public health operations using pesticides that are restricted in agricultural use. However, this strong consensus of opinion has begun to erode. The reason for this is not the result of a gradual raising of the proscriptive norms of pesticide use on the agendas of salient actors, as is the case for pesticide use in agriculture, but rather it is due to a change in circumstances which has weakened the validity of the principle that pesticides help prevent the transmission of vector-borne diseases. Any cost-benefit analysis applied by an actor when deciding on the need to use pesticides in the face of malaria and other destructive diseases used to weigh very heavily to the benefit side, but with the emergence of greater levels of insect resistance the balance has become less asymmetrical.

Pesticides widely considered too hazardous for use in agriculture are still often used for public health programmes, but this practice has recently been less free from criticism than was previously the case. The WHO had begun to meet opposition for its continued reliance on the older, organochlorine insecticides such as DDT,[27] partly prompting the virtual abandonment of pesticide use in malaria control announced at the 1992 Amsterdam summit. The epistemic community directing global public health campaigns still very much remains centred on the WHO and its various committees of experts, but the anti-pesticide lobby and proponents of biological pest control have started to have a greater impact on the political process.

4

The Killing Fields – The Issue of Human Poisoning by Pesticides

THE EXTENT OF THE PROBLEM

Chemical pesticides are by their very nature poisonous. The toxicity of such substances can never be applicable only to the targeted pest, so the fact that they need to be applied with care to avoid human poisoning is a norm of their use.

A precise understanding of how widespread human poisoning from pesticides is globally has never been possible, because of a lack of conclusive information on the issue in many countries. The inevitable result of this lack of hard facts is a tendency for the basic pro and anti-pesticides camps to swing to extremes, and make exaggerated estimates based on assumptions favourable to their own causes. In 1972 a WHO Expert Committee estimated that around 500,000 people a year are poisoned by pesticides, of which some 5,000 are killed.[1] In 1977 Copplestone, a regular member of WHO pesticide expert committees, made a more detailed survey of fatalities and estimated that the figure was nearer 20,640 a year.[2] A 1985 WHO study confirmed an annual death toll of around 20,000 whilst also claiming that the total number of unintentional poisonings was around 1,000,000 annually.[3]

These startling statistics are dismissed by the agrochemicals industry as scaremongering by the anti-pesticides lobby. The WHO figures are certainly open to question in terms of the size of the samples from which they are derived. The 500,000 poisonings estimate of 1972 was based on a survey of only 19 countries, whilst the supposedly more precise estimation of fatalities in 1977 was actually only deduced from the findings of a nine country survey and some governmental notifications. Full records of poisonings do not exist in most countries, and the WHO made some questionable generalizations in their figures, such as including deaths by chemicals not intended for pesticidal use and considering the most minor forms of skin irritation as a case of pesticide poisoning. The British Agrochemicals Association claim that there has been 'no fatal accident from a pesticide in normal use since 1974'[4] on a UK farm, and that domestic accidents involving pesticides and requiring medical attention are rarer than those involving either deck chairs or plant pots. Professor Kenneth Mellanby is amongst those who feel that the scale of human poisoning from pesticides is far less dramatic than claimed by the WHO, Oxfam, and others. In a letter to the *New Scientist* Mellanby stated that, 'the number of deaths from pesticide poisoning in 1977 and 1978 was probably measured in the hundreds and not hundreds of thousands.'[5]

This counter estimate of pesticide related deaths has in turn been criticized for being far too conservative. It is widely held that large numbers of poisonings go unreported in developing countries because workers fear it may cost them their jobs, and also because they do not associate such illnesses with their work. Added to this is the problem of actually proving a link between an agricultural worker's illness or death and his/her exposure to pesticides. The death of a man by cancer may be the long-term effect of having worked with carcinogenic sprays a number of years ago, but this is basically impossible to prove conclusively. Nicholas Hildyard is of the view that many instances of poisoning go unrecorded, even when they are reported by victims, because of the inexperience of medical staff in developing countries, who do not connect symptoms such as headaches and drowsiness with exposure to pesticides.[6] Emerging evidence that DDT and other organochlorine pesticides can be transported to a foetus via the placenta or later to the baby through the mother's milk, further bears out the fact that the extent of pesticide poisoning is an extremely difficult thing to monitor accurately.

One rare attempt to study systematically the nature and extent of pesticide poisoning in a developing country was carried out by Jeyaratnam, de Alwis, and Copplestone in Sri Lanka between 1975 and 1980.[7] The study showed that approximately 13,000 people were admitted to government hospitals for acute pesticide poisoning a year, of which around 1000 died. This would seem to suggest that Mellanby's estimation of world pesticide poisoning was indeed conservative, but the survey also revealed that only a small fraction of the Sri Lankan deaths were the result of the accidental ingestion of the chemicals. Some 73.1 per cent of the patients were admitted after having attempted to commit suicide with the aid of pesticides.

A distinction thus needs to be made between intentional and unintentional exposure to pesticides, to appreciate properly the norm that precautions should be taken to prevent poisonings.

TYPES OF POISONING

Intentional Exposure

Other surveys of pesticide poisonings back up the findings in Sri Lanka that the majority of cases are not accidental. A survey led by Jeyaratnam in 1987 found that Indonesia, Malaysia, and Thailand all had suicide levels at between 60 and 70 per cent of the total cases of poisoning.[8] The WHO has suggested a figure of two million suicide attempts annually, of which 200,000 are successful, based on Jeyaratnam's work,[9] but this clearly is highly hypothetical. It is likely, however, that the frequency of this varies widely from country to country, according to cultural attitudes to suicide, and the general availability of the particularly lethal pesticides. In Malaysia, for instance, over 80 per cent of the suicide attempts using the herbicide paraquat were made by Hindus, in contrast to only 5 per cent by Malay Muslims. Islam officially forbids suicide and Indians make up the bulk of workers on plantations using paraquat.[10] The Pesticides Board of Malaysia were so alarmed by this phenomenon that they made the addition of a foul smelling agent to paraquat compulsory, to try and deter its ingestion for suicide. The reduced availability of pesticides like paraquat to the general public in developing countries would doubtless help reduce cases of their deliberate ingestion, but this kind of precaution does not equate with the norm we are considering here, namely that people should not be innocently poisoned through the use of pesticides.

Unintentional Exposure

Accidental poisoning from pesticides can occur in a number of ways. Indirect poisoning via contaminated food and water is considered later as a separate issue, the focus here being on direct, accidental poisonings resulting from pesticide misuse.

Occupational Exposure to Pesticides
The principal victims of accidental pesticide poisoning are, predictably, the agricultural and public health workers involved in

their application. Instances of this are highest in the developing world, where workers are often ignorant of the hazardous nature of their work, and management are often negligent in safeguarding the health of their employees. Many accounts from developing countries reveal cases of workers not being provided with protective clothing or washing facilities, whilst working with highly toxic chemicals.

Jeyaratnam's survey of pesticide poisoning in Sri Lanka which, as mentioned earlier, revealed that 73 per cent of all hospitalized cases were deliberate suicide attempts, also indicated that 69 per cent of the remaining poisoning cases were of an occupational nature.[11] Copplestone considers this figure to be in line with the global pattern: 'occupational exposure usually accounts for 60–70 per cent of all accidental poisonings'.[12] Included in this category of exposure are instances of workers being contaminated whilst mixing or spraying the chemicals, those entering fields after spraying, and those working in the formulation of pesticides.

Cases of occupational exposure in developing countries are not always well documented, but it is known that 2800 workers spraying malathion were poisoned during a malaria control programme in Pakistan in 1976.[13] In this case inadequate safety measures were the primary cause of the poisoning (malathion is a relatively safe insecticide). In other cases this problem is exacerbated by the fact that the pesticides used are the particularly toxic chemicals outlawed or restricted in most developed countries. In addition to all of this, it should be appreciated that the susceptibility of developing country workers to pesticide exposure is often higher than their developed world counterparts, owing to the higher temperatures in which they work, and the higher levels of malnutrition and disease to which they are prone. It is widely accepted that occupational poisoning by pesticides can be greatly diminished once the trading of particularly hazardous chemicals is brought under control, and worker safety standards in the developing countries are implemented at levels similar to those in the developed world.

In countries with reliable statistics it is evident that injuries to workers caused by pesticides are uncommon compared with those caused by working on farms with machinery or injuries caused by falls, lifting excessive weights or manual cultivation.[14]

Long-Term Health Effects. Whilst acute[15] pesticide poisoning is largely prevented in the developed world, concern remains over the possible long-term health effects of prolonged exposure to pesticides by workers. Central to this concern are the possible cancer risks involved in exposure to particular chemicals. Many pesticides have proven carcinogenic in animal testing, and this has fuelled enough fear for some governments to restrict or ban chemicals principally on these grounds. The value of this form of testing, however, is questioned by many scientists.

> *We can observe and measure an increased incidence of liver tumours in a population of laboratory rats, exposed to 500 parts per million of a given pesticide in its food for a lifetime, but how do we use this information to assess the risk of cancer in humans exposed intermittently to 0.01 parts per million of the same pesticide in their drinking water?*[16]

Whilst it does appear that the actual hazard posed by pesticides classified as carcinogenic to people working with them is far less straightforward than might at first be imagined, studies have shown higher cancer levels amongst such people. A link between occupational exposure to arsenical pesticides and lung cancer is convincingly shown in a study by Mabuchi, Lillenfield and Snell.[17] This sort of evidence also needs to be qualified, however.

> *Epidemiological studies of pesticides for cancer risks are complicated by shortcomings in human exposure data, the multiplicity of pesticide exposures, changes in pesticide-use patterns, a rapid turnover of employees, and the latency of cancer.*[18]

There is a case to be made for pesticides as a causal factor in cancer outbreaks, but as with many suspected causes of cancer, the case remains not proven. A major breakthrough for victims claiming compensation for cancer came in July 1992, however, when a UK out of court settlement awarded Mr George Yates £90,000 after a number of doctors backed his claim that he had contracted soft tissue sarcoma after being exposed to dioxins whilst applying wood preservatives for ten years without sufficient protective clothing.[19]

Aside from their potential carcinogenicity, the other long-term health fears associated with pesticides derive from the persistence of the organochlorine chemicals. Chemicals like DDT and dieldrin are known to possess lipophilic characteristics, meaning that they dissolve in fat more readily than water, and as such they are prone to be stored as residues in human tissue. The presence of these residues has been linked to a variety of health disorders. 57 cases of neurological disease are known to have resulted from exposure to the insecticide chlordecone by manufacturing workers in Virginia,

US, in 1975, and the symptoms persisted for over four years in some cases.[20] Other ailments which have been associated with organo-chlorine deposits in body fat include immune system disorders and reproductive effects, but the evidence is generally not conclusive.[21]

The restrictions on the use of organochlorines in many countries, have not eliminated concern over long-term occupational exposure to pesticide chemicals. Organophosphate (OP) pesticides basically replaced organochlorines in sheep dips in the UK during the 1980s as a result of worries over the persistence of organochlorines, but instances of 'dipping flu' have become more common than ever. Farmers have long been known to suffer nausea and headaches after treating sheep, a practice which was legally binding until 1992. Trades unions led by the National Farmers Union (NFU) and Unison, the public service union, have made headway in the UK in gaining recognition of the problem and in securing compensation for victims. The appropriately named Robert Shepherd, who worked for the Lancashire College of Agriculture, received £80,000 in an out of court settlement in 1998 after having to give up his job due to chronic tiredness believed to be linked to dipping sheep twice a year in OP pesticides.[22]

Collateral Poisoning by Pesticides

Pesticides applied conventionally on crops may occasionally affect people other than those employed in their application. The main way in which this can occur is as a result of the drifting of chemicals sprayed on agricultural land, over residential areas. The two principal ways in which the general public has been exposed to pesticides in this manner are by the drift of chemicals used in aerial spraying, and by the drift of vapour following the evaporation of chemicals after application.

The latter form of pesticide drifting was responsible for an outbreak of skin rashes, inflamed eyes, and wheezy chests in the village of Stretton on the Fosse in Warwickshire in 1982. A volatile herbicide used on a nearby farm evaporated in a spell of warm weather, several days after application, and settled as a gas cloud over the hollow in which the village is located.[23]

The spraying of residents with pesticides despatched aerially is a commonly recorded complaint in rural Britain,[24] and has led to calls for a complete ban on this method of application. Considering that aerial spraying only accounts for around 2.3 per cent of all pesticide applications in the UK, this would seem to suggest that poisonings resulting from this practice are liable to be far more significant in developing countries, where aerial spraying is more common and generally less subject to regulation. As is the case with many aspects of the health impact of pesticides, the scale of this problem is impossible to fathom owing to the difficulty of matching conclusively symptoms of poisoning with their causal factors. This is especially so if the effects are long-term. In addition there is a lack of data in the places where the problem is likely to be greatest, the developing world.

A landmark legal case in 1997, however, appears to have transformed the legal position of people suffering from pesticide exposure of this form, at least in the developed world. A July 31st verdict of the Hong Kong High Court ordered the Swiss based multinational corporation Ciba Geigy to pay Kristan Phillips, an American musician, the equivalent of £1.9 million in compensation for illness suffered after being contaminated by the organophosphate diazinon in a Hong Kong concert hall in 1987. Phillips was forced to abandon a career as a timpanist with the Hong Kong Philharmonic Orchestra after suffering chronic exposure to the insecticide which was being sprayed on walls of the building during a rehearsal. The key witness at the trial was a British doctor, Goral Jamal, whose testimony on the various effects of organophosphate poisoning, particularly in retarding the nervous system, was accepted by the court and could open the door to claims for compensation against agrochemical producers throughout the world. The case was particularly pertinent because diazinon was at the time being cited as a potential cause of illnesses suffered by Gulf War veterans in the US and UK in long running legal battles.[25]

Poisoning by Domestically Used Pesticides
As was mentioned earlier, the BAA has defended the safety record of its members' products used in the garden, by pointing out that fewer accidents requiring attention were attributable to pesticide chemicals than to either deckchairs or plant pots. This convincing defence of the use of weedkillers, slug-pellets and the like is challenged, however, by the Pesticides Trust and others on the grounds that accidents known to result from pesticides are but the tip of the iceberg. This 'iceberg', they propose, is predominantly composed of long-term ailments of the forms already mentioned, which can not decisively be attributed to the victims' contact with a pesticide at some stage of their life.

Despite the growing popularity of organic gardening in Europe and North America, it is pertinent to remember that the household garden is by far the largest proportional recipient of pesticide chemicals. Dudley estimates that 'about a kilo of pesticide active ingredient is applied to every acre of British garden, every year'.[26] The National Academy of Sciences in the US has shown that four to eight times as much pesticide per acre is applied by homeowners as by farmers, and that this disparity is on the increase.[27] The very fact that such a density of toxic chemicals can be found in places where families live, and in particular where children play, has widened the range of the concerns over the long-term health effects, from workers using pesticides to the whole population. Some parts of Florida, Pennsylvania, and Illinois already have by-laws requiring residents to notify neighbours before using chemical sprays on lawns or trees, and moves have been made in Congress to develop Federal legislation along these lines.[28]

The representatives of the pesticide industry respond to such public concern by reminding critics that products sold over the counter in garden centres are much diluted versions of those sprayed over farm land. Since those chemicals used in agriculture are subject to rigorous testing in the industrialized world, it does seem fair to conclude that the general public need not be too alarmed about the toxicity of garden products, so long as they are used according to instructions and stored away from the reach of children.

An area of real concern over the question of garden pesticide use must still remain, however, with the alleged existence of a black market in chemicals conducted through horticultural societies. *Garden News* reported on a garden society that had a £10,000 a year turnover on pesticides such as aldicarb, which is subject to rigid safety instructions when used agriculturally and classified 'moderately hazardous' (see page 56) on the WHO Classification by Hazard scheme.[29] The potential existence of such trading merely serves to add further mist to the already murky area of pesticide poisoning.

Much evidence in recent years suggests that the main focus of concern over domestically used pesticides should not be in the garden at all, but rather in the family home. The possible health effects of various wood preservatives, used to prevent woodworm damage, have come to the fore in recent years. The British law firm Leigh, Day and Co are known to have won settlements in around 60 cases for employees of firms specializing in timber treatments. Details of such settlements have been kept confidential, but one worker is known to have died of leukaemia, whilst others have suffered from a number of ailments ranging from wide-scale paralysis and blood disorders to milder flu-like symptoms.[30] The chemicals cited as responsible for causing such disablements are tributylin oxide (TBTO), pentachlorophenol (PCP), and lindane. These same chemicals have been used in wood preservatives intended for domestic use, and in 1991 the first UK householders began suing preservative manufacturers for poisoning. TBTO and PCP have ceased to be used in the UK for wood preserving products owing, respectively, to domestic legislation and an EC directive, but lindane continues to be licensed for use in the UK. A UK government enquiry, carried out by the Advisory Committee on Pesticides, could find no link between lindane and aplastic anaemia, as had been alleged by Leigh, Day and Co on behalf of a Mr William Gaskill.[31] In Germany, prosecutors have sued a wood preservative firm for chemical negligence on behalf of 50 people, who are amongst an estimated 200,000 sufferers from diseases linked to lindane, TBTO and PCP. The chief dilemma in these cases, as in all instances of pesticide poisoning, is actually proving the culpability of the chemicals for the disease above any other potential explanations.

Poisoning due to Industrial Accidents
Accidental poisoning during the production and transport of pesticides can, of course, affect the health of the general public, in addition to those employed in the industry. This was made most dramatically evident at Bhopal, India, in December 1984 when a gas leak at a plant formulating a chemical for use as a pesticide caused the world's worst ever industrial accident.

The disaster at the Union Carbide plant in Bhopal does appear to have been the culmination of circumstances close to any worst case scenario imaginable for a chemical production site. The plant's end product, the carbamate Carbaryl, also known as Sevin, is not particularly hazardous (category II of the WHO Classification by Hazard), but the chemical methylisocyanate (MIC) which is used in its production is extremely toxic. As an intermediate chemical, however, MIC did not feature on the WHO Classification by Hazard and even failed to appear on UNEP's International Register of Potentially Toxic Chemicals. Indian authorities thus were completely unaware that the chemical was being stored.

On top of the fact that no one was really aware of the nature of a chemical used at the plant, it has since emerged that safety standards were also poor. One worker had been killed and three others injured by exposure to phosgene, another chemical used in the processing of MIC, in 1981 during Bhopal's first year as a manufacturing unit. (NB: phosgene was one of the chemicals used on the battlefields during the First World War). In the following year a visiting safety team from Union Carbide's headquarters in the US described the plant's MIC unit in an internal report as possessing 'serious potential for sizeable releases of toxic materials'.[32] Such concerns were echoed in the Indian press in a series of reports by local journalist Raj Kumar Keswani, culminating in an article for the Hindu periodical *Jansata* just six months prior to the accident. Investigations into the accident later found numerous examples of negligence which aided the tragic gas leak. A refrigeration unit used to maintain MIC at a lower and more stable temperature had been switched off to save money, while temperature and pressure gauges were routinely ignored by workers because of their unreliability. When a leak was reported by workers, it is believed that a supervisor told them it would be dealt with after a tea break, in an hour's time. There was no return to work after that tea break, however.[33]

Added to the ignorance as to the nature of MIC and the negligence over safety precautions at the plant, is a third factor accentuating the Bhopal tragedy. Bhopal is a poor city and many thousands of people lived in crowded slums near to the Union Carbide plant. These people were powerless to protect themselves from the escaping fumes which spread over the ground (MIC is heavier than air). David Weir has pieced together eye-witness reports of the Bhopal tragedy to come up with a dramatic account of the night of December 2nd 1984.

> *Hundreds of thousands of residents were roused from their sleep, coughing and vomiting and wheezing. Their eyes burned and watered, many would be at least temporarily blinded. Most of those fortunate enough to have lived on upper floors or inside well sealed buildings were spared. The rest, however, opened their doors onto the largest unplanned human exodus of the industrial age. Those able to board a bicycle, moped, bullock, car, bus, or vehicle of any kind did. But for most of the poor, their feet were the only form of transport available. Many dropped along the way, gasping for breath, choking on their own vomit and finally drowning in their own fluids. Families were separated; whole groups were wiped out at a time. Those strong enough to keep going ran 3,6 to 12 miles before they stopped. Most ran until they dropped.[34]*

Estimates of the numbers of casualties vary, but it is believed that 200,000 people were exposed to the gas and 17,000 permanently disabled as a result. The immediate death toll could have been anywhere between 2000 and 8000, as most of the victims were not formally recorded in any way, and the killing of entire families hindered any identification process. Long-term health effects include various breathing and digesting disorders along with birth defects and spontaneous abortions. After years of legal wrangling, Union Carbide US and their Indian subsidiaries were finally made liable for prosecution in 1991, opening up the way for compensation payments to 500,000 people and for the setting up of a hospital in the city to deal with ongoing ailments.

Bhopal – Titanic or Iceberg? The Bhopal disaster, as we have seen, was a consequence of a set of particularly dire circumstances. As such it has been evaluated by many within the chemical industry as a fluke, a one-off disaster unlikely to occur again. A speaker at the *Chemistry After Bhopal* conference in London in 1986 compared the disaster to the sinking of the *Titanic*, an undoubted tragedy but not justifying the abandonment of sea travel.[35] Many sceptics of pesticide production safety, however, turn the *Titanic* analogy on its head, as they believe Bhopal, rather, represents the tip of an iceberg, with a vast number of smaller accidents lying submerged from public and political view. Weir, in his book *The Bhopal Syndrome*, argues that the tragedy is continually repeated in 'mini-Bhopals' and 'slow motion Bhopals',[36] in which unseen poisoning occurs. The determination to learn the lessons of the Bhopal tragedy led to the establishment of a No More Bhopals network at a 1985 Nairobi conference on development. The network is organized by the Environmental Liaison Centre and the International Coalition for Development Action.

Whilst it is fair to consider Bhopal as a one-off accident in terms of its scale, many examples of 'mini' and 'slow motion Bhopals' can be found. In 1976 over 500 kilogrammes of toxic vapour were released after an explosion at a chemical plant in Seveso, Northern Italy, after a build up of pressure. Trichlorophenol and 2,3,7,8-tetrachlorodibenzo-p-dioxin (dioxin TCDD), a constituent of the infamous Agent Orange, pumped out to form a large cloud around the plant, although no acknowledgement of this was made to nearby villages for four days. Within three weeks pets and crops had died, 30 people were hospitalized with burns or liver pains, and one person had died. The principal health impacts at Seveso were long-term, however, owing to the highly teratogenic nature of the released gases. Accurate medical records were not kept in the aftermath of the disaster, but a Dr Alberto Columbi conducted research revealing that even by 1978 birth defects were at a rate of 53 per 1000 in the areas around Seveso, compared to an average of below 5 per 10000 in the Lombardy region as a whole.[37] The Catholic Church became involved in the issue, when some women contaminated by the poison flouted Italian law and had abortions performed.

The fact that tragedies can occur outside the glare of the sort of media interest shown at Bhopal is seen in the case of the PT Montrose DDT plant at Cicadas, Java. Suspicions that the plant had been secretly burning off waste at night were confirmed by an investigation, conducted by WALHI (Indonesian Environmental Forum) and KRAPP (Indonesian Network Against the Misuse of Pesticides), in 1985. It emerged that, over time, 25 villagers had been killed as a result of this action.[38]

Man as the Pest – The Military Application of Herbicides

A further means by which people have been poisoned by pesticides is as a result of their use by wartime enemies as defoliants. Investigations into the potential military applications of herbicides began in the USA in 1941, although stocks of 2,4,5-T and 2,4-D earmarked for use against the Japanese were never used during the Second World War. Prior to the Battle of Britain success, the Royal Air Force had a plan to utilize De Havilland Tiger Moth aeroplanes unsuited to air combat to drop quantities of the old, presynthetic insecticide *Paris Green* on invading German troops.

The British were the first to actually undertake such a strategy in wartime in the early 1950s during the Malayan emergency, when 2,4,5-T and 2,4-D were used to clear lines of communication and wipe out food crops in the struggle against the communist uprising.[39] ICI provided the technical advice for the UK and Malayan governments, and in 1952 fire engines spraying sodium trichloroacetate (STCA) and Trioxane, mixtures of the aforementioned herbicides, were sent along a number of key roads. After seven months, however, studies suggested that it was more effective, both economically and practically, to remove vegetation by hand and the spraying was stopped. In 1953 the use of herbicides as an aid to fighting the guerillas was restarted, as a means of destroying food crops grown by the communist forces in jungle clearings. Helicopters despatched STCA and Trioxane, along with pellets of chlorophenyl n' n' dimenthyl urea onto crops such as sweet potatoes and maize.[40] Studies which highlighted the environmental and health damage resulting from similar spraying operations ten years later in Vietnam have never taken place in Malaya.

The use of herbicides was far more widespread in Vietnam, with an estimated 17 million gallons of 2,4,5-T, 2,4-D, picloram, and cacodylate sprayed, in a variety of mixtures, on jungle foliage and enemy crops by the US Air Force between 1962 and 1971. American scientists have estimated that 10 per cent of Vietnam's inland forests, 36 per cent of mangrove forests, and 3 per cent of cultivated land have been affected by the programme codenamed Operation Ranch Hand.[41] This scale of ecological disruption indirectly affected the health of the Vietnamese populus by reducing the quality of their nutritional intake and creating refugees who were susceptible to disease, but most dramatic were the alleged cases of direct toxification by herbicides.

Dioxin, which arises as a contaminant in the manufacture of 2,4,5-T, is known to be extremely toxic to humans. An estimated 170 kilograms of this poison was sprayed over Vietnam and the neighbouring countries of Laos and Cambodia, amidst the applications of Agent Orange.[42] Dioxin, as has already been shown in the Seveso disaster, is believed to be teratogenic, hepatoxic, mutagenic, carcinogenic, a skin irritant, and responsible for increasing cholesterol levels in blood. Many studies have linked instances of such symptoms amongst South Vietnamese residents and their offspring with the Agent Orange sprayings between 1962 and 1971. However, as is in the nature of toxicology, and particularly carcinogenicity and teratogenicity, proving what are the causal factors is extremely difficult, if not impossible. Numerous instances have come to light of spontaneous abortions and infant deformities in the last 20 years,[43] but a conclusion from the 1983 International Symposium on Herbicides and Defoliants in War was that:

No study published to date seems to be conclusive in either proving or disproving an association of phenoxy herbicide/dioxin exposure with adverse outcomes of pregnancy in humans.[44]

The evidence is more conclusive with regards to liver damage resulting from dioxin exposure. A paper from the same symposium found that:

Chronic hepatitis was more than ten times as prevalent among those subjects who had been directly exposed to military herbicides (more than a decade previously) than among those who had not.[45]

Whether or not Vietnamese birth deformities, liver damage or any other ailments can be attributed to Operation Ranch Hand, no compensation has been forthcoming for any of the victims. The Cambodian government attempted to claim compensation for damage done to the Kompong Cham province during the US herbicide campaign, but the case dissolved with the overthrow of that government in 1970. The only people who have been compensated for illnesses attributable to Operation Ranch Hand are soldiers who fought on the same side as those responsible for the spraying. War veterans in the US, Australia, and New Zealand, who have suffered subsequent skin and liver disorders or birth defects in their offspring, won a long battle for compensation in 1979, when a US Federal Judge ruled that they could sue the companies responsible for manufacturing Agent Orange, led by Dow Chemicals. Over 45,000 people have since claimed a share of the US$180 million in damages from Dow and six other chemical firms. Dow agreed to the settlement in the face of public pressure and mounting legal costs, but have always maintained that the various illnesses incurred by the veterans are not related to the Agent Orange sprayed in Vietnam. Much scientific data do appear to support this view, and show that troops could not possibly have been exposed to levels of dioxin sufficient to cause any permanent damage.

> *A soldier directly sprayed would attain an internal body concentration of 7×10^{-5} microgrammes per kilogramme or 1/1750 of the minimum toxic dose; soldiers moving through previously sprayed areas would ingest much less. . . the dioxin sprayed with Agent Orange in Vietnam cannot have caused systemic illnesses in Vietnam veterans or birth defects in their children.*[46]

Despite the inconclusiveness of scientific data relating to Agent Orange exposure, the US defoliation campaign in Vietnam, Cambodia, and Laos was roundly condemned by the US scientific community and many international statesmen. Continued pressure by the Herbicide Assessment Commission (HAC), including a petition signed by 5000 scientists (of whom 17 were holders of Nobel prizes), led to the termination of the campaign in 1971 amidst public horror at evidence of horrific birth defects occurring in the South Vietnamese population.[47] In 1972 at the UN Conference on the Human Environment in Stockholm, Swedish Prime Minister Olaf Palme denounced the use of herbicides in war as 'ecocide'. Palme made no explicit reference to US actions in Vietnam, but the implied criticism caused grave offence to the Nixon administration, who responded by withdrawing the US ambassador from Stockholm. Full diplomatic relations between the two countries were suspended for over a year (January 1973 to May 1974).

The US government had always considered herbicides (along with riot control agents) to be outside the Geneva Protocol on Chemical and Biological Weapons, and hence considered that their actions in the Vietnam War were not contrary to international law. When the US finally became signatory to the Protocol 50 years into its life in 1975, it did not refer to herbicides, but subsequent announcements have denounced their use as agents of warfare, except in routine situations (such as in clearing vegetation around US military base camps).

In circumstances similar to the pay out to Vietnam veteran troops involved in Operation Ranch Hand, in 1994 the US government began paying compensation to troops suffering illnesses purported to be the effect of taking part in the Gulf War in Kuwait in 1990 and 1991. The symptoms experienced by the claimants vary widely and the causal factors have not been as clear cut as in the Operation Ranch Hand case, with pesticides only one of a number of suspected causes.

Symptoms reported by Gulf War Syndrome sufferers include: memory loss, headaches, skin complaints, leukaemia and birth defects. Organophosphate pesticides used on troops to combat sand flies and scorpions have been cited as culpable for this, alongside various other forms of exposure to chemicals including: medical innoculations against diseases and biological weapons, the inhalation of toxic smoke from bombed Iraqi chemical plants and the effects of any gas attacks the Iraqis may have carried out. One prominent theory to explain the range of complaints experienced by Gulf War veterans is a cocktail effect created by simultaneous exposure to the various chemicals.

The UK government's delay in admitting the scale of pesticide use in the war, alongside failing to compensate the alleged victims or recognise Gulf War Syndrome as an illness, fuelled speculation in the UK media of a conspiracy to cover up incidents of pesticide poisoning. The main pesticides used were malathion, used as a delousing powder on Iraqi prisoners, along with diazinon, dimenthyl-phosphorothonate and azamethiphos used to protect allied troops in their sleeping quarters.

THE POLITICS OF PREVENTING HUMAN POISONING BY PESTICIDES

Whilst the extent to which pesticides affect human health is unclear, and subject to dispute by environmentalists and the chemical industry, the fact that the chemicals are potentially hazardous and that safety standards are needed to regulate their production and use is accepted by all. Most actors involved in the politics of pesticides, including governments, international organizations (IOs), and NGOs representing industry and environmentalists alike, have at some time proposed guidelines for pesticide production and use with the intention of safeguarding human health.

Governments

All national governments have some laws or guidelines concerned with the safety of workers dealing with pesticides, though of course these vary greatly both in terms of their scope and in the extent of their implementation. The US has had pesticide legislation since the 1910 Insecticide Act, and today has probably the world's most extensive regulatory system based around the Federal Insecticide, Fungicide and Rodenticide Act of 1947 (FIFRA). FIFRA basically amounts to a licensing system in which all persons involved in selling pesticides are compelled to register the chemical with the Environmental Protection Agency (EPA), an independent body responsible for ensuring registered pesticides have passed stringent safety standards. At the other end of the scale is Senegal where, despite the existence of a government commission designated to formulate pesticide laws, actual regulation is reported to be negligible. A report compiled by the Pesticide Action Network (PAN) and other environmentalist groups, coordinated by the Environment Liaison Centre, concluded that: 'Essentially, no pesticide control exists in Senegal due to weak regulations for dealing with violations of the law'.[48]

The world pattern for national pesticide regulation roughly corresponds with the examples of the US and Senegalese systems, with developed countries possessing far tighter controls than their developing counterparts.[49] The far greater levels of human poisonings in developing countries are a reflection of this situation.

Pressure Groups

Pressure groups have been active on pesticide issues since the early 1950s, when concerns as to the growing resistance of insects to DDT and its possible effects on wildlife began to be aired by the International Union for Conservation of Nature and Natural Resources (IUCN, now the World Conservation Union), which was established in 1948.[50] As has already been shown, however, the real catalyst for political responses to pesticide matters was the publication of Rachel Carson's *Silent Spring* in 1962. Most concern over pesticides was at this stage concentrated on environmental side-effects of the sort articulated by Carson, and consequently they became the focus of US conservation organizations, such as the Sierra Club and the National Wildlife Federation. The impact upon humans of pesticides was also considered by such groups, but this did not become the predominant pesticide issue until the effects of Operation Ranch Hand on Vietnamese citizens began to be seen in the late sixties. The work of the Herbicide Assessment Commission, an offshoot of the American Association for the Advancement of Science (AAAS), which led to the abandonment of Operation Ranch Hand in 1971, also gave impetus to groups to act against the dangers of pesticides used in conventional settings.

Up until the 1980s, a variety of pressure groups lobbied industry, government, and international organizations over pesticide matters alongside other concerns. Friends of the Earth (FoE), the International Organization of Consumer Unions (IOCU), and Oxfam were amongst the most prominent of NGOs to propose guidelines for pesticide use. Oxfam's 1982 publication *A Growing Problem – Pesticides and the Third World Poor*, explicitly set out safety standards it recommended governments, IOs and the agrochemical industry to observe.[51]

The Pesticides Action Network
A May 1982 conference of NGOs addressing the issue of global pesticide trade at Penang, Malaysia, finally brought about the creation of an international body dedicated solely to campaigning on pesticide issues, the Pesticides Action Network (PAN). The conference was co-hosted by the IOCU and the Malaysian branch of FoE (Sahabat Alam Malaysia), and these groups, along with Oxfam and many others, agreed to coordinate efforts in a broad based coalition, organized through six decentralized regional headquarters (Dakar, Nairobi, Penang, London, San Francisco, and Palmisra in

Colombia). PAN naturally assumed the forefront of the world movement to regulate pesticide use and distribution, but from early on it supported the FAO's right to act as the international regime for these issues.

> *The Pesticide Action Network (PAN) International recognizes the pivotal role that the Food and Agriculture Organization (FAO) plays in formulating and promoting major advances in agricultural policies and practices around the world.*[52]

PAN were very active in the instigation of the FAO *Code of Conduct on the Distribution and Use of Pesticides* (see below), and from then on have fulfilled a watchdog role, monitoring its implementation and lobbying for new, more stringent provisions to be included.

Interest Groups

The chief sectional interest within the issue of pesticides and their health impact is clearly that of the chemicals manufacturers, which is represented by GIFAP/GCPF. GIFAP has a permanent Toxicology Working Group, which regularly publishes guidelines and technical information derived from the work of ad hoc working parties. Sets of guidelines include: safe uses of pesticides, protective clothing standards, and the safe transportation and storage of chemicals. These booklets generally come in four languages, and are worded simply in order for them to be easily understood by farmers and other agricultural workers. At the same time, the working group has been involved in assessing the toxicity of pesticides and producing technical papers to defend many products against contrary toxicological evidence. In 1991, for instance, much work was done to refute claims by the International Agency for Research on Cancer (IARC) that pesticide spraying constituted a serious cancer risk, and in countering the estimates of the WHO/UNEP Working Group on the Public Health Impact of Pesticides Used in Agriculture on the actual incidence of pesticides poisoning cases. The IARC indeed can be seen as another interest group within this issue, albeit with a far more limited focus of interest.

United Nations Agencies

The effects that pesticides can have on human health have also stimulated a number of UN agencies to produce guidelines, aiming to minimize poisoning incidence. The WHO, FAO, ILO, UNEP and even the World Bank have attempted, with varying levels of success, to establish internationally accepted standards for the regulation of this issue.

The World Health Organization (WHO)

The WHO has a long history of involvement in the issue of pesticides and their health impact, having begun its series of publications on the toxicity and specifications of particular chemicals in 1953, following the report of an Expert Committee on Insecticides. The WHO has continued to be a source of technical information for pesticide toxicity over the years, with its expert committees functioning as focal points for the epistemic community within the issue-system.

The Expert Committee on the Safe Use of Pesticides, for example, in 1973 devised the idea of a standard worker exposure protocol, with the intention of it becoming a definitive reference for those concerned with the safety of workers applying new organophosphorous pesticides, which were beginning to replace DDT. In 1975 the Standard Protocol was published in the guise of the *Survey of Exposure to Organophosphorous Pesticides in Agriculture*. This document outlined the techniques which could be used to determine when levels of exposure to OP pesticides became hazardous, and included a variety of means by which pertinent medical data could be collected to assess the health of spraymen. In 1978 the Expert Committee on the Safe Use of Pesticides recommended an extension of the protocol to include other types of pesticide, and in 1982 a revised and updated protocol was republished, applicable to all types of pesticides.

Undoubtedly the WHO's most influential work in the area of pesticide poisoning prevention is the Classification by Hazard scheme, which is today widely accepted as the authoritative guide to pesticide toxicity. The scheme was begun in 1975 after approval by the 28th World Health Assembly. The scheme was proposed in 1973 by the WHO Executive Board and prepared over the next two years on the basis of recommendations by the WHO Expert Advisory Panel on Insecticides. Full guidelines, classifying individual pesticides into four categories in terms of their potential hazard to man, were first published in 1978 and have continued to be periodically revised and re-issued over subsequent years.

Table 4.1 demonstrates how the four categories are determined. Both the oral and dermal toxicity of each pesticide are considered in the assessment, and account taken of the fact that solid formulations are inherently less hazardous than liquid. The LD_{50} figure

Table 4.1 *WHO classification of pesticides according to degree of hazard to human beings*[54]

Hazard Class		LD_{50} (rat) (mg/kg of body weight)			
		Oral		Dermal	
		Solid	Liquid	Solid	Liquid
Ia	Extremely hazardous	5 or less	20 or less	10 or less	40 or less
Ib	Highly hazardous	5–50	20–200	10–100	40–400
II	Moderately hazardous	50–500	200–2000	100–1000	400–4000
III	Slightly hazardous	over 500	over 2000	over 1000	over 4000

is a statistical representation of the amount of the pesticide per kilogram of body weight that it is believed would kill 50 per cent of rats in testing. In addition to these four classifications by hazard, the WHO publishes a fifth table of pesticides which in their estimation 'are unlikely to present any acute hazard in normal use'.[53]

The WHO recommendation does not specify any symbols for use in labelling pesticides according to their hazard classification, implying that they envisage their role within the issue system of pesticide poisoning as principally epistemic, and that the functions of regulating the issue and implementing any rules lie elsewhere. The scheme has been accepted by most of the salient actors, however, and in many cases used as the basis for regulations with legal effect. The EC's 1978 *Classification, Packaging, and Labelling of Dangerous Preparations (Pesticides) Directive* was based on the WHO classification scheme, and formally implemented in 1985. The EC classification has only three categories rather than four, 'very toxic', 'toxic', and 'harmful', but these are almost identical with the WHO's categories Ia, Ib, and II. The UK's Pesticides Safety Precautions Scheme adopted in 1983 follows the EC Directive, and hence also follows the WHO classification. Some countries have adopted the WHO classification, but placed some pesticides in a different category, on the basis of their own research and experiences. Malaysia, for example, classifies paraquat as highly hazardous rather than moderately hazardous, probably as a consequence of the popularity of this chemical as a means of committing suicide.

The WHO and EC classification schemes are widely accepted around the world, but a number of states do employ their own, distinct schemes. The US, Bulgaria, Brazil, Canada, and Japan, for instance, operate different numbers of categories, different testing procedures, and/or place different emphasis on the distinctions between dermal and oral toxicity or between liquid and solid pesticides.[55] The Canadian system, in particular, is unique in that pesticides are classified according to their intended use, as well as by their toxicity. All pesticides, regardless of their toxicity, receive a 'restricted' classification, if they are intended for use in environmentally sensitive locations such as forests, or around lakes and rivers. On top of this, provincial governments in Canada can apply their own versions of the federal classification scheme.

The International Programme on Chemical Safety

From 1980, the work of the WHO on the safety aspects of pesticides has been channelled through the International Programme on Chemical Safety (IPCS). The IPCS arose out of the collaboration of the WHO, ILO, and UNEP, when it became apparent to them that areas of their work overlapped. The WHO's regional office in Europe had from the 1970s been researching the area of preventing accidents involving toxic chemicals, whilst the ILO was devising an alert system to aid occupational safety. Both of these operations saw the advantage of absorbing the work of UNEP's International Register of Potentially Toxic Chemicals (IRPTC), and the IPCS was born.

The IPCS clearly sees its role as epistemic, defining itself as 'providing the internationally evaluated scientific basis on which Member States may develop their own safety measures'.[56] The WHO is the executing agency for the programme,[57] and the central unit of the IPCS, responsible for day-to-day activity, is located in the Division of Environmental Health, in Geneva. Membership of the programme is open to both states and NGOs. 27 countries are represented in the programme, sometimes through designated national agencies, and also two international institutions, UNEP's IRPTC and IARC. IPCS's budget of around US$9 million biennially is 20 per cent derived from the WHO's regular budget, with the rest coming from voluntary donations by UNEP and the member states.[58]

The WHO had already been cooperating with UNEP on an Environmental Health Criteria (EHC) programme since 1973, producing a series of documents on the health and environmental impact of individual pesticides, and in 1980 this was brought under the IPCS umbrella. The EHC programme forms a central part of the IPCS. WHO task groups regularly meet in a variety of locations to consider particular chemicals and produce a report. One of the group acts as a chairman, a secretariat is made up of IPCS staff and civil servants from the host country, and observers are usually present, including a GCPF representative. Other output from the IPCS includes Health and Safety Guides, International Chemical Safety Cards, and poisons information monographs. The 1992 United Nations Conference on Environment and Development (UNCED) boosted the role of the IPCS by prescribing it the central role in its proposal for an intergovernmental mechanism to coordinate chemical risk assessment and management. The proposal also advocated that the FAO and OECD Chemicals Programme be involved in the IPCS.[59]

Intergovernmental Forum on Chemical Safety (IFCS)
In 1994 the IPCS was joined by a sister body, the Intergovernmental Forum on Chemical Safety, following a decision of the International Conference on Chemical Safety in Stockholm. The IFCS was charged specifically with the task of implementing the UNCED proposal (Chapter 19, Agenda 21) which it duly adopted as the chief of its priorities for action at its first meeting. The harmonization of chemical risk assessments is thus IFCS's raison d'être.

> *The forum is a non-institutional arrangement whereby representatives of governments meet together with intergovernmental and non-governmental organizations with the aim to integrate and consolidate national and international efforts to promote chemical safety.*[60]

As with the IPCS, the WHO administers the IFCS and acts as its secretariat. The fora themselves are held irregularly but ongoing work is undertaken by the Intersessional Group made up of IFCS officers and 26 governmental representatives coordinated into a bureau of one President and four Vice-Presidents and five regional groupings. The ISG makes recommendations to the IFCS and studies implementation strategies.

The United Nations Environment Programme (UNEP)

Aside from its role within the IPCS, UNEP also independently operates the International Register of Potentially Toxic Chemicals (IRPTC) which is signatory to that programme. The IRPTC represents another input into the complex epistemic community that is concerned with the wider issue of human poisoning by chemicals, of which the issue of pesticide poisoning forms a part. IRPTC provides an international source of knowledge on the potential hazards of chemicals, utilized by other UN agencies and states. It has adopted a more regulatory orientated stance on the issue of chemical trading, which will be examined in the later chapter on the trade in pesticides.

The World Bank

In 1985 the World Bank announced a set of guidelines aiming to avert any damage to human health or the environment from pesticides when used in development projects funded by the bank. The guidelines were drawn up with the assistance of the United States Agency for International Development (USAID), and in general give advocacy to the work of the FAO and WHO on the issue of pesticide poisoning. The guidelines call for adherence to FAO guidelines on *Good Labelling Practice*, and for the WHO Classification by Hazard scheme to be the benchmark in the choice of appropriate pesticides for a project.

The FAO's Code of Conduct

Whilst the roles of the WHO and the IPCS can be summarized as basically epistemic, the FAO can be seen as having taken the initiative in terms of regulation setting, with its *Code of Conduct on the Use and Distribution of Pesticides*. This broad document aims to establish international standards for pesticide safety and trade by which governments and companies may be judged.

> The code is designed to be used . . . as a basis whereby . . . any citizens concerned may judge whether their proposed actions and the actions of others constitute acceptable practices.[61]

The code was drawn up after the FAO Second Government Consultation on International Harmonization of Pesticide Registration Requirements in Rome in 1982, which formally endorsed a working paper of the FAO Panel of Experts called *Pesticide Specifications, Registration Requirements and Application Standards*. This action represented a response by the FAO to NGO pressure for action to be taken on the issue of human poisoning by pesticides. David Bull of Oxfam was even given the task of drawing up an initial list of proposals for the code.[62] The consultation assigned the FAO to draw up an appropriate code in consultation with other UN agencies and relevant international bodies.

The code basically aspires to regulate the issues of both human pesticide poisoning and international pesticide trade. The provisions dealing with trade are considered in Chapter 7, as this issue, while clearly interlinked with that of safety, involves different questions and different stakes for the actors concerned. Regulating the export of the more hazardous pesticide formulations will of course contribute to the goal of minimizing human poisoning, but ultimately that goal is only achievable by the domestic implementation of measures to ensure the safe use of such products. This is explicitly recognized in Article 3.1 of the code which states:

Governments have the overall responsibility and should take the specific powers to regulate the distribution and use of pesticides in their countries.[63]

Articles 4, 5, 6, 7, 10, and 11 are of particular relevance to the issue of minimizing human poisoning by pesticides. Article 4 calls on the agrochemical industry to ensure that all products have been satisfactorily tested in accordance with 'good laboratory practice',[64] before being made available. Reports of these tests should be granted to any government authorities of the country where they are sold, if requested. Articles 5 and 6 request that governments should implement a registration scheme for pesticides, based upon the FAO *Guidelines for the Registration and Control of Pesticides*. Article 7 further recommends that governments ought to develop these schemes in accordance with the WHO's Classification by Hazard categories.

The agrochemical industry, both in the guise of GCPF and the separate companies, does regularly test products for toxicity and, as we have seen, GCPF/GIFAP position papers are available on request. The industry does also, in principle, support the notion of national registration schemes meeting international standards. GIFAP and GCPF have long campaigned for this, although their motivations are somewhat different from those which drove the FAO to include this provision in the Code. GCPF's interest in harmonizing registration schemes is based on cutting costs for pesticide manufacturers.

In similar markets, absence of harmonization frequently represents a considerable cost factor. A small local formulator or manufacturer, for example, could find himself faced with a government requirement to carry out a test on a product which no other government requires – and such tests are rarely inexpensive.[65]

Surveys suggest that all states do possess registration schemes, proscribing the domestic uses of certain pesticides on the basis of toxicity testings. These schemes differ greatly in rigour and style, as was highlighted in the previous examples contrasting US and Senegalese legislation, and the variations from the WHO scheme in classifying pesticides by hazard. The FAO Code of Conduct has as its goal the levelling-up of national regulation standards, and whilst the interests of industry do not coincide with stringent restrictions, it does have a stake in the closer approximation of standards, producing something of an international consensus on the issue. GIFAP was very active in promoting harmonization at the 1977 and 1982 Consultations on International Harmonization of Pesticide Requirements, the second of which spawned the FAO Code of Conduct. Governments, at the two international consultations and elsewhere, have tended to have little sympathy with the agro-chemical industry's appeal against non-tariff barriers created by independent registration schemes. The consultations did not greatly advance the harmonization of national registration schemes. Governments reaffirmed the feeling that setting their own standards for testing and registering pesticides was a facet of their sovereign rights, in spite of industry appeals that harmonization was 'a prerequisite for solving the world's food problem'.[66]

The one striking exception of countries agreeing to bring their registration policies closer together comes predictably from the part of the world where national sovereignty has been most eroded or pooled, Western Europe. The first set of guidelines for pesticide registration to be produced with the idea of developing international consensus came from the Council of Europe in 1962. This set of guidelines was derived from a 1959 agreement which set up a Public Health Committee, whose task it was to investigate questions related to hazardous chemicals.[67]

The European Community followed the example of its largely ineffective counterpart institution, and in 1978 produced the Directive for Common Registration of Agrochemicals. After extensive debate between member states on the familiar lines of sovereignty versus common interests, the directive was finally approved by the Council of Ministers in August 1991.[68] By 1993 the 12 member states had adjusted their national laws and implemented a common registration scheme. A 'positive list' of approved active ingredients to be allowed free movement throughout the community was established. A follow up Uniform Principles Directive standardized the testing and evaluation of pesticides whilst taking into account variations in climate and agriculture throughout the community.[69]

This system, however, was thrown into confusion in 1997 when the European Court of Justice upheld a protest by the European Parliament and annulled The Uniform Principles Directive (Case C-303/94). The European Parliament challenged the directive not through any disapproval of a common EC registration scheme but for reasons of internal EC politics. The Parliament has had a long standing power struggle with the Council of Ministers and objected to the Council adopting the Uniform Principles Directive without consulting them first. The Council had believed that the Directive did not require Parliamentary consent since it was one of a number of follow up Directives still covered by the 1991 Directive decision. Parliament, however, succesfully proved that the Uniform Principles Directive did require their consent since it differed in its interpretation of ground water from the 1991 directive. The irony of the case, of course, is that the Parliament almost certainly would not have objected to the directive if they had been consulted and the registration system was an unfortunate victim of internal squabbling. The European Commission has vowed to introduce a new Uniform Principles directive to fill the legal vacuum that has been created and the possibility remains that a new set of tighter testing standards may now be introduced bearing in mind the fact that three new member states, all renowned for stringent safety and environmental standards, Austria, Sweden and Finland, have joined the European Union since 1994.

Alongside registration, the key means by which safety measures for those producing or using pesticides can be implemented is through the standardization of labelling and advertising information for the chemicals. Article 10 of the FAO Code of Conduct clearly spells out a set of acceptable standards for the labelling of pesticide containers. Producers are called upon to ensure that instructions for using the product are in an appropriate language, give the storage life of the chemical, show how to dispose of it safely, warn against reusal of the container, and most importantly display the hazard classification of the pesticide as defined by the WHO. Article 11 deals with advertising practices, charging companies with the responsibility for ensuring that: any claims made for a product can be properly validated, any pictures used show full safety precautions being observed, and that advertisements should not be made for restricted products without clearly stressing that they are restricted.

GCPF and the agrochemical firms claim that these FAO code provisions are being implemented on their behalf, but the verdict of a report by the Environment Liaison Centre (ELC) in Nairobi, from where PAN operates in East Africa, is that the code has had little impact on safety standards in developing countries. The ELC report collects evidence from 12 developing countries and gives numerous examples of pesticides being repackaged into new containers without warning labels once imported, and highlights the fact that the labels frequently are ignored, because of illiteracy. In this instance it seems that the problem lies not in the agrochemical industry failing to observe the FAO guidelines, but in the guidelines themselves not being sufficient to counter the problem. In the case of advertising practices, however, the evidence does point an accusing finger at the agrochemical industry.

In the mass of advertisements and promotional leaflets collected in Latin America, Africa, Asia and the Pacific, it is virtually impossible to find a single one which satisfactorily follows the provisions of the FAO code.[70]

The report provides examples of pesticides classified by the WHO as highly hazardous being advertised as safe for human beings, and photographs of people demonstrating spraying techniques without wearing protective clothing. An overt example of such an advertisement is a photograph used by the Solo Technology Company of Germany, depicting two scantily clad models smiling gleefully whilst carrying spraying equipment.

A further provision related to the issue of limiting human poisoning by pesticides is found under Article 8.1.9 of the code, which calls on industry to ensure that, 'persons involved in the sale of any pesticides are trained adequately to ensure that they are capable of providing the buyer with advice on safe and efficient use'. GIFAP itself admitted that the agrochemical industry has failed to comply with this provision: 'Detailed observations in various developing countries have revealed however that we continue to fall far short of the standards of the FAO Code of Conduct'.[72]

It seems fair to conclude that the pesticide industry has failed to observe the FAO code on a number of occasions with respect to

Table 4.2 *Advertising Infringements of FAO Code in Ecuador (1987)*[71]

Code Article		No	%
	Promotion material surveyed	*45*	*100*
11.1.13	No warning about hazards or symbols	30	66.7
	No manufacturer's name	11	24.7
11.1.11	Guarantees profits	18	40
11.1.1, 11.1.7	Claims of efficiency without validation	25	55.6
11.1.12	Dangerous practices shown	10	22.2
11.1.17	No reference to need to read labels	14	37
11.1.2, 11.1.8	Invalid safety claims	9	20

advertising, but it should be acknowledged that it has generally fulfilled its obligations in terms of correctly labelling its products for export. Whereas pressure has been maintained on the industry to improve its advertising standards, the focus in terms of the labelling problem has been to develop a new, more stringent set of guidelines.

The Globally Harmonized Scheme (GHS)

Hopes in terms of establishing new standards for labelling and marketing pesticides and other potentially hazardous chemicals now rest on the Globally Harmonized Scheme, which has received the endorsements of both UNEP and the IFCS. As with the IPCS and IFCS, the GHS represents the output of a number of international organizations cooperating where their work overlaps. The architects of the scheme have set a target of the year 2000 for the implementation of a global system of classifying chemicals according to both their human and environmental hazards and harmonizing labelling and other forms of information accordingly.

Three international organizations are central to the GHS. The OECD is responsible for managing the development of health and environmental hazard information for developing a classification scheme. It has set up an expert advisory group towards this end. The United Nations Committee of Experts on the Transportation of Dangerous Goods have the task of determining criteria for classifying the physical hazards of chemicals (for example, the flammability of chemicals). The ILO have assumed responsibility for the overall coordination of the system, acting as its secretariat, and have also set up a working group containing governmental and worker representatives charged with the task of producing the means of communicating the classification scheme. As well as labelling standards, this will include data sheets for workers involved in chemical transport and guidance information for governments on how to implement the scheme.[73]

CONCLUSION – A REGIME?

It has been established that there is sufficient consensus amongst actors on the importance of safeguarding human health from pesticide poisoning for this to constitute an international norm, but is it possible to conclude that an international regime exists within the issue system? The chief aspirant to this role is clearly the FAO with its Code of Conduct on the Use and Distribution of Pesticides. Chapter 7 details how other provisions of this code eventually became the basis of a regime regulating the issue of the international trade in pesticides, but its impact on the issue of human poisoning is less dramatic. Registration schemes still vary greatly in scope throughout the world, with many states falling well below the standards promoted by the FAO. Advertising practices continue to flout the Code's recommendations, and the industry admits that it has failed to observe the provisions on training pesticide salesmen. The Code's labelling provisions have had an impact on industry behaviour, but have proved so inadequate in curbing the problem of poisonings in developing countries that they have not gained the respect of many of the salient actors.

Thus it seems that the FAO's Code of Conduct provisions relating to the issue of human poisoning by pesticides have not developed to a status whereby they are universally accepted as appropriate for authoritative allocation to salient actors. The key factor in this failure was the rejection of the Code's labelling provisions in 1991 by the pesticides protest lobby for being too lenient. Up until this point there had been consensus amongst the actors in the issue system that the FAO Code was the focal point for rule formulation, even if those rules were not being widely implemented. GCPF continues to treat the FAO as the legitimate source of decision making within the issue, but this view is no longer shared by all actors.

The epistemic community, centred on the WHO, has attained a widely respected position within the issue system, as is evidenced by the worldwide impact of the Classification by Hazard scheme and the fact that the pesticide protest lobby turned to the WHO for leadership in its campaign to develop new pesticide labelling standards. However, this epistemic community, as we have seen, does not aspire to regime status and has continually abdicated rule setting and implementation to others. In effect, the question of preventing human poisoning by pesticides has been transformed from being an issue regulated by an ineffective regime towards becoming an issue without a regime at all. The recurrent problem within pesticide politics is at the heart of this. There is sufficient consensus for a norm to exist amongst actors, but their divergent interests have so far prevented the development from this of specific rules that are acknowledged by all and have behavioural effect.

5 When a Weapon Misses the Target – The Issue of Environmental Pollution by Pesticides

INTRODUCTION

The fact that all pesticides are by their nature toxic substances means that any contamination of unintended targets with them is potentially hazardous, and so undesirable. Thus the prevention of environmental pollution by pesticides has become a norm of conduct, guiding the behaviour of all actors. Once again, however, it can be seen that there are different levels of adherence to this norm. To some actors, the evidence of environmental damage due to pesticide use is enough to warrant the outright abolition of their use in any capacity, whereas others merely wish to see them used with some consideration for their ecological consequences. The basic premise that environmental pollution from pesticides is a negative consequence of their use and should be limited, does however represent a universal norm by which all are guided to some extent.

As with human poisoning, the actual extent of pollution by pesticides is unclear and disputed by scientists and political actors alike. Traces of pesticides can be found in the soil, in the water, in the air, and unintentionally in crops and animals, but there is little consensus as to when this equates to pollution at a level at which we should be concerned.

FORMS OF PESTICIDE POLLUTION

Pesticides in the Soil

The soil is the principle recipient of pesticides, the source of which may be deliberate or accidental. The direct application of pesticides to the soil is a common practice in agriculture, particularly in the use of herbicides. It has been estimated that 25 per cent of all agricultural land in the US is treated with pesticides in this way, every year.[1]

In addition to this, however, a significant amount of pesticides continually enter the soil unintentionally due to the drifting of these chemicals when sprayed and their fallout from the atmosphere. Unlike with the intentional entry of pesticides into the soil, this source is indiscriminate and affects a much wider land area, including areas where their presence may be wholly undesirable. Much of the pesticides intended for crop application clearly will miss their target or run off the plants into the soil beneath. A report by Beasley, Rohrbach, Mainland and Meyer in 1983 demonstrated that around 65 per cent of an insecticide spray used on blueberry bushes found its way into the soil.[2] To this can also be added the entrance of pesticides into the soil from crop residues, leaf fall and root deposits. A less voluminous but more widespread source of pesticides which enter the soil is by atmospheric fallout. Small amounts of pesticides have been detected in raindrops and atmospheric dust, which are absorbed into the soil on reaching the ground.

A number of possible fates await pesticides on entering the soil:

Once in the soil, pesticides can be absorbed onto soil particles, chemically bonded to other compounds in the soil, volatilized from the soil surface into the atmosphere, moved through the soil by molecular diffusion, leached or run off into water, taken up by plant roots or ingested by soil fauna (thus entering the food chain), or degraded.[3]

Whether the presence of a pesticide in the soil constitutes an environmental problem or not depends somewhat on its persistence. A quickly degrading pesticide will not be likely to disrupt the ecosystem greatly, but a highly persistent chemical may have biological effects beyond the period of its usefulness. A GIFAP report identified four types of such biological effects which could be environmentally damaging. These effects concern the capacity of chemical residues to:

1 survive long enough to affect succeeding crops;
2 affect soil organisms;
3 leach into water used for human consumption; and
4 cause long-term damage to soil fertility.

The effects of residues on living organisms can be summarized into four categories. They may:

1 be directly toxic;
2 cause genetic resistance;
3 be passed on to other organisms; or
4 have sub-lethal effects on behaviour or reproduction.[4]

Pesticides in Water

As with the soil, pesticides may enter water sources either deliberately or accidentally, although instances of the former are far fewer. Relatively tiny amounts of pesticides are applied to streams, ponds, and reservoirs in order to protect fish, attack weeds and algae, and control insects which breed in water. These sorts of practices are generally restricted in the developed world by firm legislation. In the UK, for example, the local water authority is required to be contacted before any spraying operations in or around freshwater areas can be undertaken. In developing countries, however, the deliberate adding of pesticides to freshwater is more common and often more haphazard. The use of pesticides for fishing has been reported on a number of occasions. Bull found it to be a common practice in Ghana.

> *The fishermen or farmers then use the insecticides by pouring them into the water of small shallow streams, following the flow downstream until the fish begin floating to the surface.*[5]

The unintentional contamination of groundwater remains the more serious problem, however. Pesticide residues can enter water through drift and atmospheric fallout in the same way as they do the soil, but also in a number of other ways. Chemicals in soil may enter nearby water through runoff or be carried there with eroded soil particles. Pesticides also may make up some of the industrial effluent regularly pumped into streams and rivers. This could be the wastes from fabric plants practising moth proofing or from the manufacturing, formulating, and packaging stages of production in an agrochemical firm. Similarly, sewage will often contain pesticide traces such as the bactericides found in some soap and cosmetic products.

On top of this, spills of pesticides into rivers have been known during the storage and transportation of the chemicals. Hundreds of tonnes of pesticides and other chemicals were washed into the Rhine at a Sandoz warehouse in Basle, Switzerland, in November 1986, after a fire was brought under control with hoses. Similarly, the derailing of a railway tanker in California in July 1991 caused severe contamination of the Sacramento River, which runs alongside the railway line. This river feeds the local water supply at Lake Shasta and as a consequence nearly 200 residents of the area required immediate hospital treatment for nausea and dizziness.[6] Animals may also suffer in this way if pesticides contaminate their drinking water. Oxfam reported on such an incident in Bangladesh in 1981 when the runoff of pesticides from waterlogged bogland caused hundreds of cattle deaths.[7]

The effects of a cumulative input of pesticides into groundwater can also be lethal to the organisms which inhabit it. An increase in the mortality of bacteria, fungi, algae, aquatic invertebrates, amphibians, reptiles or fish will disrupt the food webs which exist between them and therefore upset the ecosystem. The fact that pesticides concentrate in the tissues of aquatic organisms more readily than in terrestrial life forms exacerbates this problem.[8] Of most concern to man is the effect of such pollution on some fish populations, both directly through poisoning and indirectly due to a depletion of their traditional prey. Large-scale declines in the numbers of paddy field fish in Malaysia in the early 1980s due to a mysterious disease termed as 'wabak kurdis' (scabies epidemic) was found to be directly attributable to the increased use of pesticides on rice plants.[9] Any precise estimate of overall losses of fish due to pesticide poisoning is difficult because of the complex nature of marine habitats.

The presence of pesticides in groundwater can also have sub-lethal effects on aquatic life. The raising of the water temperature due to pesticide presence, or the entry of the chemicals into fish brains or nervous system, can impact the behaviour and reproductive capacities of them.[10] The most serious consequence of behavioural change occurs when a species of fish develops a resistance to the pesticide it has been exposed to. When this happens, these fish become capable of carrying previously lethal levels of chemicals, which can then be passed on to the next organism in the food chain. As a result of this, traces of pesticides have even been found in polar bears.[11] Of course, the next organism in the food chain could also be man.

Pesticides in the Air

Pesticide droplets have been detected in the atmosphere over most parts of the globe. Clearly, therefore, they are capable of falling many miles from the areas where they were originally intended to be applied.

Pesticide vapours enter the atmosphere in many ways. A significant proportion of pesticides may be lost during spraying, through drifting in the wind, or evaporation. A 1978 Canadian survey found that up to 35 per cent of the herbicide 2,4-D volatilized on application to prairie soils.[12] Volatilization can also take place on secondary deposits of pesticides. Some particularly persistent substances, such as DDT and dieldrin, remain long enough as surface residues after falling with rain that they are subject to evaporation again. Other routes by which pesticides enter the atmosphere include the escape of vapours from pesticide manufacture and formulation plants, and the introduction of residues within dust storms originating in agricultural areas.[13]

Though the density of pesticides which fall to earth from the air is far less of a hazard to man and the environment than the pollution of soil and water, concern remains at the build up of toxic vapours in the atmosphere. Wheatley estimated that one-sixth of all DDT produced up until 1974 was contained in the atmosphere.[14] The extent of this contamination has decreased over the years, however, with the decline in the use of DDT and the use instead of less persistent chemicals.

A different form of environmental hazard due to the existence of certain pesticides has emerged in recent years. The soil fumigant methyl bromide was in 1992 confirmed as a significant agent in the depletion of the ozone layer. A UNEP report concluded that around half of all methyl bromide applications to the soil are ultimately emitted into the atmosphere, and that once there their capacity for ozone destruction is at least 30 times greater than that of organochlorine compounds, such as the infamous CFCs (chlorofluorocarbons). The report estimated that between 5 and 10 per cent of annual global ozone depletion was attributable to methyl bromide.[15]

Pesticides and Wildlife

The effects that the presence of pesticides in water can have on aquatic organisms have been considered, but many other forms of wildlife can also be affected by exposure to these chemicals. A 1983 UK Ministry of Agriculture, Fisheries and Food (MAFF) *Approved Products for Farmers List* stated that the proportions of pesticides which are 'harmful' or 'dangerous' are: 88 per cent for fish, 46 per cent for bees, 43 per cent for livestock, and 42 per cent for wildlife and game. In developing countries, where broad spectrum pesticides are still widely favoured to the more pest specific varieties, because of their comparative cheapness, these proportions will undoubtedly be higher.

Insects, birds, mammals and plants may become contaminated with pesticides directly on spraying, through the soil or water, or by directly or indirectly consuming them in food. In the UK, MAFF has a policy of warning all farmers intending to use herbicides about the potential ill effects on neighbouring susceptible crops. One such susceptible crop is believed to be the wild rose found in rural hedgerows, whose numbers have rapidly declined as a result of spraydrift from various herbicides.[16] The technique of spraying pesticide droplets contained within minute plastic spheres, known as microcapsules, is known to have had dire consequences for bees. The capsules attach themselves to hairs on the bee in the same way as pollen does, and can then be taken into the hive and possibly eaten. The realization of this problem has led to the addition of latex to the capsules in the US, reducing the likelihood of their take-up by bees.[17]

Pesticide residues in the soil can directly poison the organisms which inhabit there, or indirectly poison the organisms feeding on them. The effects on organisms within the soil have been well researched, as this obviously has repercussions for the quality of the soil and its role in crop production. The general conclusion of most research is that the effects of pesticides on soil organisms are usually short lived and that populations will return to normal quickly after a decrease. One exception to this is the persistent insecticide dieldrin, which has been used to control termites and beetle larvae for numerous seasons at a time. Beneficial soil arthropods have been unintentionally reduced in number for long periods by the application of this chemical to the soil.[18] The decreased usage of persistent organochlorine pesticides in the developed world has minimized the hazards to soil habitats, but the problem persists in developing countries.

The greatest route by which wildlife come into contact with pesticides is through the contamination of their food sources. It may be the case that the effects of pesticides on soil-inhabiting organisms are limited, but the impact on some predators of these organisms can be far more profound. Birds are far more subject to taking in pesticide residues in this way as their bodies break down harmful chemicals less readily than do mammals. The birds most vulnerable are those at the top of the food chain, the birds of prey. Persistent chemicals such as DDT and dieldrin end up deposited in these creatures via small birds who feed upon contaminated insects in the soil. The birds of prey are left with the biggest deposits from having accumulated the toxic residues of all organisms below them in the food chain. This process is known as biomagnification. In the UK the sparrowhawk was declining for 25 years because of direct poisoning from its prey and the thinning of its egg shells due to pesticides. The bird began to reemerge in the late 1970s once the residues of organochlorine pesticides used in the 1950s had finally begun to disappear.

Birds are also prone to a more direct poisoning from organochlorine pesticides when feeding on treated seeds, or when their habitats become contaminated. Aldrin and dieldrin were widely used in the UK in the late 1950s and 1960s as a seed treatment to protect cereal grains from insects, and it is now widely accepted that this contributed to the temporary lessening of sparrowhawks and a decline in kestrels generally. The lethal component of aldrin and dieldrin for the kestrels is the chemical 1,2,3,4,10,10-hexachloro-6,7-epoxy-1,4,4a,5,6,7,8,8a-octahydro-1,4,5,8-dimethamonaphthalene (HEOD). A 1992 report from the Institute of Terrestrial Ecology reviewing this subject concluded that:

> *In the period 1963–75, HEOD probably accounted for about 50 per cent of all recorded Sparrowhawk deaths and 39 per cent of all recorded kestrel deaths in eastern arable districts.*[19]

The higher mortality rate in the East of England is explained by the more intensive use of dieldrin and aldrin in this area, while further evidence of the culpability of these pesticides comes from the resurgence of kestrels when they began to be restricted by legislation.

> *The proportion of deaths attributed to HEOD declined between 1963–75 and 1976–86, following a marked reduction in aldrin-dieldrin use, and fell to nil in 1987–90, when aldrin and dieldrin were withdrawn altogether.*[20]

The fact that the hawks were contaminated via seeds as well as through biomagnification was borne out by the sight of dead birds around recently sewn fields in the early 1960s. The Royal Society for the Protection of Birds (RSPB) has also reported deaths of geese and swans in the East of England due to the consumption of treated wheat grain.[21]

The spraying of a bird's habitat, a practice common in the control of vector-borne diseases, has also been shown to affect their mortality. Woodland areas treated with pesticides with the intention of controlling disease transmitting insects, can cause local bird populations to suffer poisonings. Surveys in north-western Zimbabwe have demonstrated this to be a side-effect of the use of DDT to control tsetse-flies in operations to restrict the spread of trypanosomiasis in cattle. A comparison between areas of treated and untreated woodland showed up a considerable impact by DDT on chat songbirds.

> *In the 1987–89 treatment area, numbers fell by 88 per cent over 33 months. . . Numbers in the unsprayed area fell by 13 per cent over the same period... In a second study area, a further treatment of DDT one year after the first, was followed by a 74 per cent decline in numbers over nine months.*[22]

Physiological explanations have been offered to explain the fact that birds, and falcons in particular, appear to be far more susceptible to pesticide poisoning than other animals. A link between DDT and the thinning of egg shells is well documented, and this problem has been shown to be most acute amongst falcons. Also, the fact that organochlorines are highly lipophilic gives credence to the theory that they assume greater toxicity in falcons and migratory birds, because these creatures tend to burn off more stored fat than other birds and animals owing to their lifestyle, which allows the pesticide residue to enter the nervous system.[23]

The evidence of pesticides affecting other animals is less conclusive. As with human health, the impact of organochlorines and other pesticides on mammals in normal exposure situations tends to be minimal. The carcinogenicity, teratogenicity, and mutagenicity of pesticides to rats in laboratory experiments has only been proven on the exposure of the creatures to amounts of the substances far in excess of natural encounters. Two cited exceptions to this general pattern for mammals, however, are those of the bat and the mink which, studies suggest, have a greater propensity to accumulate organochlorines.[24]

Pesticides and Crop Losses

Pesticides may also be responsible for damaging farm crops when the chemicals become volatile, or unintentionally come into contact with crops other than those they are intended to protect. The drift of vapour from neighbouring crop fields, the effects of herbicide residues which have remained in the soil after application on a different crop in a previous season, or changes in the nature of the pesticide due to the climate can all be causes of crop losses.

In the UK Friends of the Earth and the National Farmers Union have lobbied the government for action to provide farmers with greater information on the problem of persistent herbicides after taking up the complaints of farmers who have suffered damage to crops due to the effects of residues from applications on preceding crops.[25]

In 1992 American farmers in Florida suffered great losses in vegetables such as cucumbers and broccoli apparently because the Du Pont fungicide Benlate (benomyl) had turned poisonous due to heat and humidity.[26] The fact that pesticides can become volatile in the face of high temperatures obviously has significant implications for importers in the South, though the extent of this problem is unclear. Pimentel has estimated that the cost of negative pesticide effects on crops in the USA is about US$70 million a year.[27]

Summary

It can be proven that pesticides sometimes pollute the environment and poison the organisms that inhabit it, but the overall significance of this to the natural world is still open to debate. The influence of pesticides is one of many inputs determining the balance of nature, alongside far less contentious human practices such as building reservoirs and dams or fishing.

> *Nature is not static and . . . the balance of nature is a shifting one, the result of countless influences and an endless struggle among the inhabitants of any particular community. Pesticides add elements to the struggle and, at least temporarily, shift the balance. Whether this results in a better or worse environment cannot be determined until we learn what better or worse means. The concept that any change is bad can be embraced only if we assume that evolution has, in 1979, finally reached an optimum stage for all.*[28]

Whilst the wholesale contamination of the environment by carefree pesticide application is clearly undesirable, minor changes to an ecosystem need not necessarily be viewed as ecologically damaging. Judging whether the net result of such change is desirable, however, is of course difficult to discern and subject to dispute by the political actors within the issue-system of environmental pesticide pollution.

THE POLITICS OF ENVIRONMENTAL POLLUTION BY PESTICIDES

The issue of pesticide induced environmental pollution was the catalyst for the appearance of all pesticide issues on the international political agenda, and also to some extent the emergence of the wider issue of environmental degradation itself. Rachel Carson's *Silent Spring* in 1962, whilst considering human poisoning, focused primarily on the effects of pesticides on wild animals, vegetation and rivers. As is well documented, the book had a profound influence on many people and, despite numerous attacks on its scientific authenticity by industrialists, it is recognized as having helped fuel the take-off of environmental politics in the 1960s.

It would seem reasonable to conclude, however, that since the early 1960s environmental pollution by pesticides has ceased to be the most contentious issue within pesticide politics, falling behind the issues of human poisoning and food contamination. This is reflected by the fact that no international bodies deal solely or specifically with pesticide pollution. The FAO Code of Conduct, as we have seen, basically deals with human safety and pesticide trading, the WHO Classification by Hazard scheme fixes its toxicity measurements in relation to humans and not other ecological considerations, and there are no inter-agency working groups within the UN system concentrating entirely on pesticide pollution.

This is not to say, however, that ecological considerations are absent in pesticide politics. Pressure group influence has aided the banning or restriction of many pesticides principally on ecological grounds, and visible improvements in the biodiversity of some countries have been seen in recent years due to such action.

The politics of environmental pollution by pesticides generally operates at the state or regional level, and not directly on a global scale. A potential breakthrough in terms of global policy, however, has emerged with the 1998 Rotterdam Convention dealing with the pesticide trade, where it was agreed that the definition of a hazardous pesticide would include environmental considerations as well as human health. The Convention decrees that for a substance to come within the scope of the convention it must be:

> *... a chemical formulated for pesticidal use that produces severe health or environmental effects observable within a short period of time after single or multiple exposures, under conditions of use. (Article 2 (d))*

This represented something of a breakthrough, as opposition to including the word 'environmental' was evident in the negotiating of the Convention. How much regard will be given to environmental factors in deciding whether to regulate the trading of certain pesticides remains to be seen, but it is likely that they will be secondary to human health considerations.

National Regulation

The testing procedures for registering new pesticides nationally, referred to in Chapter 4, normally incorporate environmental criteria as well as toxicity to man. The US FIFRA system, for instance, was in 1972 augmented by the Federal Environmental Pesticide Control Act (FEPCA), which decreed that a chemical should not be registered unless it could be shown that 'it will not cause unreasonable adverse effects on the environment'.[29] In reality, human health concerns have generally predominated in the US registration of pesticides, especially with concern to the suspected carcinogenicity of particular chemicals.

In line with the two FAO government consultations on the International Harmonization of Pesticide Registration Requirements in 1977 and 1982, expert meetings on the environmental criteria for registration took place in 1977, 1979 and 1981. The difficulties inherent in setting universal standards for registration were made explicit at the 1981 meeting.

> *The balance between risk and benefit may differ greatly under different socio-economic systems. Under a highly developed well resourced system, harm to a rare bird species may be sufficient reason to avoid or restrict the use of a particular chemical. In situations where vector-borne human diseases, starvation, or malnutrition are possible factors, however, the risk/benefit analysis may lead to a different decision.*[30]

This assessment is borne out by reality. It is difficult for governments in many developing states to prioritize environmental issues such as pesticide pollution, when they are seen to be counter to their immediate and basic interests. Hence the environmentally hazardous organochlorine pesticides are still frequently used in much of the developing world, despite their reduced use in much of the developed world. The advent of 'Prior Informed Consent' (PIC) as a rule of the international trade in pesticides has, however, at least ensured that importing authorities are now made aware of products that have been restricted on ecological or health grounds in other countries. The impact that PIC will have on environmental pollution still remains to be seen, but ultimately the decisions relevant to the issue are still being taken at the level of national government, often according to a perceived national interest.

Regional Regulation

Exceptions to this general pattern of independent national regulation within the issue system of pesticide pollution are found in the nature of regional intergovernmental arrangements. These come in two forms. Firstly, there exist regional regimes set up when neighbouring states share a common stake in a particular policy question, such as the avoidance of polluting common stretches of water. The second form of regional regulation occurs due to the effect of political cooperation between states in other issues, what is known as 'spillover' in the neo-functionalist model of regional integration.[31]

Common Stake Regional Regimes

A number of intergovernmental agreements have been signed throughout the world which aim to delimit the amounts of pesticides discharged into particular seas or other tracts of water. 16 governments have signed the Mediterranean Action Plan (MAP) which is attempting to cut levels of discharge into the Mediterranean, whilst nine countries are signatories to the North Sea Conference which aims to do likewise for that sea. The MAP dates back to the 1976 Barcelona Convention for the Protection of the Mediterranean Sea Against Pollution. This convention committed the signatories to the general principle of protecting the environmental quality of the sea, and was proceeded by three protocols considering particular forms of pollution. The third of these, adopted in 1980, was the Land-Based Sources Protocol, which included regulations to control pesticide pollution. The most significant agreement concerning pesticides under the Barcelona Convention came in 1991, when the signatory governments committed themselves to a phase-out of organophosphate pesticide use by 2005.

The North Sea has been subject to a number of multilateral agreements concerning various forms of pollution. Of most relevance to pesticide pollution is the 1974 Paris Convention for the Prevention of Marine Pollution from Land-Based Sources. This corresponds with a sister convention, the 1972 Oslo Convention on Control of Dumping from Ships and Aircraft, and together they have spawned the Oslo and Paris Commission (OSPARCOM) which has regularly met to monitor the implementation of the provisions of the twin conventions. This system was augmented in 1984 by the inauguration of ministerial conferences dealing with the problem of North Sea pollution. These conferences have worked closely together with OSPARCOM and a further homogenization of the system was completed in 1992 when the Oslo and Paris Conventions were formally merged 'into a single Convention under which all sources of pollution which may affect the maritime area covered by the convention can be addressed.'[32]

The regime formed from these conferences and conventions in fact covers the North East Atlantic, Norwegian Sea and parts of the Arctic Ocean, in addition to the North Sea. The focal point of the regime is a 'black' and 'grey' list of chemicals according to which the dumping or runoff of certain substances into North Sea bound rivers or pipelines is either banned outright or restricted. Chemicals on the black list are completely prohibited, whilst those on the grey list are limited by permits granted by the appropriate national authorities.[33]

A similar regional regime is operated for the Great Lakes in North America by the International Joint Commission of the US and Canada (IJC), which dates from the United Anglo-American Boundary Waters Treaty of 1909. Specific consideration of pesticide pollution came about in 1978 when the Great Lakes Water Quality Agreement adopted various recommendations from the Pollution from Land Use Activities Reference Group (PLUARG). In 1992 the IJC called on the Canadian and American governments to phase out the production of organochlorine chemicals, which of course includes a number of pesticides.[34]

Numerous other bilateral and multilateral agreements aiming to control pollution are in operation throughout many of the world's rivers, lakes, seas and oceans. The Commission for the River Rhine, which now comprises one part of a series of arrangements on the Rhine basin, was indeed the world's first intergovernmental organization, having been established at the Congress of Vienna in 1815. Figure 5.1 shows the locations of the many regional agreements which deal, at least in part, with environmental pollution, including that caused by pesticides. The action plans listed all utilize the expertise of UNEP staff on their secretariats, and are coordinated with UNEP's Regional Seas Programme. Although not all rivers, lakes, and coastlines are subject to some form of pollution regulation, international lawyers have recognized that there is movement towards an international norm on this question.

> *A consistent tendency is observable towards the formation of an* opinio juris *which makes the prevention of pollution in international rivers and lakes obligatory for riparians.*[35]

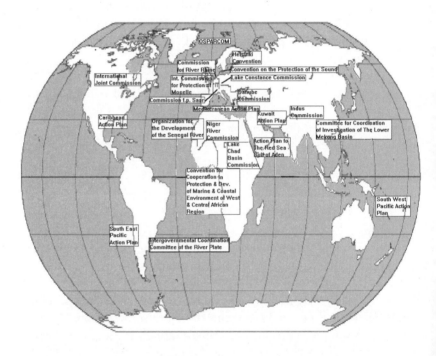

Figure 5.1 *Regional regimes which regulate pesticide pollution*

Spillover Regimes

The primary example of the 'spillover' form of environmental cooperation comes from the home of normative functionalist theory, Western Europe. Reference has already been made to the European registration scheme (see Chapter 4), which aims to standardize the national pesticide licensing systems. The follow-up Uniform Principles Directive which aims at standardizing the testing and evaluation of pesticides was preoccupied with environmental criteria in its drafting stages.

> *The drafters have already decided that more experience is needed about the impact of pesticides on non-target aquatic flora, and the fate of pesticides in air, before the draft can be fully achieved.*[36]

EC involvement in environmental issues such as pesticide pollution has evolved gradually since the mid-1970s. The first EC Directives with relevance to pesticides to be issued were concerned with the quality of drinking water (1975) and the disposal of polychlorinated biphenyls (PCBs) (1976). Since 1973 EC environmental policy has been guided by four Action Programmes (1973–76, 1977–81, 1982–86, 1987–92), which have set out basic goals concerned with controlling pollution and managing natural resources. In addition, the EC has acted as signatory for some of the regional regimes already referred to. The Commission has exercised its supranational authority by committing all 15 member states to the North Sea agreements, the Mediterranean Action Plan, and the 1976 Bonn Convention on the Protection of the Rhine Against Pollution by Chlorides.[37]

Environmental policy was not envisaged for the EC by the Treaty of Rome, but its incorporation into that framework treaty from 1973 onwards has been justified on the grounds of it being a facet of the moves towards ensuring fair competition and a single market. Differing national environmental legislative standards represent an uneven playing field and a barrier to free trade, it is argued. The development of such policies represents a classic enactment of the functionalist scenario of economic integration spilling over into other policy sectors.

Global Regulation

We have seen that the issue of environmental degradation by pesticides is predominantly dealt with at the national or regional level, and usually only at the latter level when states are forced into bilateral or multilateral arrangements through the existence of common stretches of water. EU environmental policy relevant to pesticides is an exception to this, but then the EU is very much a unique case in international politics as a whole. Within much of the wider issue of environmental degradation, the EC can best be conceptualized as having superseded its constituent member states as a chief international actor. This is explicitly recognized in international environmental diplomacy, such as at the 1998 Rotterdam Convention, where the term Regional Economic Integration Organization (REIO) is used to signify that the EU is the legal signatory rather than its constituent countries. The EU has acted in the traditional manner of a state in establishing a registration scheme for pesticides and signing regional environmental agreements with nearby countries. By and large, therefore, pesticide politics in the environmental sphere is basically conducted at the governmental level, albeit with the input of environmental pressure groups and an epistemic community.

The explanation for this is that pesticide pollution is fundamentally a localized problem. The problems of contaminated and poisoned wildlife are not transferred significantly across state boundaries, and although the question of contaminated water does frequently become a cross border problem it never really takes on a global dimension. To put it another way, the ecologies of the US or the EU countries are never greatly affected by the misuse of pesticides in African or South American countries.

Methyl bromide

An outstanding exception to this general situation has emerged in recent years, however, with the findings about the effects of the presence of the soil fumigant methyl bromide on the atmosphere. Methyl bromide is used extensively in the farming of tomatoes and strawberries, particularly in the US. The fact that organohalogen[38] chemicals accumulate in the atmosphere and do indeed have a global environmental impact has long been known. However, this has never been considered to pose a significant threat to global security until the discovery that methyl bromide is a significant ozone-depleting agent.

Hence a global agreement concerning methyl bromide use and production was reached in November 1992 in Copenhagen in a follow-up meeting of the Montreal Protocol, a treaty dealing with the issue of ozone depletion. The Copenhagen meeting decreed that methyl bromide production and consumption levels should be frozen at 1991 levels from the start of 1995. Concerns had been voiced about the health and local environmental effects of methyl bromide for years (the Netherlands government phased out its use in 1992), but it took the realization that the chemical posed a threat to global security for it to be made subject to any international regulation.

The 1987 Montreal Protocol on Substances that Deplete the Ozone Layer arose out of the 1985 Vienna Convention for the Protection of the Ozone Layer, by which the 28 signatories basically just confirmed the existence of ozone depletion as a global problem and agreed to increase research and the exchange of information. The Montreal Protocol added substance to the Convention, agreeing to the progressive phase out of CFCs by 50 per cent and paved the way for further agreements. By 1989, 81 governments had agreed to the Helsinki Declaration on the Protection of the Ozone Layer which called for a complete phasing out of CFC use and production by the year 2000. The Copenhagen agreement represented a continuation of the process started in Vienna in 1985.

In September 1997 the 9th Meeting of the Parties to the Montreal Protocol committed 160 governments to a timetable for a complete phase out of methyl bromide production and use. Developed countries agreed to end use of the chemical by 2005 after a series of intermediate cuts, whilst developing countries were given a deadline of 2015 to eliminate its use following a freeze in 2002. This agreement brought forward by five years the deadline for developed countries agreed at the 7th Montreal Protocol meeting in Vienna in December 1995 and committed developing countries to a full phase out date for the first time. The agreement disappointed the 25 NGOs present at the meeting however, who had campaigned for phase out dates of 2001 and 2006, for developed and developing countries respectively, and were optimistic of success following the US unilateral commitment to a 2001 phase out of methyl bromide under the Clean Air Act.[39]

Persistent Organic Pollutants (POPS)

The methyl bromide treaty may soon, in time, be joined by another global regime, dealing with a range of organochlorine pesticides. UNCED instigated a process of research which culminated in a UNEP declaration in support of a treaty similar to the methyl bromide Convention dealing with particularly persistent and environmentally damaging chemicals (POPS).

UNEP's governing council in 1997 endorsed the opinion of the UNCED-born Intergovernmental Forum on Chemical Safety that an international, binding treaty be set up to phase out the production and use of 12 POPS including: aldrin, chlorodane, DDT, dieldrin, endrin, heptachlor, hexachlorobenzene, minex, toxaphene and dioxins in their various forms (Decision No: 19/13c). UNEP proposed that an international negotiating committee should hold its first session in 1998 with a view to establishing a legal instrument by 2000, accompanied by an expert group charged with the role of determining further POPs to add to the initial list of 12. The UN Economic Commission for Europe took a lead in proceedings when 28 of its members from Europe and North America agreed to enact a regional treaty banning at least 10 of the 12 specified chemicals by 1998.[40]

Pressure Groups

Although the regulation of pesticide pollution remains a predominantly governmental concern, international non-governmental actors do play a role within the issue. Environmental pressure groups such as Greenpeace and Friends of the Earth include pesticide pollution on their agendas, and the Pesticide Action Network is as active on the ecological aspects of pesticides as it is on the other pesticide issues. PAN's 'Dirty Dozen' campaign was backed by Greenpeace and Friends of the Earth, and indeed was adopted from a similar domestic campaign organized by Environmental Action in the US. Launched on World Environment Day, June 5th 1985, the Dirty Dozen campaign does appear to have been influential in encouraging a reduction in the use of persistent organochlorine pesticides in the developed world.

The Worldwide Fund for Nature (WWF) also takes an interest in pesticides because of their environmental impact, as is evidenced by the employment of a Chemicals and Consumer Policy Officer. In this capacity, WWF's Peter Hurst, in collaboration with the Pesticides Trust and the Copenhagen Centre for Alternative Social Analysis, produced in December 1992 a report calling on governments to reduce pesticide use on environmental grounds. The report was particularly aimed at the member states of the OECD, appealing for them to follow the example of the Dutch, Danish, and Swedish governments and implement national pesticide reduction schemes.[41]

Similarly, IUCN has long maintained an interest in pesticide pollution matters. In 1966 the General Assembly of IUCN passed a resolution which, besides noting the environmental hazards posed by pesticides, called for greater control over the trade in these chemicals.[42] In 1980, IUCN collaborated with WWF, FAO, UNEP, and UNESCO (United Nations Educational, Scientific and Cultural Organization) to develop the World Conservation Strategy, a general outline of global guidelines for nature conservation. This strategy encouraged the wider introduction of non-chemical methods of pest control, arguing that:

> ... *excessive pesticide use promotes resistance ..., destroys natural enemies, turns formerly innocuous species into pests, harms other non-target species, and contaminates food and feed.*[43]

Pressure groups specializing in particular areas of wildlife protection have also been known to have an input into pesticide regulatory politics. The RSPB is, of course, principally a domestic organization, campaigning to safeguard the interests of wild bird species in the UK, but at times its work has had international ramifications. The 1991 banning of strychnine for controlling foxes in the Republic of Ireland was encouraged by the RSPB by the advancement of information linking the use of this poison and the decrease in numbers of birds of prey. The RSPB has also managed to exert an influence on the issue of human poisoning by pesticides through the use of its expertise on toxicity. The Pesticide Exposure Group of Sufferers (PEGS) was set up by Enfys Chapman in 1988 to counsel victims of sprayings after she had been provided with technical information concerning organophosphate poisoning, collated by the RSPB in the US.[44] This provides an interesting example of functional issue linkage, with the power of the RSPB, in terms of its resources and access to epistemic knowledge, giving it the capacity to influence a policy question, which seemingly is not salient to the group.

UN Agency Involvement

Within the UN system, although there are no commissions or working groups set up to deal specifically with pesticide pollution, a number of groups do have competence on the issue in an epistemic capacity. The Environmental Health Criteria Programme under the International Programme on Chemical Safety umbrella (see Chapter 4), includes environmental considerations in its reports on the toxicity of specific chemicals which are used by the International Register of Potentially Toxic Chemicals and other relevant organizations.

The UNEP/WHO Global Environmental Monitoring System (GEMS) has also been involved in producing information related to pesticide pollution. Set up after a recommendation at the 1972 UN Conference on the Human Environment at Stockholm, GEMS was intended 'to do the "earthwatching" and to provide the monitoring data needed for assessment of the state of the environment and for its environmentally sound management.'[45] In effect, Gosovic asserts, GEMS has never really developed as a truly coordinated system, claiming that this was always 'more of a wish and a verbal assertion than a reality'.[46] Instead, he summarizes the system as a 'series of discreet environmental monitoring projects carried out by agencies and partly or fully funded by UNEP'.[47] Moves to establish a permanent intergovernmental machinery were rejected at a 1974 Intergovernmental Meeting on Monitoring and any coordination has rested with the governing council of UNEP.

GEMS' brief is clearly wide, but it has taken part in some monitoring of DDT and other organochlorine pesticides in the biota. The most significant work of GEMS in the field of pesticide pollution has been in collating data on the contamination of drinking water sources, most recently in 1988.[48] An earlier assessment by GEMS was used by the WHO in publishing guideline values for drinking water sources. These guideline values were found to be exceeded in rivers in five countries and in lakes in three countries, and in one instance by a factor of 1000.[49]

Another relevant UN programme is the International Referral System for Sources of Environmental Information (INFOTERRA), organized by UNEP. Established in 1975, INFOTERRA is basically a network designed to be able to refer enquiries on a vast range of environmental topics to relevant registered institutions. Information on pesticides and their impact on the environment is obtainable through the network, which in 1984 became interlinked with the UNEP IRPTC (see Chapter 7). The IRPTC was designated as one of an original four INFOTERRA 'special sectoral sources' which were intended to provide 'comprehensive substantive information on priority environmental topics'.[50]

CONCLUSIONS

It is clear that the issue of pesticide induced environmental degradation is not subject to regulation by a single and specific regime as a subset of the issue system, in the way that we have seen for the issue of international pesticide trading, and is demonstrated in the following chapter on food contamination by pesticides. In effect it appears that, internationally, the issue is deeply integrated into the issue system of land source marine pollution and other areas within the wider issue of environmental degradation, such as ozone depletion and the survival of specific animal species. Policy questions within the issue of pesticide pollution thus are dependent on the perceived significance of related environmental questions for their placing on the international agenda. Methyl bromide was long recognized as a hazard to birds, bees and other wild animals,[51] but it took the recognition of its connection with the more high profile subject of ozone depletion for the chemical to become regulated globally. Epistemic consensus, in this case, needed to be allied to a sense of crisis before regulation could occur. This is a theme explored in the final chapter.

The issue system of pesticide pollution also greatly overlaps some of the other issues within the pesticides policy system, in terms of the epistemic community and, for the issue of pesticide trading, the regime. The national and European pesticide registration schemes and aspects of the International Programme on Chemical Safety, which were considered in Chapter 4, also incorporate environmental considerations, as we have seen. At the same time, the Prior Informed Consent procedure on which the international pesticide trade regime is centred can, of course, be seen indirectly as a regulatory body for the issues of both human poisoning and environmental degradation by pesticides. Under PIC, as we shall later see, the fact that a particular pesticide has been banned or severely restricted in one country on human health or environmental grounds is automatically made known to potential importers.

The point made at the start of this section, that the issue of pesticide induced environmental degradation is generally less contentious than other pesticide issues, is borne out by these isolated examples of international regulation. Only where the issue system overlaps either vertically with another issue within pesticides politics, or horizontally with another issue in the wider issue of environmental degradation, does any form of international regulation occur. Hence we see the importance of the placing of an issue on the international agenda, as perceived by actors, in influencing regime creation. This is a theme very much at the heart of international pesticide politics and is something that will be explored in Chapter 9.

6 The Secret Ingredient – The Issue of Food Contamination by Pesticides

INTRODUCTION

Chapter 4 considered the problem of human poisoning by pesticides resulting from a direct exposure to the chemicals. Human poisoning by pesticides can also occur indirectly, through the consumption of contaminated foodstuffs or drinking water. This form of poisoning adds an extra dimension to the more direct human poisoning considered earlier, because of the strong international dimension to the issue. Whereas exposure to pesticides through occupation or accident is basically a localized problem, capable of being countered by national legislation or education, the contamination of food must inevitably become a matter of worldwide concern because of the extensive international trade in this commodity. Any norm that food should not be traded if it is dangerously contaminated with pesticides needs to be adhered to equally by all participants in the world economy, if it is to have behavioural effect. Merely regulating imports nationally is insufficient as a means of upholding the norm, because if the regulations of a state are not in line with the export regulations of their trading partners, the supply of an essential commodity will disappear.

This reciprocity must in some way be responsible for the unique formalization of this norm on the international agenda. Clearly, the issue of food contamination is functionally related to that of pesticide trading but, as we shall see, the issue has developed its own distinct political process.

THE EXTENT OF THE PROBLEM

As with all areas of pesticidal pollution, the extent to which the presence of pesticide residues in food represents a threat to human health is unclear and hotly disputed between the actors to whom the issue is salient. High doses of agrochemical toxins have been responsible for a number of acute poisonings and even deaths of people eating the contaminated produce. The worst food poisoning epidemic of all time occurred in Iraq in 1971–72, due to the consumption of bread made from wheat grain treated with an organo-mercury fungicide. 6530 local farmers and members of their families were admitted to hospital with varying symptoms, and 459 died. The fact that the symptoms took at least 60 days to appear contributed to the size of this catastrophe.[1]

Direct poisoning of this sort results from an ignorance of the hazardous nature of pesticides. Reports from developing countries abound with stories of farmers continuing spraying right up until harvesting time, in the face of heavy pest infestation.[2] Pesticides are even known to have been used for fishing, as was illustrated in Chapter 5. There have even been cases of criminally fraudulent uses of pesticides, of which one of the most infamous concerned the doctoring of Italian wine in 1992. Four million litres of wine produced in the Veneto region of Northern Italy were seized by police and four men arrested for lacing the wine with pesticides, with the intention of slowing down the process of it turning to vinegar.[3]

Alongside the effects of such wanton misuse of pesticides, food produce can also be contaminated accidentally by spray drift or by a leakage of the chemicals during storage. 17 people were killed in 1976 due to being poisoned by the insecticide parathion, which had contaminated wheat flour in a warehouse storing the two together.[4]

Such cases represent extreme instances of poisonings resulting from malpractice, but the subtler health impact of pesticide residues remaining in foodstuffs after their normal application has emerged as a major consumer and health issue in the last 20 years.

A 1991 Report by the UK Working Party on Pesticide Residues found that 48 per cent of potatoes, 32 per cent of cereals and 29 per cent of fruit and vegetables that were sampled contained some traces of pesticides.[5] The rise to prominence in North America and Europe of organic food, grown without the aid of any chemical pesticides or fertilizers, is a testament to the public concern over the presence of potentially toxic residues in their food. However, even organic food has occasionally been found to contain traces of pesticides. In some instances this is likely to be a result of unscrupulous producers, but some minor contamination by pesticides in rain or groundwater is also possible.

The significance to human health of traces of pesticides that remain in foodstuffs from conventional pest control applications, or arrive there by environmental pollution, is subject to great debate. As was made clear in Chapter 4, many uncertainties exist in relation to the possible long-term effects on human health of pesticides. GCPF/GIFAP are unequivocal in defending their produce against charges of making foods carcinogenic or hazardous in some other way. 'The question is "Are we poisoning the very crops which we are seeking to protect?" The short answer is "No"'.[6]

The agrochemical industry point to their own testing procedure for new products which can often take over seven years and result in only 1 in 10–15,000 chemicals actually reaching the market. On top of this, they argue that government studies of pesticide residue levels in imported and home grown food, plus the national legislation dealing with this, provide an extra check that ensures consumer safety.[7]

However, although industry testing procedures and national regulations are generally quite stringent, in the North at least, poisonings by pesticides contained in food do occur. In the Republic of Ireland in 1992, 29 people suffered acute poisoning after eating cucumbers illegally treated with aldicarb, a carbamate classified as 1(a) in the WHO hazard scale.[8] Similarly, in 1985 108 people in the US were poisoned by aldicarb contained in Californian water melons.[9] The use of aldicarb was not approved nationally in either case, indicating that domestic inspection and control procedures are often inadequate guarantees of consumer safety. Senator Pat Upton, speaking in the wake of the Irish aldicarb poisoning outbreak, estimated that only 2000 samples of food were tested each year in Ireland out of a total of 2.5 million tonnes that are consumed.[10]

In addition to this problem of enforcing food safety standards, there remain questions as to the integrity of the corporate and national testing of pesticides, designed to determine their likelihood of remaining as residues in food. In September 1992 the President and three other employees of Craven Laboratories in Texas were found guilty of falsifying tests on pesticides, in order to get them approved for use by agrochemical companies. Craven's evaluations of pesticides had been accepted by the US Environmental Protection Agency, the UK Ministry of Agriculture and other national authorities for a number of years, and this revelation obviously created concern for the safety of foodstuffs treated with pesticides approved by the laboratory.[11] This was not the first time that a contracted testing laboratory had been found to have supplied bogus information relating to pesticides. Three executives at Industrial Bio Test (IBT) in the US were jailed after a trial in 1983, when it was discovered that they had concocted laboratory tests on animals in order to get certain pesticides and pharmaceutical chemicals registered.[12] IBT had apparently conducted around 800 tests on animals for 140 pesticides, most of which proved to be invalid. The fraudulent testing had been going on for a number of years and it is believed that the US government had been aware of it from as early as 1977.[13]

Aside from such cases of fraudulent testing, the findings of the scientific community concerned with the issue of the pesticide food contamination are often subject to much debate. Little epistemic consensus exists as to the effects on human health of small traces of various pesticides in food, despite the existence of global guidelines delimiting acceptable levels of the residues.

The carcinogenicity of certain pesticides is a particularly moot point, as was shown in Chapter 4. In the US the Delaney Clause – a provision of the Food, Drug and Cosmetic Act – effectively outlaws the presence of any suspected carcinogen from human food. This contrasts with most other national legislation schemes which generally accept that it is unnecessary to go to the trouble of prohibiting food on the basis of the presence of infinitesimally tiny traces of a suspected cancer-inducing chemical. Cancer scientist Bruce Ames, Director of the Environmental Health Sciences Centre at the University of California in Berkeley, has added his weight to the sceptics' camp. Ames' core argument is that it is hypocritical to show concern over the presence of pesticide traces in food, because such food invariably contains far greater levels of natural toxins. Ames has estimated that the average American consumes 1.5 grammes per day of 'natural pesticides', produced by all plants as a defence against predators, which amounts to 10,000 times the daily consumption of synthetic pesticides. Very few natural toxins have been tested on animals for carcinogenicity in the way that synthetic pesticides have, but of those that have been tested over half were found to cause cancer.[14] Ames goes further to argue that banning pesticides would actually result in an upsurge in cancer in the general public, as the resultant increase in fruit and vegetable prices would worsen the dietary intake of the poor, a factor known to increase the risks of cancer. He concludes by savaging the pressure groups who have campaigned to have stricter limits on pesticide use. 'The rich lawyers who are running environmental organizations may not care, but the poor care.'[15]

Ames' views have, of course, proved controversial. Pressure groups including The US Consumers Union, Parents for Safe Food, and the Pesticides Action Network, have criticized Ames for undermining their efforts to highlight dangerous food residues.

> *No one will dispute that there are natural toxins. The point is that pesticides are a controllable and avoidable extra burden to our bodies. People have little control over natural toxins, but can control – and expect controls on – artificial pesticides.*[16]

A similar lack of consensus exists over the potential for birth defects to ensue from the consumption in food of pesticides suspected to be teratogenic.

Another area of contention concerns the possibility of a so-called 'cocktail effect' of different pesticide residues in food. Pesticides are often used in combinations, and it has been shown that pesticides that are comparatively safe individually may acquire more dangerous properties when mixed with other chemicals (a process known as synergism).[17] In the UK, the Pesticides Trust has called for more testing of pesticide mixtures and *Which?* magazine has concluded that 'The possible effect of these mixtures on our health hasn't yet been fully assessed'.[18]

Aside from the divergence of opinion concerning the dangers of pesticide residues in foodstuffs, there is also some controversy over the actual need for chemical control in the case of some fruit and vegetables. It is well established that a certain percentage of pesticides is used not to save a crop from pest destruction, but merely to maintain its appearance to a particular standard. Customer expectations ensure that retailers demand blemish free products from farmers and exporters, although there are no discernible health risks inherent in partially brown bananas or lettuces containing a few holes in their leaves. Maintaining the cosmetic value of products leads to the spraying of crops until close to harvesting time, a practice which increases the likelihood of residues in the final product.

Similarly, consumer demand for fruits and vegetables out of season means that chemicals are often used on stored produce to avoid insect or fungus attack.

> *...now consumers are 'hooked' onto regular supplies of beautiful looking foods 365 days of the year. The increased risk of high pesticide residues is probably an inevitable side effect of this process.*[19]

Contamination of Drinking Water

A key route by which pesticides can enter the human body is via drinking water. Contamination of drinking water by pesticides occurs in two ways. Pesticides applied intentionally or accidently to rivers and lakes may be carried into aquifers, or secondly they may gradually be leaked into groundwater supplies through the soil. The latter process is very slow, and as a consequence it is the more persistent chemicals which tend to be found as contaminants in drinking water. More dramatic contaminations can occur when pesticides are dumped or spilled in large quantities. The section on water pollution in Chapter 5 described how a Californian drinking water supply was poisoned after the derailing of a railway tanker. A similar contamination occurred in Peterborough in 1992, when an aquifer serving the city was infected by waste produce from a weedkiller manufacturer dumped nearby. The scale of contamination was massive, but was prevented from reaching households by newly installed water filtration technology. No human harm resulted from this incident, but the fact that such a large scale contamination of an aquifer could occur obviously highlights a potentially widespread danger to human health, particularly in countries lacking modern water treatment technology.[20]

THE POLITICS OF PESTICIDE RESIDUES

The norm that food contamination by pesticides should be limited, it will transpire, is the one of the proscriptive norms of pesticide politics that has proved itself most salient to the actors in the policy system and travelled furthest down the road of international regulation. The desire for international standards, delimiting acceptable levels of pesticide residues, has proved more widespread than that for more general human exposure and for environmental pollution.

This consensus on the need for global rules, however, emerges despite wide differences in opinion on the actual threat to human health posed by traces of pesticides in food. The basic premise that the presence of toxic chemicals in foodstuffs is undesirable is of course unquestionable, but a wide divergence of opinion exists as to how far to go to safeguard human health. In the US, as we have seen, the Delaney Clause of the Food, Drug and Cosmetic Act effectively outlaws the presence of any suspected carcinogen from

US foodstuffs, even in minute amounts. This sort of absolutist stance is also adopted by some pressure group activists. Lang and Clutterbuck conclude their chapter on residues in food in *P is for Pesticides* by stating bluntly 'there should be **no** contamination of food by pesticides'.[21]

This strand of opinion is rejected, predictably enough, by the chemical industry, but also by much of the epistemic community. Bruce Ames, as we have seen, is very much opposed to this approach, and many other scientists have argued that it is folly to worry about inconceivably small traces of chemicals in everyday food. GCPF and GIFAP have made full use of such scientific opinions, in producing reports dismissing the threat to human health of pesticide residues in food.

> *The foundation of modern toxicology rests on the tenet that 'the dose makes the poison'. Indeed, without specifying amounts, the word 'toxic' is meaningless. Many dietary compounds which at small levels are harmless or even essential to health can be toxic at higher levels – Vitamin A is a particularly well known example.*[22]

A rather more eccentric approach to demonstrating the lack of danger posed to health by ingesting pesticides was adopted by the well known entomologist, Dr Ronald Fennah. Dr Fennah, who was to later become Director of the Commonwealth Institute of Entomology, whilst working in the West Indies in the 1940s is reported to have inhaled daily 100mg of DDT powder, and drunk water dusted with the insecticide for 13 months. This bizarre ritual was carried out to demonstrate the safety of the only recently discovered chemical. Fennah apparently suffered no ill effects and lived to the age of 77.[23]

GIFAP Residue Working Group

GIFAP set up a group to represent the interests of the pesticide industry on questions arising within the issue of residues in food. As has already been mentioned, the agrochemical industry has frequently utilized favourable scientific opinion in producing papers countering claims made about the potential harm resulting from pesticide residues in food. The Residue Working Group made an effort to provide personnel for any FAO trials concerning residues in food, and for all Codex Committee on Pesticide Residues (CCPR) meetings. No specific group deals with residues under the GCPF system but experts are still utilized to promote the industry's position.

Pressure Groups

The issue of pesticide residues in food is a concern of many of the aforementioned environmental and consumer organizations such as Greenpeace, Friends of the Earth, and the International Organization of Consumers Unions, as well of course as PAN. PAN has facilitated links between these groups on the issue of residues in food, particularly in the context of the Dirty Dozen campaign. This campaign, which touched upon all of the proscriptive norms in pesticide politics, included an effort to raise public awareness of the potential hazard to health posed by the presence of certain pesticides in foodstuffs. The IOCU, along with the US based pressure group the National Resources Defense Council (NRDC), collaborated on an article entitled *Your Daily Dose of Pesticide Residues* promoted as part of PAN's *Dirty Dozen Information Packet*.[24] This article warned that the existence of national and UN acceptable daily intake levels (ADI) and maximum residue limits (MRLs) for residues in food is not sufficient to guarantee human safety.

> *There is no foolproof way of ensuring an absolutely safe universal ADI given the diversity of food products consumed and different vulnerabilities of individual consumers, especially young children and malnourished people, who are more susceptible than the 'average' person, assumed in tests to be a well-fed adult man.*[25]

Abraham and Mott also highlighted the difficulties in implementing MRLs and ADIs, citing that only one in fifteen shipments of fruit and vegetables crossing the US/Mexican border is inspected, and that residue testing in much of the developing world is negligible.

The Regulation of Drinking Water Contamination

The problem of pesticide residues in drinking water is often treated as separate from the general issue of food contamination, and has attracted some distinctive actors and rules. The Codex Alimentarius Commission, which serves as a multi-regime for the whole wider issue of food contamination, does technically include drinking water within the definition of its subject matter. 'Food means any substance, whether processed, semiprocessed, or raw, which is intended for human consumption, and includes drink. . .'[26]

In practice, however, Codex's guideline standards, including those of the Codex Committee on Pesticide Residues (CCPR), have generally not been applied to drinking water. An exception to this exists for bottled mineral water, as this is a traded product, but as standard drinking water is transported and consumed within state boundaries it is not considered within the Codex's sphere of interest.

Clearly, drinking water contamination is linked functionally to the issue of environmental pollution by pesticides, and some of the organizations referred to in Chapter 5 are also active in the area of residues in food. GEMS, as was outlined in Chapter 5, has been involved in setting global standards for the contamination of drinking water sources since 1976, research which led to the WHO establishing a figure of ten microgrammes of pesticides per litre of water as a global safety standard.[27] Friends of the Earth have become involved in this area through their work on river pollution. In 1988 FoE reported the UK government to the European Commission, over levels of 12 different weedkillers in tap water in a number of parts of the country. The Commission took up the case and in 1991 Carlo Ripa di Meana, the Environment Commissioner, chastised the government for permitting regional water companies to exceed EC standards.

Throughout the late 1980s and 1990s the EC established maximum admissible concentrations (MACs) for pesticides which have been adopted by member states. The EC standards are stringent, the MAC for the presence of any pesticide in water being 0.1 microgrammes per litre and 0.5 microgrammes per litre for mixtures of pesticides, a level 100 times lower than the WHO standard.

This delimitation has met with opposition throughout the EC for being excessively cautious and expensive to implement. Representatives of the water industry in the UK responded to Commission criticism of standards in Southern England by claiming that the Directive had no scientific basis. Derek Miller of the Water Research Centre reasoned that: 'Often you cannot even measure such low amounts... The directive amounts to a statement that we do not want any pesticides in our water', and concluded that 'there is no toxicological basis for trying to do it'.[28]

In 1992, UK water industry representatives and scientists coordinated with like-minded colleagues in other EU countries to form Eureau, an international lobby group aiming to revise the Drinking Water Directive. Eureau held the first in a regular series of campaigning seminars in London in July 1992. Whilst cost-cutting is undoubtably one aim of the group, they deny that this is their sole objective.

> *We are not trying to weaken the Directive, but only to bring it up to date with current scientific knowledge. We want to weed out the redundant bits, add new parameters in some places – for example, to include bromine compounds – and to make others more specific. We want to spend money where there is good evidence of a risk to health.*[29]

The Codex Alimentarius Commission's Role in Regulating Pesticide Residue Levels in Food

Very much at the heart of the issue system of pesticide residues in food, and the wider issue of food contamination, is the Codex Alimentarius Commission, the implementing machinery of the Joint FAO/WHO Food Standards Programme (Figure 6.1). The Commission began life in 1963 following the recommendation of an FAO/WHO Conference on Food Standards in the previous year.

> *The purpose of the Programme is to protect the health of consumers and to ensure fair practices in the food trade; to promote coordination of all food standards work undertaken by international governmental and non-governmental organizations; to determine priorities and initiate and guide the preparation of draft standards through and with the aid of appropriate organizations; to finalize standards and after acceptance by governments publish them in a Codex Alimentarius either as regional or worldwide standards.*[30]

The membership of Codex is open to any member state or associate member of the FAO and WHO that wishes to join. Regular sessions of the Commission are held once a year at the headquarters of either the WHO or FAO, in Geneva and Rome respectively. The member states of the Commission vote on a majority basis for the adoption of a draft standard for a particular issue concerned with food quality. An allowance is also made, within the rules governing Codex, for regional standards 'on the proposal of the majority of members belonging to a given region submitted at a session of the Codex Alimentarius Commission'.[31] In most instances, the draft standards voted on at the Commission are prepared by subsidiary bodies specializing in a particular issue.

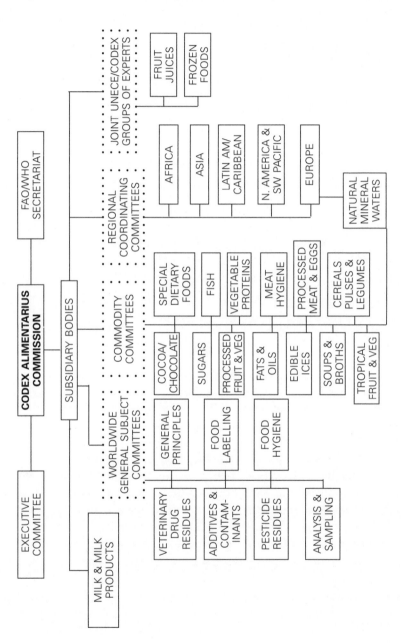

Figure 6.1 *Organizational structure of the Codex Alimentarius Commission and subsidiary bodies*[32]

The Codex Committee on Pesticide Residues

The Codex Committee on Pesticide Residues (CCPR) consists of delegations of the member states of the Commission who meet normally once a year, for a week, in The Netherlands. The main part of these meetings is taken up designating MRLs for particular pesticides in food. The MRL is a figure denoting the maximum permissible amount of a pesticide in a food. It is calculated by estimating how much of a particular produce a person could consume without exceeding the acceptable daily intake (ADI) of residues. The ADI can be defined as:

> *The amount of a chemical which can be consumed every day for an individual's entire lifetime with the practical certainty, on the basis of all the known facts, that no harm will result.*[33]

The ADI, in turn, is established by deducing the level at which the chemical has 'no observed effect' on animals and dividing this by a safety factor of 100. Another means of deciding this figure may be used as 'determined by toxicologists in the light of all relevant facts known at the time'.[34] The MRL also tries to take account of regional variations in pest control practices, as the standard figure is based on trials conducted according to good agricultural practices (GAPs), by which FAO guidelines for safe and optimal pesticide use are observed.

This technical work is undertaken by the CCPR's sister group, the Joint Meeting on Pesticide Residues (JMPR),[35] an annual grouping of experts from the FAO and WHO, who meet alternately in Rome and Geneva in September every year. Meetings are composed of government scientists and leading academics in the field, without any corporate representation. The CCPR's deliberations are very much reliant on the findings of this body, whose task it is to respond to its technical queries and devise appropriate MRLs for it to consider.

The establishment of MRLs for pesticides is a lengthy and multi-faceted procedure, summarized in Figure 6.2.

Government acceptance of Codex MRLs is encouraged by permitting two degrees of compliance – 'full acceptance' and 'free distribution'. A government giving full acceptance to a Codex MRL undertakes to ensure that any imported or home produced food conforms with the relevant specifications and that it will not enact legislation to hinder the distribution of any food conforming with the limit. A government agreeing to free distribution with regards

i	CCPR arrange priority list for consideration by its annual meeting (often after a recommendation by member).
1	JMPR prepare recommended limits.
2/3	Secretariat distributes the MRL recommendations to governments and IOs for comments/proposed amendments.
4	CCPR formulates recommendations for proposed DRAFT CODEX MAXIMUM LIMITS.
5	Proposal submitted to Commission via secretariat with view to adoption as a DRAFT STANDARD.
6*	DRAFT STANDARD sent out to all members and any interested IOs for comment.
7*	CCPR considers comments and decides whether to amend draft standard.
8	Draft standard submitted to Commission by Secretariat with view to adoption as a CODEX STANDARD.

a	CODEX STANDARD circulated to governments for acceptance.
b	Standard published as APPROVED CODEX MRL.

* These stages may be omitted if CCPR decides a pesticide is non-controversial

Figure 6.2 *Codex Alimentarius Commission decision making process for the establishment of maximum residue limits*

to Codex MRLs commits itself only to the second of the two requirements.[36] In addition, governments which do not accept a Codex MRL are requested to state the reasons why.[37] Boardman, using data collated in 1981, estimated that government acceptance of Codex MRLs, either in full or partial, was just under 70 per cent.[38] By 1992 over 2,000 MRLs had been set for 80 pesticides.[39]

The CCPR conducts much of its work through *ad hoc* working groups, which meet separately and report back during the Committee's session. The Ad Hoc Working Group on Priorities and Ad Hoc Working Group on Acceptances have specific roles to play in the formulation, dealing respectively with sections (i) and (a) of the above diagram. Two other *ad hoc* groups also meet during a CCPR session, working on the questions of residue problems in developing countries and the methods of analysis. Hence, the CCPR has also been involved in making recommendations to the Commission on the means of providing technical assistance to developing countries to aid the testing for residues in food. The Commission can then pass on such information to the FAO or any other organizations involved in an aid programme.

EC Residue Regulation

Whilst it can be seen from the figures of government acceptances of Codex MRLs that a certain level of international harmonization has been achieved, the most extensive consensus has occurred within the European Union, as is the case in other areas of pesticide politics.

The EU has a number of directives which adopt MRLs for a variety of foodstuffs and pesticides. The directives draw on the work of the CCPR and JMPR, but do not set identical MRLs, in general favouring more stringent limits. The UK Ministry of Agriculture has acknowledged the role of the CCPR by stating that 'Codex MRLs are taken as presumptive standards in the absence of a UK MRL'.[40]

The EU's involvement in the issue of pesticide residues in food derives from the 1986 Single European Act, Article 100a of which commits the European Commission to ensure the member states apply a high degree of environmental, consumer and public health protection.[41] The 1990 Directive on Residues in Fruit and Vegetables[42] updated an earlier non-mandatory directive setting MRLs for a wide range of fruit, vegetables and animal foodstuffs.[43] In addition, directives exist covering cereals,[44] meat, and dairy products.[45] Member states are permitted to enact lower national MRLs but products within the EU standard should be allowed free movement across national borders. MRLs can be periodically amended by a majority vote in the Council of Ministers, but new standards require unanimity.

The International Impact of a Codex MRL

Aside from the EU, the setting of legally binding residue limits for pesticides in distributed food has remained the preserve of national authorities. The US, for instance, has in general set far more vigorous limits for its foodstuffs than those set by Codex, largely due to the catch-all Delaney Clause. However, the existence of international guidelines has at least provided standards by which governments may be judged and lobbied. Monitoring of international food contamination standards with the aid of the benchmark Codex ADIs and MRLs has been undertaken by the UN, the chemical industry, and pressure groups alike.

GEMS coordinated an extensive survey of 11 countries (Australia, Austria, Canada, Guatemala, Hungary, Ireland, US, UK, New Zealand, Sweden, Japan), with data derived from 12 years of research (1971–1983).[46] The findings from the 11 collaborating centres show that the intake of organochlorine and organophosphorous pesticides was always within JMPR ADI standards where they existed, although some samples contained aldrin, dieldrin and lindane levels close to the limit.

GIFAP's Residues Working Group conducted a monitoring of national food contamination levels, the findings of which have been published as the periodically updated report *Pesticides in Food*. The reports serve to show that residue levels are invariably found to be within Codex limits but some discrepancies are reported. For example, a survey of Swedish food contamination standards, using data derived from the Swedish National Food Administration, found that 0.5 per cent of domestic food commodity samples and over 3 per cent of imported food samples exceeded maximum legal levels. The report accounts for this by stating that:

> *(Sweden's) . . . maximum allowable levels are based on ADIs from the JMPR which are conservative and that occasional samples over these tolerances are not considered to represent any serious health hazard.*[47]

Pressure groups concerned with the issue of residues in food have also been known to use Codex standards to highlight cases of contamination, even though these groups are generally critical of such standards (as emerges later in this section). Greenpeace in Brazil in 1991 conducted spot checks on foodstuffs in several cities and found that, on average, between 2 and 5 per cent contained pesticide residues over the MRLs of the government or Codex.[48]

In general then, it appears that monitoring and testing operations have found that Codex standards for residue levels are only very occasionally exceeded. However, as was illustrated earlier in this chapter, concern has been raised about the quality of such testing. Evidence that only tiny fractions of food are routinely tested in a developed country like the Republic of Ireland and that major testing laboratories in the US have been proved to be fraudulent raises the question of how much impact global guidelines standards can have, particularly in developing countries, where the problem is clearly going to be most acute.

The Future of Codex

Codex pesticide MRLs have developed as a significant set of global guidelines for the issue of residues in food, despite their essentially voluntary character, and clear problems in their implementation as even non-compulsory standards. They serve as a yardstick by which governments may be judged in the absence of national standards, and as a guide for governments as to what is internationally acceptable when setting such national standards.

The status of Codex standards, in pesticide as well as other food contaminants have, however, been the subject of debate concerning their establishment as legally binding global demarcations. This arose out of the efforts of GATT and a number of actors supporting it, to liberalize world trade in as many commodities as possible. National differences, in the levels of contaminants permissible in food produce, create obstacles to the free trading of such produce, contrary to the ethos of GATT (now World Trade Organization (WTO)), who favour globally agreed standards.

In October 1989, the Bush administration in the US presented the 'double zero' plan at the Uruguay Round of GATT talks, which aimed to curb domestic agricultural subsidies and the right of states to limit the importing of food on non-scientific grounds. The criteria deemed not to represent scientific evidence included social, economic, cultural, and religious grounds for limiting food imports. In effect, the basis of the plan was that a state would be required to prove scientifically the need for a particular restriction on food imports. The plan advocated the legitimizing of Codex food standards as the source of acceptable scientific evidence on which the international trade in foodstuffs should be governed. GATT took on board this idea in 1990 and hence it could have become internationally binding law on the completion of the Uruguay Round.

Had this occurred, any attempt by a country to enforce domestic
MRLs on food stricter than those advocated by Codex would have
led to them being challenged to justify the legislation on health or
environment grounds, or else facing the penalty of either GATT
sanctioned trade retaliation or the payment of compensation to
exporting countries.

Environmental and consumer groups were alarmed at this prospect
because, as we have seen, Codex standards are often lower than those
set nationally (or by the EU). A worldwide lowering of standards
was thus seen as the likely scenario of the international harmonization of food standards, including those limiting pesticide residues.

> *If Codex standards become a 'ceiling' on the regulations that can be enforced
> on imported goods, farmers in countries with stricter standards will find
> themselves competing with imported foods produced under much less strict
> environmental regulations. If this situation begins to threaten their economic
> survival, they may feel compelled to lobby for lower standards to create a
> level playing field.*[49]

The underlying fear of environmental and consumer groups is that
Codex standards cannot be relied upon to guarantee consumer safety
because the body is not impartial in its judgements.

> *Under the provisions of the draft GATT treaty, responsibility would be handed
> over to a small group of supposed experts, many of whom have vested interests
> in the companies whose products they are judging.*[50]

The evidence that Codex committees are populated more by
industrial and corporate representatives than those representing
consumers is incontestable. The UK based pressure group National
Food Alliance in 1993 published a report based on two years of
monitoring Codex Committees (1989 to 1991), which was endorsed
by 47 other groups worldwide, and highlighted this apparent bias.
The report found that of the 2578 participants in the various
meetings only 26 came from consumer organizations with none from
environmental groups. In contrast, 660 of the participants came from
the food industry.[51] The report goes on to call for a reform of Codex
to increase the representation of public interest groups. However,
the selection of participants is made by governments when compiling
a national delegation to send to the Codex Commission and various
committees, so this imbalance can not really be blamed on Codex
itself.

It is clear, however, that the adoption of Codex MRLs in place of national limits would, in general, represent a loosening of safety standards in many countries. In the US, for example, the adoption of Codex MRLs would greatly increase the acceptable levels of DDT residues (EPA Action Thresholds) in the following foods: Broccoli (×33), Carrots (×10), Grapes (×20), Lettuce (×33), Potatoes (×50), Apples (×10), Bananas (×50), Peaches (×50), Pineapples (×33), Strawberries (×20).[52] Standards would also be relaxed in Europe and many other developed countries.

It is an interesting illustration of the incoherence of the state an as actor in modern international politics that the US government should have campaigned internationally for rulings that would undermine its own domestic legislation and with it American sovereignty. Bush's Double Zero plan can be construed as having been a continuation of a long running power struggle between the president and the Environmental Protection Agency. In the 1980s the Reagan administration attempted to dilute the EPA's pesticide standards with the intention of reducing the regulatory burdens on the food industry. EPA officials sympathetic to the industry were appointed and an attempt to change the science of toxicology was made by altering the safe factor by which residues are divided in calculating the legal limit and encouraging less emphasis to be placed on data derived from animal testing.[53] Reagan's changes failed to get off the ground, however, owing to disapproval by the courts and Congress, creating a simmering feud between the executive and EPA which re-emerged in 1989 despite a change in President, with Bush replacing Reagan.

The overwhelming conclusion which can be drawn from this domestic political struggle, and from the composition of national delegations to Codex meetings, is that corporate interests often seem to predominate over those of environmental and consumer groups in the eyes of governments. Hence, the international legitimation of Codex standards is feared by environmentalists as a global corporate conspiracy riding roughshod over the interests and rights of consumers. In an intriguing twist to the traditional dialogue between Governments and pressure groups, the issue of food safety has seen environmental and consumer organizations citing the threat to national sovereignty posed by government backed action.

Food standards should be set openly, their main purpose being the protection of consumers and the environment. Individual nations should not be obliged to sacrifice high standards in order to facilitate world trade and the movement of global capital.[54]

CONCLUSION

The role played by the Codex Committee on Pesticide Residues within the issue of food contamination by pesticides does appear to fulfil the criteria of an international regime as defined by Krasner, and adopted for this study. The CCPR, in fact, can best be conceived as a regime within the multi-regime of the Codex Alimentarius Commission, which regulates the whole wider issue of food quality standards. The Codex Alimentarius Commission has some 30 subsidiary bodies, five of which act as Regional Coordinating Committees, one of which deals with general principles, whilst the rest deal with a particular foodstuff or contaminant.

Despite the levels of dispute as to the actual threats to human health posed by the presence of pesticide traces in food, the norm that such contamination needs to be in some way delimited seems to meet near universal acceptance. Although their motives may be different, environmentalist and consumer groups, the food and chemical industry, and governments acknowledge the need for standards governing the issue.

Codex deliberations over pesticides and other questions of food quality have been subject to criticism, particularly by pressure groups, but its standards have had an impact internationally. The work of the JMPR concerning pesticides is a strong source of international technical expertise, which we have seen is drawn upon by governments, as well as the CCPR in setting rules governing the distribution of food. Thus, the JMPR represents the focus of the epistemic community within the issue, whereas the CCPR is part of a multifaceted regime, setting rules to be approved by the decision-making machinery of the Codex Alimentarius Commission.

The behavioural effect of the regime on related actors is seen in the high level of acceptance of its rulings by member governments, and the fact that its standards are widely accepted as applicable in the absence of comparable national standards. Thus there is at least a partial implementation of its rules, which is sufficient to consider it as fulfilling the functions of an international regime.

The possibility remains, however, of the CCPR, and Codex as a whole, strengthening its role by having its rules becoming binding on all members and enforceable with sanctions. If the wishes of many vested interests in politics are ever realized, Codex could actually acquire genuine supranational authority, backed by WTO as the enforcer. This would be a real case of a world government for food standards, a true regime rather than a quasi regime, as the present arrangement could in the circumstances be conceptualized.

This strengthening of the regime, if it were to come about, would represent a classic case of international bargaining, of governments realizing the collective benefits of collaboration. Such a development would open up a significant amount of international trade, netting governments anything between US$200 billion and US$5.2 trillion in total.[55] A cynical view of this, in the context of the empowerment of a non-elected global body to govern food standards, is that even the sacred cow of state sovereignty may be sacrificed on the altar of profit.

In effect, the increased authority of Codex would reflect a change in its underlying principle. Rather than fundamentally being guided by the motive of safeguarding the quality of food commodities, as Codex was in its foundation and still is today, the regime would in this instance be more geared towards the goal of standardizing the regulation of food commodities in order to facilitate trade. The regime and its salient actors in this scenario would undergo a shift in their values, becoming more informed by the desire to maximize economic gains in comparison to the value of minimizing human suffering. This would not be to say that the latter value would be necessarily subserviant to the former, but it would certainly be in competition with it in shaping the aspirations of the actors.

Codex standards are presently almost certainly sufficient to safeguard human health. The work of the JMPR is impartial and well respected. Codex standards, despite the levels of corporate influence, reflect their work to a large extent. The fear exists however that with an inexact science like toxicology, judgements could over time become too informed by the value of maximizing economic gains and less so by that of minimizing human suffering. The lack of epistemic concensus on the issue, as highlighted earlier in this chapter, could allow the purpose of the regime to become blurred or even, some fear, to be hijacked by the free trade ethos of big business.

When scientists do reach agreement, it can be a powerful force that can even overcome political and national differences. However, when science is uncertain, as is typically the case is assessing the risks of toxic chemicals, there is more room for political factors to shape the way different countries interpret science in making policy decisions.[56]

Governments are prepared to override the value of maximizing economic gains when scientific evidence of a threat to human welfare or the environment is presented clearly, as seen in the agreement to cut methyl bromide production and use (see Chapter 5) and various other environmental regimes, but when evidence is less clear cut they are less inclined to do so.

7 Peddling Poisons – The International Trade in Pesticides

THE PROBLEM DEFINED

The introduction into developing countries of Northern agricultural technology in the 1960s and 1970s, known commonly as the 'Green Revolution', created a dependence on pesticides produced in the North and opened up a massive new trade, flowing from North to South. Over 90 per cent of all pesticides are produced in the industrialized North and, while most of the trade in these products is within these countries, some 20 per cent of pesticides are sold to the South to the tune of around £2.4 billion per year.[1] With increased public consciousness of pollution and the merits of organic farming in Europe and the US, the developing country market looks set to continue to expand and become increasingly attractive to the big agrochemical firms in the North.

International regulation of the trading of pesticides has, until recently, been extremely lax and certainly not kept in step with municipal law in the developed states. Awareness of the hazardous nature of many substances used for pest control has gradually seen the most toxic chemicals becoming banned or restricted, with rigorous safety guidelines for their application developed. Many pesticides banned and withdrawn from use domestically in the developed world, however, have continued to be marketed to developing countries where most states have weak regulatory procedures or lack the resources to efficiently enforce those that do exist. The response of many agrochemical firms to greater scrutiny of their produce by health and environmental groups has been to redirect their goods to such less restrictive markets. Following the banning of DDT in the US because of its carcinogenic qualities, some chemical companies turned to Southern trading partners to stave off losses from accumulated stocks of the chemical. Possibly as a result of this, DDT levels in the average Nicaraguan and

Guatemalan citizen in 1981 were reported to be over 30 times that of the citizens of their major trading partner.[2] Many reports show that pesticides banned in the US such as dieldrin, aldrin, heptochlor, and chlordane have been freely marketed abroad, along with the particularly lethal leptophos, a chemical never registered in the US.[3] In 1981 Weir and Schapiro revealed that over 25 per cent of the US's exported pesticides were unregistered, with their destination invariably being a developing country.[4] Often the main importers of such products are subsidiary bodies of the companies manufacturing them in the first place. A Costa Rican offshoot plant of Standard Oil of California was in 1979 reputed to be the principal importer of pesticides restricted in North America.[5]

The flood of particularly toxic pesticides into the South, backed up by persuasive advertising, has accentuated the problems which arose when such products were used widely in the North, as specialized knowledge on pesticides is much more scarce and high levels of illiteracy prevent workers from even reading safety instructions printed in their own language. A clear theme which emerges is that the side-effects of pesticide use – human poisoning, environmental pollution and food contamination – are at their most damaging in the developing world. As these costs have become apparent, the development of the norm that the international trade in pesticides needs to be controlled has occurred.

It is probably not being over cynical to argue that acceptance of this norm has been influenced by the realization in the North that trading in deadly toxins is also ultimately hurting itself. Pesticides profitably dumped on the Southern market can return to Northern consumers in their food imports from the same countries, in a process which has been labelled the 'circle of poison'.[6] In 1967, for example, 300,000 lbs of beef from Nicaragua were refused entry into the US, because of excessive DDT levels. Central America had been one of the chief recipients of restricted US pesticide exports during this period.[7] The consumer demand for products such as coffee, sugar, and particularly cotton ensures that this circle cannot be broken without acting on the problem of the trade in dangerous pesticides. The US government in 1981 estimated that 5 per cent of imported food contained levels of pesticide residues illegal under domestic restrictions.[8] Around 50–70 per cent of all food produced in the South is exported to developed countries, rather weakening one defence of the agrochemical corporations that their trade helps improve living standards in the less developed countries by increasing food production levels.

REGULATING THE INTERNATIONAL TRADE IN PESTICIDES

Whether their motivations are genuinely altruistic or purely those of self-interest, it is evident that there is some consensus amongst the actors within pesticides politics that the international trading of the chemicals needs to be subject to some form of control. GCPF have acquiesced to the norm of regulating the trade in pesticides on the basis that greater uniformity in the limits of residues in food will at least simplify the process of trade, even though trading standards may be tightened.

International Register of Potentially Toxic Chemicals

The first organization to take steps towards establishing guidelines for international pesticide trading was UNEP. The idea of an International Register of Potentially Toxic Chemicals (IRPTC) was first aired at the 1972 Stockholm Conference on the Human Environment, and came into existence in 1976. UNEP's initial aspirations in this area were ambitious, seeking to develop rules 'as a first step towards a global convention',[9] but ultimately the IRPTC developed more humbly as a body for facilitating information exchange.

The register is coordinated from the Programme Activity Centre in Geneva and its two chief services are the running of an extensive data bank providing hazard assessments and regulatory information on chemicals and the operation of a global network which facilitates collaboration on such matters with other organizations. The recipients of such technical information are varied.

Although IRPTC is designed primarily to aid national authorities responsible for the protection of human health and the environment, its services are currently available to everyone at no cost.[10]

UN Consolidated List

After a series of resolutions in the UN General Assembly which raised alarm about the trading of toxic chemicals, a Consolidated List of Products Whose Consumption and/or Sale Have Been Banned, Withdrawn, or Not Approved by Governments[11] was compiled in 1982. The vote to compile the list was carried by 146 votes to one, with the US as the sole opponent. This directory has been regularly updated and contains details of over 500 hazardous products, of which around a third are pesticides.

FAO Code of Conduct

The most comprehensive attempt to establish a framework of guidelines for the international trade in pesticides is found within the FAO's Code of Conduct on the Distribution and Use of Pesticides.[12] The Code's guidelines relating to the safe use of pesticides, such as labelling and registration standards, have been discussed earlier. What will now be considered are the provisions relating to the distribution of pesticides. The two most relevant articles in this regard are Article 8 'Distribution and Trade' and Article 9 'Information Exchange'.

Article 8 calls upon the agrochemical industry to ensure all products are fully tested before being exported and that the results of these tests are submitted to the importing country's authorities before the products arrive. A further provision requests that pesticides intended for export be properly packaged and labelled in accordance with the guidelines set out elsewhere in the Code. Article 8.1.5 attempts to address the problem referred to earlier, whereby subsidiary bodies of big multinational chemical companies within developing countries are responsible for importing pesticides restricted in the country of the parent company. The provision requires companies to ensure that the subsidiary bodies employ the same standards in producing or manufacturing pesticides as are required in their own countries.

Article 9 deals with the question of notifying importing countries as to the nature of traded pesticide chemicals. It is suggested that governments of exporting countries should inform the authorities of the importing state if they have restricted the use of the pesticide domestically. Article 9.5 acknowledges the role of UNEP's IRPTC and calls on governments to provide information on pesticide control legislation prior to the implementation of the FAO Code, in the form of an inventory for the IRPTC. A further provision in the article charges the governments of importing countries with the responsibility of establishing procedures for receiving and dealing with such information exchanges.

The evidence from studies monitoring the FAO Code, in the first few years after its introduction, was that the provisions dealing with pesticide trade and information exchange had little impact in the underdeveloped countries. A detailed report of several non-governmental organizations coordinated by the Environmental Liaison Centre which examined implementation in 12 countries in Africa, Asia and South America concluded that:

> *In each of the countries surveyed, pesticides containing ingredients classified by WHO in class 1A or class 1B were found to be freely available and being transported, sold, and used in extremely unsafe manners.*[13]

The explanation for this was that:

> *It is clearly beyond the capabilities of the governments in these countries to provide the massive inputs necessary to control the trade in these products.*[14]

Similarly, an FAO questionnaire distributed to all UN members in 1986 evaluating the impact of the Code of Conduct found that over 40 per cent of governments in Africa, Asia and the Pacific region had not been receiving any notification from exporters when importing banned or highly restricted pesticides.[15]

PAN from the outset were unequivocal in their belief that the Code's 'haphazard prior notification scheme' was inadequate:

> *Even countries with adequate regulations in place find that notification arrives all too often after a dangerous chemical has already entered the market.*[16]

Prior Informed Consent

PAN and the other pressure groups critical of pesticide trading practices were adamant that the shortfalls of the FAO Code's distribution provisions could be remedied by the inclusion of a requirement that importing countries give 'prior informed consent' (PIC) before receiving pesticides. According to PAN, PIC means that:

> *Before a pesticide that is banned or restricted in its country of origin can be exported to another country, an authorized government in the importing country must (1) be notified about the pending import along with the reason the pesticide is restricted in the country of origin, and (2) agree to the pesticide's importation.*[17]

The FAO Code's notification requirements in Article 9 were always very much a compromise measure designed to avoid antagonizing the chemical industry, and never satisfied the demands of the various pressure groups lobbying for trade regulations. The OECD, hardly a vociferous campaigner against developing country exploitation, in 1984 adopted a notification scheme which though falling short of PIC went further than the FAO Code. The Guiding Principles on Information Exchange Related to Export of Banned or Severely Restricted Chemicals[18] revolved around the idea of a two-tiered notification procedure, under which the initial information exchange on exporting a restricted chemical can be supplemented by further information at the request of the importing country.

UNEP adopted a similar two-tier notification scheme[19] but only after more ambitious 'prior authorization' guidelines proposed by a Working Group of Experts had been dropped in the face of pressure from GIFAP and representatives of the exporting countries. Similar pressures were responsible for the last minute withdrawal of PIC from Article 9 of the FAO Code of Conduct during its ratification in 1985. Despite appearing on seven of the eight drafts of the Code, PIC was removed for the final draft, apparently in the face of strong UK and US persuasion.

> *The FAO, already preoccupied with famine issues, was politely reminded that its sister organization, UNESCO, lost 25 per cent of its budget when the United States, angered by its policies, withdrew funding.*[20]

No national delegation officially requested the deletion of the PIC provision and 30 countries protested at its removal, but it appears that covert pressure convinced delegates at the ratifying conference that the Code as a whole would be at risk if a compromise over Article 9 was not accepted.

> *The majority expressed deep concern that the principle of 'Prior Informed Consent' no longer appeared in the present version of the Code... These members, however, recognized the need not to delay the adoption of the Code.*[21]

Led by PAN and Oxfam, the campaign to incorporate PIC into Article 9 of the FAO Code carried on regardless of the 1985 ratification. Oxfam's attempts to incorporate PIC into UK legislation via the 1985 Food and Environment Protection Act was rejected by the government on the basis that it was unnecessary because 'Britain will honour all of its international obligations'.[22] A few weeks later the UK's 'international obligations', in the shape of the FAO Code, emerged minus PIC. In other arenas, however, the PIC proponents did make some headway. The Netherlands became the first country to formally embrace PIC into domestic legislation in 1985 and the

EC made moves towards adopting the procedure for all its member states before eventually absorbing the whole FAO Code of Conduct, including PIC, into European Law in the 1990s.[23]

Some international progress towards the legitimization of PIC was made in June 1987 with the adoption by UNEP's Governing Council of the 'London Guidelines for the Exchange of Information on Chemicals in International Trade.'[24] These guidelines expanded the scope of the IRPTC by requesting that states notify the IRPTC of domestic chemical restrictions with the idea that the information could then be transmitted to the relevant authorities of other countries. In addition, a working group was set up to investigate the possibility of including PIC provisions into the IRPTC system. Despite such developments, PIC failed to be included in Article 9 of the Pesticide Code when revisions to the Code were debated at the November 1987 session of the biennial FAO General Conference.

By 1989, however, PIC finally gained international legitimization, as a rule governing international pesticide trading. The US, UK and German representatives at the 1987 UNEP Working Group meeting had continued to resist the inclusion of PIC in the London Guidelines. However, this stubborn resistance had the effect of galvanizing support for PIC from developing country delegates at UNEPs Governing Council. PAN were instrumental in mobilizing all representatives from countries party to the Group of 77 developing nations lobby to campaign for PIC's inclusion in the London Guidelines. As a result, the 1987 UNEP Governing Council, whilst not officially incorporating PIC into the London Guidelines, passed a pledge that the provision would be included at the next Council session in 1989.[25] Hence in 1989 a voluntary PIC procedure was established in which the IRPTC served as the body responsible for transmitting the relevant information between importing and exporting countries. 75 countries joined the scheme in its first year of operation. UNEP's provisional acceptance of PIC in 1987 prompted similar action at the November 1987 FAO Conference. A Resolution was passed ensuring that PIC be added to the FAO Code by the next FAO Conference in November 1989.[26]

PIC has, in fact, developed as a two-pronged rule. On the one hand, the procedure operates around a globally applicable list of chemicals which should not be exported without the expressed approval of the appropriate importing authority. On the other hand, PIC requires that exporters should make importing authorities aware of the fact that a traded chemical is banned or severely restricted in their own country. The PIC list, derived from the first of these two facets, is the focal point of the procedure by which governments can prohibit the import of particularly dangerous pesticides. All designated national authorities are asked to make a prior decision on the future importing of chemicals on the list, which exporters are obliged to respect. For any countries which have failed to give such a decision:

> . . . *the status quo with respect to importation shall continue, ie the chemical should not be exported without the explicit consent of the importing country, unless it is a registered pesticide or a chemical for which use or importation has been allowed by government action in the importing country.*[27]

The implementation of PIC since November 1989 has proved to be a lengthy and complicated procedure. Initially for an exported pesticide to require the PIC procedure to be enacted, it had to be in Category 1 A of the WHO Classification by Hazard and be banned or severely restricted in at least five countries. Determining when a pesticide can be classed as having been severely restricted by a government proved controversial and resulted in far fewer chemicals becoming subject to PIC restrictions than was first anticipated. Decision Guidance Documents (DGDs) have been produced by the FAO/UNEP Working Group on the implementation of PIC to clarify the details of the PIC procedure, and inform importing countries of their rights.[28] From the beginning of 1992, any ban or severe restriction on a pesticide has automatically led to its addition to the PIC list.

The establishment of the principle of PIC as an international rule was enhanced by GIFAP's acknowledgement of its legitimacy. GIFAP's annual report for 1991 announced as one of its aims for 1992 that it would 'continue to cooperate with FAO/UNEP on the implementation of PIC'.[29] The reason for this apparent U-turn on PIC appeared to be a fear of the alternatives, such as an outright prohibition of the export of certain pesticides. The drafting of a bill in the US during 1991–92 proposing to introduce export controls for pesticides raised alarm in the agrochemical industry and prompted GIFAP to take the extraordinary step of criticizing the bill on the grounds that it was contrary to the FAO Code of Conduct.

> *A major concern . . . is the appearance of a draft Bill on pesticide export control in the USA which is very much at variance with PIC in the FAO Code, namely that this draft legislation is export rather than import control orientated.*[30]

GIFAP here opportunistically interpreted PIC as recognition that trade regulations for pesticides should be based only on import rather than export restrictions. In a choice between PIC and export restrictions of the sort discussed in the US Congress, PIC is the lesser of two evils for the pesticide industry. It is a fact that some developing countries are still only too happy to accept dangerous pesticides.

PIC's central role in an international pesticide trade regime was confirmed by UNCED, which included within its Agenda 21 Programme for Action a call for governments to participate in and implement the UNEP/FAO scheme (Chapter 19.38). The possibility of transforming the voluntary scheme into a binding international convention was also aired at the Rio summit and this was taken up by the FAO and UNEP in the following three years. The 107th FAO Council meeting in 1994 charged its secretariat with the task of initiating the drafting of such a convention. UNEP's Governing Council then in 1995 concurred with the FAO decision (UNEP Decision 18/12) and instigated the convening of a UNEP/FAO Intergovernmental Negotiating Committee (INC) to set up a mandatory PIC Convention by a target date of 1997.

UNEP's target proved a little optimistic but, after five INCs, the most profound international agreement on pesticides was eventually signed in 1998. The Rotterdam Convention on the Prior Informed Consent Procedure for Certain Hazardous Chemicals and Pesticides in International Trade effectively transforms the voluntary scheme into a mandatory scheme and opens up the possibility of expanding the scope of the procedure.

By 1998 22 pesticides had become subject to the voluntary PIC scheme (Table 7.1), along with four other industrial chemicals, and this list was agreed as the starting point for the new instrument.

Progress at the first four INCs (Brussels March 1996, Nairobi September 1996, Geneva May 1997 and Rome October 1997) proved slow, but a sustained effort at a fifth INC in Brussels in March 1998 proved decisive and managed to erase the numerous brackets inserted into the negotiating text on matters unable to be resolved at Rome.

In a push to finalize the Convention text by the end of the session, delegates met during the evenings and on Saturday. Over one hundred conference room papers were produced during the six-day session.[31]

Table 7.1 *Pesticides subject to the PIC procedure in 1998*

Date	Chemical
1991	Aldrin DDT Dieldrin Dinoseb & dinoseb salts fluoroaetamide HCH (mixed isomers)
1992	Chlordane Chlordimenform 1,2-dibromoethane (EDB) Heptachlor Mercury compounds
1997	2,4,5-T Captafol Chlorobenzilate Hexachlorobenzene Lindane Pentachlorophenol Methamidophos Methyl-parathion Monocroptos Parathion Phosphamidon

Much debate at INC 5 surrounded the question of how many notifications of a chemical's banning or severe restriction should be required to instigate consideration of the chemical for the list of those automatically subject to the PIC procedure. Some delegates favoured limiting this procedure to chemicals banned in five countries in three distinct regions, others favoured requiring only one notification. Either of these extremes threatened to undermine the procedure.

> *The Chair noted that too many notifications would paralyze the process and too few notifications could drown the CRC (Chemical Review Council) and the Secretariat with work.*[32]

PAN's Barbara Dinham has highlighted the implications of this debate by pointing out that records from the voluntary scheme indicate that the five notifications proposal would lead to a list of 30–40 chemicals as opposed to around 220 chemicals under the one notication scheme.[33] In the end a compromise was agreed at Brussels that one notification from two different regions would trigger the process. The composition of the regions has yet to be finalized, however. The FAO's seven regions will be used as the basis for this, but many countries party to the new convention are not members of FAO and need to be allocated appropriate regions. This matter will be resolved at the first conference of the parties following the ratification of the Rotterdam Convention.

Notifications from governments subject to the new convention must include information about chemical properties and how the formulation is used, along with details of domestic regulatory actions. This information is to be submitted to the Secretariat who will then forward it to the Chemical Review Committee (CRC) which will consider the case for including the chemical in the automatically triggered PIC list (Annex III). The CRC will consider the reliability of the evidence provided, the significance of reported effects in comparison to the quantities used and discern whether any reported ill-effects could be prevented by proper application of the chemical. The Secretariat are able to take up reports from NGOs in addition to those from governments. This practice was established under the voluntary scheme when in 1997 PAN action highlighted health problems peculiar to developing countries resulting from the use of five pesticides (the final five pesticides in Table 7.1).

Under the new convention the CRC will prepare a DGD for each chemical it recommends for inclusion in Annex III and the final decision on whether to include it will be taken at a conference of the parties (CoP). If the CoP approves, the Secretariat, in the form of the FAO's Director General and UNEP's Executive Director, will then communicate this information to all parties to the Convention.

The composition of the CRC has not yet been determined but it will be a subsidiary body of the CoP, possibly with 21 nationally appointed experts selected on the basis of geographical quotas. A decision on this will be taken at the first CoP along with the question of how to finance the instrument. NGOs will be permitted as observers alongside the government representatives at the CoPs although opposition to this was voiced at INC 5. China's delegate at Brussels, clearly unfamiliar with the notion of civil society or with the transnational nature of major NGOs, suggested that '. . .any NGO of a contracting party shall not be admitted if that contracting party objects.'[34] The Chinese proposal was eventually withdrawn in the face of unified opposition and it was agreed that NGOs could attend provided that not more than one-third of the parties register an objection.

Voting in the CRC will be on the basis of a two-thirds majority, whilst any amendments of the convention will require the agreement of three-quarters of the CoP. A Conciliation Committee will serve to resolve disputes, which may also be arbitrated by the International Court of Justice, but in both cases only after the agreement of all parties. This clearly opens up the possibility of parties failing to fulfil convention obligations, but such an arrangement has proved adequate in other international regimes and is as much as could realistically be expected for such an instrument.

The contentious issue of whether the rules of the Convention could be overruled by World Trade Organization (WTO) provisions on free trade in the event of any clash was fudged by removing a get out clause to this effect, which was supported by the US government. In its place a number of governments were permitted to include in the preamble a statement that the Convention will not 'prejudice their respective positions in other international forums and negotiations addressing issues related to the environment and trade'.

The export notification scheme, whereby governments are required to provide information on a pesticide severely restricted domestically before exporting it, also was the subject of much debate at the INCs. The vexed question of how frequently an exporter need provide such information was finally resolved with an agreement that 'export notification shall be given before the first export and subsequently before the first export in each calendar year' (Article 12 (2)). The exporter is further required to provide notification in the event of a tightening of domestic laws regarding the chemical concerned and it was also established that such notifications are no longer required once a chemical is in Annex III, when the provision of information rests with the convention's secretariat.

The convention will come into force 90 days after 50 governments have ratified it. Considering that 95 national delegates came to agreement at INC 5 and some 154 countries participate in the voluntary scheme, this should not provide an obstacle to its passing into international law.

CONCLUSIONS

The presence of the PIC rule since 1989 for the trade in the most hazardous pesticides since 1989 has confirmed the existence of an international regime, located within the issue system of pesticide trading and the wider issue system of chemical trading. Krasner's benchmark definition of a regime as featuring 'principles, norms, rules and decision-making procedures',[35] is met by the combined work of the FAO and UNEP's IRPTC in this 'given area of international relations'. The norm that the international pesticide trade needs to be regulated is near universally accepted, with even the chemical industry acquiescing, and the rule that PIC be given by importing countries before hazardous chemicals can be exported has been established to ensure that this norm is respected. The decision-making procedures within this issue system are embodied in the newly established CoP and CRC set up by the Rotterdam Convention.

Krasner's use of the term 'principles' in his regime definition basically mirrors what are in this study considered as values. Finlayson and Zacher, in Krasner's landmark publication *International Regimes*, describe principles as 'prevailing beliefs that underlie states' policy orientations to a variety of issue areas',[36] and go on to describe as an example, 'a belief that free trade enhances the welfare of all countries'. The principle (or value) underlying the norm of regulating the trade in pesticides/toxic substances, namely the desire to avoid human suffering, can be understood as having superseded the value of free trade in this particular issue. The arguments of the chemical industry when originally opposing the implementation of PIC were based on the need to uphold the principle of free trade. Its eventual acceptance of PIC was not so much a shift in values, however, as a reorientation in the light of new circumstances. The realization that the alternative to an international trade regime based on the PIC rule could be a scenario with greater restrictions on free trade forced the industry to rethink their strategy and retreat a few yards in order to defend itself from a more damaging attack. The industry lost the battle over PIC in order to ensure that they did not lose the war over free trade. The new cease-fire line between the two values delimits the norm that has generated the regime now in operation in this particular issue.

A further criterion for determining when an international regime is in operation, not explicitly articulated by Krasner, is evidence of a behavioural effect, through the implementation of defined rules or at least from observable compliance with a particular norm. List and Rittberger include such a criterion in their classification of a regime.

The identification of a regime requires the observation of norm and rule guided behaviour, ie some minimal effectiveness which can be measured by the degree of rule compliance.[37]

Measuring the implementation of PIC is not as straightforward as it might be for other international rules. This is firstly because its details are still evolving, and secondly because it is a rule which need not have a direct effect on the problem that it is designed to help remedy. Measuring the impact of the rule is also complicated by the fact that there could, in theory, be 100 per cent compliance with it but, at the same time, a negligible effect on the trade in hazardous pesticides. The rule can only serve to make importers more aware of what they are importing. The final decision still lies with such authorities on whether or not to import.

Ultimately, the successful implementation of PIC can only be gauged by evidence that importing authorities are being provided with documentation detailing regulatory information on any product that is on the PIC list entering their country. Prior to the 1998 convention, for chemicals not yet on the official PIC list there was a reliance on the goodwill of the exporter, as the requirement for information exchange for these chemicals is only bilateral. Neither the FAO Code of Conduct nor the London Guidelines required that such records are kept by the secretariat. The practice did appear to be followed, however. The Canadian designated national authority (DNA) have made it known that they have received notifications from the US and the EU for particular pesticide compounds and constituent ingredients and that they are 'not aware of any violations of the notification rule'.[38] However, Canada's importing regulations have always been advanced enough to safeguard the country from importing dangerous chemicals and the conclusion of their DNA was that, 'in Canada, the PIC procedure has had very little or no effect on the importation of pesticides'.[39] Similarly, the DNA for Sweden has stated that 'the PIC procedure has no significance for the importation of pesticides to Sweden'.[40] Sweden, in fact, by February 1993 was alone in having made the final import decision to permit the entry of the first six chemicals restricted by the PIC provision, subject to its own inspectorate's advanced approval. With the Rotterdam Convention in place, governments are obliged to give appropriate notification and will be exposed if they fail to do so.

For chemicals included on the PIC list the relevant information comes centrally in the form of the DGDs, and implementation of the PIC rule can be seen to have begun once the DGDs on the first six pesticides on the PIC list were distributed to all governments taking part in the voluntary procedure in September 1991.

FAO and UNEP have also strived to try to make the PIC rule go further in countering the problem of the trade in hazardous pesticides by empowering developing country importers with greater knowledge of their rights under the procedure. Various training schemes in the South have been initiated by FAO and UNEP/IRPTC in the past three years to strengthen the regulatory capabilities of developing countries. In 1991, UNEP/IRPTC and the UN Institute for Training and Research (UNITAR) combined to create a training programme for implementing PIC.[42] This programme initially concentrated on Asia, with the first FAO-UNEP/UNITAR Regional Workshop on the Implementation of PIC held in Manila, The Philippines, in August 1991. Collaboration with FAO has continued in similar workshops in Africa and Latin America. A central theme of these workshops is the encouragement of countries to develop National Registers of Potentially Toxic Chemicals (NRPTCs), and foster links with the IRPTC. Extra budgetary support for these training programmes is to be provided by the governments of the US, Switzerland, the Netherlands and Finland. Undoubtedly, pressure groups led by PAN will also play a key role in the implementation of the Rotterdam Convention, both in terms of alerting the secretariat of new pesticides to consider for Annex III's PIC list and in ensuring governments are thorough in fulfilling their obligations.

It is clear that implementation of the PIC rule has occurred since 1991 and from 1998 will be more rigorously enforced. In light of this, it is fair to conclude that the PIC procedure is a rule that has had observable behavioural impact and that the final criterion for determining the existence of a regime has been met by the combined work of UNEP and FAO within the issue system of international pesticide trading.

8 Steering a Middle Course: Avoiding the Overuse of Pesticides – The Concept of Integrated Pest Management

INTRODUCTION

The norm that pesticides should not be overused is unusual in that it is not derived from a single value and hence not part of a wider issue system cross cutting other policy areas. The norm, in effect, represents a compromise between the competing norms and values that guide actor behaviour within the pesticides politics. Integrated pest management (IPM), the offspring of this norm, is a concept which aims to balance the values of avoiding human suffering, avoiding environmental degradation, and maximizing economic gains.

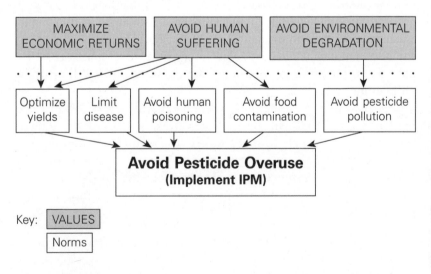

Figure 8.1 *Relationship between the norm of avoiding pesticide overuse and the other norms and values within pesticides politics*

In light of the damage that can be done to the environment and human health by the misuse of chemical pesticides, many people have called for a more limited use of these substances in general, going beyond the sort of trade restrictions considered earlier. A body of opinion has steadily emerged which would like to see all uses of manufactured pesticides ended, in favour of alternative practices of pest control. Even more conservative voices within pesticides politics have come to aspire towards a situation in which reliance on chemicals is replaced by a multifaceted approach to the problem of crop protection in agriculture. Some governments have implemented legislation reducing pesticide use. The governments of Denmark, The Netherlands and Sweden in the late 1980s launched schemes to cut pesticide use by 50 per cent before the end of the century.[1] The inclusion in the FAO's Code of Conduct of Article 3.8 stating that 'governments and the pesticide industry should develop and promote integrated pest management',[2] seems to signify that the principle that pesticide usage be kept to a minimum has developed the status of an international norm. The agrochemicals industry has noted this, and made efforts not to appear out of line with such opinion. A Shell report on their agrochemical business acknowledges that:

> *Environmental and economic arguments as well as sound biological principles support a trend to integrated pest management (IPM), by which is meant the coordination of agricultural practices and biological and chemical control of pests.*[3]

The report goes on to stress that IPM ultimately must still be dependent on chemical applications. The acceptance of the role of other methods of pest control, however, indicates a tacit acknowledgment of the norm of minimizing chemical use. GCPF, as we has seen in Chapter 3, have a working group dealing specifically with IPM implementation.

The development of this norm has its roots not only in the problems of environmental and human poisoning referred to earlier, but also in the growing realization that over-reliance on chemicals in agriculture has its own pitfalls. Whilst crop yields undoubtedly improve with the initial application of pesticides, these yields are difficult to sustain because pests often develop resistance to a particular toxin after prolonged exposure to it. The number of insects known to be resistant to pesticides rose from around 50 in the 1950s to over 400 in the 1980s.[4] The physiological adaptation of insects to a pesticide can take on a number of forms. Some insects have been known to evolve a layer of their body which is impenetrable to a pesticide, whilst others develop systems which can store insecticides and then detoxify them. The *Aedes aegypti* mosquito in Malaysia has developed the capacity to excrete an insecticide, which was once fatal to it, before it can be absorbed.[5] Research in Malaysia has also revealed that pests can sometimes develop resistance to types of insecticide other than the one which has actually been used against it. The diamond back moth is now immune to the effects of both organophosphate and carbamate pesticides, despite never having been exposed to the latter form of chemicals.[6]

On top of this problem of pest resistance is the phenomenon of pest resurgence in the face of continued exposure to pesticides. Pesticides often eliminate natural predators of the targeted pest, which can lead to the pest actually flourishing after a while.

The response of farmers to pest resistance and resurgence is often to increase the dosages of pesticides, which merely serves to exacerbate the problems of pollution, poisoning and food contamination, whilst ultimately not improving yields. The development of resistance to pesticides can cause even more direct harm. The resurgence of malaria in much of the developing world in the 1980s was due principally to the widespread resistance of mosquitoes to chloroquine, which for years had successfully suppressed their numbers. Disease carrying pests may also indirectly become immune to chemical control, as has been identified in the Cameron Highlands of Malaysia where house flies are now resistant to a number of insecticides, owing to the fact that they tend to hatch their larvae in vegetable beds.[7]

The effect of this growing problem of pest resistance has been to make the issue of minimizing the use of pesticides salient to the industry that manufactures them. The realization from the agrochemicals industry that it is in its own interests to discourage the overuse of their products is, of course, a position far removed from that of the environmentalists, some of whom call for an outright end to pesticide use, but the common ground between them can be seen to constitute a genuine international norm.

THE ALTERNATIVES TO CHEMICAL PESTICIDES

Biological Control

The most widely used alternative to chemical pesticides in agriculture is the practice of mobilizing the natural predators of a pest in order to control it. This usually involves the introduction of a natural enemy somewhere where it does not naturally occur. For such predators to become established in their new habitat, however, a small pest population must be maintained in order for them to continue suppressing the pest. Careful research is required before such action is taken in order not to upset the ecosystem and create new, unforeseen problems. If a predator is introduced which also attacks crops or beneficial insects it can become a pest in its own right, as happened when Sri Lankan crows were introduced to Malaysia with the intention of controlling coffee caterpillars.[8] An alternative to introducing new species to a habitat is to augment an already present pest predator by providing it with food and facilities for breeding.

The most common form of biological control is the use of insects to control other insects. This technique has been employed successfully in the protection of cassava crops in Central Africa by the International Institute of Tropical Agriculture (IITA), an internationally funded centre based at Ibadan in Nigeria. IITA research discovered a number of predators to the mealy bug, the cause of a considerable depletion in cassava yields, and launched the world's largest ever biological control programme based around the parasitic wasp *Epidocrasis lopezi*. The parasite quickly became established in much of the cassava belt which stretches from Senegal to Mozambique, and helped reverse a crisis which was costing around US$2 billion annually in losses.[9] The mealy bug is now under control in all 19 countries in which the wasp was released and crop losses have fallen from 50 per cent to below 20 per cent.

Biological control can also include the use of microbes as pathogens against a variety of pests. Some well known examples of this include *Bacillus thuringiensis*, used by organic gardeners to control caterpillars, and *Trichodermavinide* which attacks silver leaf fungus on fruit trees. The advantage of microbes over insects in biological control is that they are usually more specific predators and are less prone to infest beneficial crops or insects. The field of biopesticides has been boosted by the development of a technique to increase genetically the capacity of microbes to kill their insect hosts.

Research by Tomalski, Miller and Stewart at the Institute of Virology and Experimental Microbiology in Oxford has succeeded in implanting genetic fragments from the venom of scorpions and mite into the genome of insect specific baculoviruses, greatly increasing their deadliness when infecting insect hosts.[10]

Resistant Plants

Another means of reducing dependence on pesticides in agriculture is to breed strains of crops which are inherently resistant to their normal predators. Many voices within agriculture are now appealing for a switch from the traditional practice of breeding plants for maximizing yields, as the green revolution had taught developing countries, to focusing on producing hybrid species requiring less chemical protection. Once again, economic arguments have been critical in altering perspectives within the agricultural community. The risks to human health and the environment from excessive pesticide use have been well documented, but the appeal of this form of crop protection lies in the fact that it reduces production costs and offers better guarantees of regular, albeit smaller, yields. In the UK the National Institute of Agricultural Botany has introduced minimum standards of resistance for new cereal crops, and has a policy of refusing to recommend any crop failing to meet this standard, however high yielding it may be. It has been estimated that two-thirds of the UK's annual 4.5 per cent rise in wheat production in recent years is the result of varietal improvements in the crop.[11]

Much current research in the field of plant resistance is concentrated on isolating the genetic traits responsible for this, so that they can then be bred into other plants not possessing such a facility. The pioneer in this new era of genetically engineered crops is a strain of tomato which has been inter-bred with a gene from the bacterium *Bacillus thuringiensis*. This bacterium kills caterpillars and its toxin, if introduced into a plant's genetic make-up, can make the plant resistant to caterpillars and other common pests.

Probably the most significant research in developing resistant strands of plants is being carried out by the IITA on the banana and its close relative the plantain. These fruits, which represent a staple food for over 60 million Africans, have increasingly fallen victim to a fungal disease known as Black Sigatoka, first discovered in 1973 in Zambia. The natural resistance of bananas to disease is negligible, owing to a continual history of selective breeding which has produced extremely low levels of genetic variability between fruits. Big plantations, responsible for providing the North's supply of bananas, have overcome this problem with the aid of chemicals, but this is an option not open to Africa's many subsistence farmers.

The IITA have promoted the use of cooking bananas, resistant to Black Sigatoka, as an interim solution but these are less popular than plantains and research has concentrated on producing resistant versions more similar to the traditionally popular fruit. The search for such a fruit led scientists from the IITA to South-East Asia, where varieties of fertile, wild banana can be found. Resistant genotypes of this wild banana have been collected and propagated in the laboratory to produce new hybrid species of banana. A process of evaluation is now going on to determine which new strain of banana/plantain is most appropriate to be bred for agricultural use.[12]

Non-Fatal Chemical Controls

There exist a number of ways to help protect crops from pests involving chemicals, but which fall short of directly killing the pest. The chemicals used are less toxic and consequently less hazardous to man and the environment than traditional pesticides.

Probably the best researched of these chemical control methods involves the use of insect sex pheromones. Either the natural substance or a synthetic version can be applied so as to disrupt the mating of insects or lure them into traps. One such product is the synthetic sex hormone Sellbate, which trials show can be as equally effective as organophosphorous insecticides in keeping stem borers away from rice crops.[13] A different method of controlling insects by disrupting their reproductive activities is to use chemicals, known as chemosterilants, to sterilize the males of a pest species. These chemicals have the disadvantage of being mutagenic to the pest, so permitting the target organism genetically to develop resistance in the same manner as many have to conventional pesticides. A means of sterilizing insects without chemosterilants does exist, however, involving the exposure of the pest to radiation. An FAO sponsored project has successfully controlled Mediterranean fruit flies in this way.[14]

Other forms of non-fatal chemical control have been researched but, as yet, with little success. Insect repellents are openly marketed for use in protecting people from irritation and bites, but their application in agricultural situations has not been developed. A similar idea is to use anti-feeding compounds to make a host plant distasteful to an insect.[15] Research into this is also at an embryonic stage. Some progress has been made on the use of chemicals as growth regulators to either retard the development of the insect or, conversely, to accelerate the ageing process. This is clearly a sophisticated process and it will require a great deal of research before it represents a viable means of everyday insect control.

Cultural Controls

Not all of the non-chemical forms of crop protection are procedures rooted in technology, however. Cultural controls, limiting pests by affecting their habitats, are in general based on the techniques employed by farmers to protect their crops before dependence on pesticides set in, in the latter part of this century.

Returning to the age old practice of crop rotation is one such form of cultural control. With the advent of the green revolution, crop rotation was basically abandoned in favour of monoculture. Monoculture allows for more economical harvesting and sowing, but at the same time permits pests to flourish. Multi-cropping, on the other hand, provides pests with only small areas of host crops to inhabit, while the practice of having fallow seasons within the cycle breaks up any pattern of gradual pest proliferation.

Another traditional farming practice which can be rediscovered as a means of culturally controlling pests is the destruction of crop residues after harvesting. Burning or ploughing fields after they have been harvested removes any remaining pest habitats and eggs, otherwise free to flourish when the new growing season comes around. Interplanting a cash crop with plants or flowers which deter its pests is another old fashioned agricultural technique which is beginning to find favour again, with the rise in consumer demand for organic produce in the North. Planting orange marigolds amongst crops of green peppers, for example, attracts pollinating insects to the flowers whilst simultaneously repelling other potentially harmful insects with their scent.[16] Similarly, the application of natural products such as lemon rind, tobacco plant stems, and ash can be effective in killing some insects or at least in deterring them. Farmers in northern Ghana are known to use the liquid derived from boiling seem leaves as a pesticide against caterpillars and weevils, which infest soyabean crops.[17]

The use of physical controls against pests can sometimes be an effective means of limiting their damage without resort to chemicals. Placing metal barriers in the ground around a crop field is a way of deterring termites or rodents, for example, while utilizing yellow boards covered in glue can serve as a means of trapping whitefly. Projects in the UK, Norway and Sweden in the early 1990s explored the benefits of creating banks of grass in the middle of crop fields, providing habitats for spiders and beetles which are the natural predators of aphid pests.[18] The thinking behind this simple procedure, created by exempting tracts of the field from ploughing, is to reverse the effects of a gradual increase in the size of crop fields which has resulted in fewer hedgerows, and with it fewer predators to the aphid. The costs of creating the banks and sacrificing a small area of cultivation have been calculated at initially about £85 per 50 acres, falling to only £30 per year thereafter. How much pesticide can be saved from this procedure is as yet unclear, but the evidence so far is promising. Rhone-Poulenc have supported Dr Wratten of Southampton University in his campaign to develop wider research into this form of cultural pest control, providing further evidence of the chemical industry's own commitment to reducing dependence on its produce.[19]

Integrated Pest Management

Integrated pest management (IPM) utilizes the various pest control techniques mentioned previously, in line with the norm that chemical pesticide use should be optimized. The FAO/UNEP Panel of Experts have defined the concept as follows:

> *A pest management system that in the context of the associated environment and the population dynamics of the pest species, utilizes all suitable techniques and methods in as compatible a manner as possible and maintains the pest population at levels below those causing them injury.*[20]

This represents very much an holistic approach to pest control, as the whole ecosystem of which the plant and pest form a part is always considered. This is a total change in approach to traditional pest control, where each pest is treated as a separate problem, and any interrelationships are not considered. Thus, for instance, a fundamental principle behind IPM is the idea that the targeted pest should never be completely eliminated but rather maintained at an acceptable level whereby damage to the crop is not economically significant.

The conception of this economic threshold indicates that IPM is rooted in more than merely the desire to restrict pesticide use for the good of the environment and human health. It becomes apparent that what are at first seemingly contradictory norms form the framework on which the system is operated. The value on which traditional pesticide use is guided, namely the optimization of profit by increasing yields and decreasing damage, is still influential under IPM, but is reconceptualized. By operating a system in which the aim is to satisfy all of these norms, the idea of an optimum yield becomes understood both in terms of economic profit and the human and environmental costs. Balancing these disparate aspirations requires that systematic research be undertaken before the appropriate remedies are integrated into the economically deficient ecosystem in question. At a simple level this may just mean taking time to estimate levels of pest infestation in a region prior to applying appropriate crop protection techniques, rather than applying pesticides immediately as a preventative measure. This sort of action will be likely to cut the farmers' input costs, whilst simultaneously lowering the risk to the environment. The ultimate projection of this idea is to refine the deduction of the optimal yield with the aid of computer technology. Computer models can be made of the complex ecological interactions making up the system under consideration, to determine which measures of pest control represent the most appropriate long-term methods of obtaining an optimal yield.

This idealistic IPM system has yet to be fully practised, but examples of successful programmes based on the principles discussed can be found. The first well documented implementation of an IPM programme occurred in the cotton plantations of the Canete Valley in Peru in 1956. After a decade of successfully controlling pests in the area through the use of organochlorine insecticides, farmers suddenly began to lose around 70 per cent of their crops to the original pests. This situation arose from the widespread development of insect resistance to the pesticides and the simultaneous demise of the natural enemies of the insects due to indiscriminate spraying. Entomologists asked to look into this problem came up with a radical package of measures. Applications of insecticides were drastically reduced from up to 40 sprayings per season to only one or two, quarantine measures were introduced, and planting times became regulated. These measures proved successful, and after two seasons cotton yields returned to their previous levels.[21]

Another IPM success story is the case of a trial conducted in the 1970s in Alabama to find an alternative to relying on DDT spraying on cotton crops. The conventional production practices were compared to a new short season technique, which used a higher plant density with controlled inputs of fertilizer and irrigation to limit plant size. The application of pesticides was done in accordance with information derived from scouting, to find the levels of pest population and with it the economic threshold for spraying. The total amounts of pesticide used were at only around a quarter of the traditional method, but after three years of similar results for the two methods, yields became substantially better from the IPM system. With the accompanying reduction in insecticide and irrigation costs, it became clear that the new production methods were far more economically viable for the area, as well as being more productive and less hazardous.[22]

Problems Associated with IPM

Whilst the attraction of a scheme in which the environmental and human hazards of pesticide use are reduced at the same time as economic profits are maximized is obvious, IPM is not without its drawbacks as a pest control scheme. The proposed alternatives to pesticides for use in crop protection also possess flaws which can become apparent if they are not carefully operated. Intensive research is required before biological control schemes can be enacted, to ensure that the ecosystem is not undesirably disrupted by the introduction of a pest predator. It needs to be ensured that the predator is specific to the pest it is intended to control, or else it may become a pest in its own right by attacking crops or beneficial insects. The introduction of cane toads to Australia and of crows to Malaysia to control coffee caterpillars are cases in point. In both instances the introduced species are accepted as having caused more harm than good to the crops they were intended to protect.[23]

The augmentation of advances in genetic engineering to the field of biological control, creating what are known as biopesticides, has created great excitement in the scientific world but has also brought with it concerns as to their usefulness and possible side-effects. Biopesticides by 1991 had only secured around 1 per cent of the pesticide market, which an article in *Nature* summed up as being the result of 'technical snags with their development'.[24] The article, which heralded new advances in the area of biopesticides, still admitted that:

Formulated insect pathogens often break down quickly on plant surfaces; they may be costly to produce; and they kill pests more slowly than chemical insecticides.[25]

The research being considered promises to overcome the third problem by genetically strengthening the pathogens of microbes and also making them adaptable in the face of pest resistance, but a number of concerns over this technology remain. Fears exist among some scientists that engineered viruses could be capable of replicating and migrating to other, unintended hosts.

Developing a means of pest control without resort to chemicals or pest predators, by breeding pest resistant crops, also has its weaknesses. For a start it is possible that the crop variety with the best resistance may have a yield that is too low to make it economically viable, or that its quality may be below what is expected by consumers. Only a limited number of resistant crops will be able to match these essential criteria. It is also known that a side-effect of increasing a crop's resistance to a particular pathogen can be to reduce its resistance to another. As with the debate on genetically modified organisms (GMOs), concern has also been aired as to the ramifications of manufacturing genetically engineered crops that are resistant to pests. Recent evidence that some insects have become resistant to *Bacillus thuringiensis*, the toxic genes of which have been incorporated into tomato plants, suggests that this form of pest control is prone to the same Achilles' heel that has basically called pesticide use into question.[26]

Perhaps the biggest fear concerning this technology, however, is that ultimately it may actually provide a new, and bigger stage for pesticides to act on and thrive. It should be remembered that it is agrochemical businesses that own the vast majority of plant breeding companies, and the possibility remains that far from using resistant crops as an alternative to chemicals, they will be exploited as a means of allowing more intensive pesticide use. Crops have already been developed which are resistant to particular herbicides rather than weeds, allowing greater quantities of such herbicides to be used against the weeds without harming the crop.[27] The potential environmental consequences of this do not need spelling out, suggesting that the technology of inducing greater crop resistance is in the wrong hands and could exacerbate a problem it was hoped it could help solve.

The mutagenic effects of chemicals used to sterilize male pests have already been discussed, and it is clear that all forms of indirect pesticides are still very much in their infancy as crop protection alternatives. At the same time, it is a common delusion that natural chemicals are inherently safer than their synthesized counterparts, and so more preferable for use as pesticides. The use of tobacco-based solutions is frequently cited as a traditional pest control agent which can be rediscovered as an alternative to modern insecticides, but nicotine is as equally hazardous as most synthetic chemicals owing to its high mammalian toxicity.

The use of IPM as a package of pest control measures has had its successes, as has been illustrated, and has the potential to thrive once successfully harnessed to computer technology. Extensive national pesticide reduction schemes have thus been implemented in Denmark, Sweden and The Netherlands, three of the world's wealthiest countries. IPM's applicability as an antidote to all the ill-effects associated with pesticide use does need to be qualified, however. The bulk of environmental and human tragedies occur in developing countries where the application of such substances is comparatively unregulated. IPM does not always represent a viable alternative in these states because ultimately it is rooted in advanced technology. Returning to age old methods of pest control may be less hazardous for developing country workers, but it should be remembered that it was the inadequacy of such measures to protect crops that led to the green revolution and chemical control in the first place. An economically viable IPM system requires sophisticated technology and a well-trained workforce able to analyse the ecology, geology, and agronomy of a region and prescribe the appropriate solution. These prerequisites are clearly not to be found in most developing countries (the farmers of the Canete Valley example were wealthy and well educated). This problem is recognized by the epistemic community. A paper presented at the 1989 FAO/UNEP Panel of Experts on IPM appealed to Northern universities to make their databases available to institutions promoting IPM in the developing world, but this appeal has not met a great response as yet.[28] There may well be an international norm prescribing that the use of pesticides be kept at a minimum level, but it seems that the people to whom this is most pertinent cannot afford the prescription charges.

THE POLITICS OF AVOIDING PESTICIDE OVERUSE

The norm that pesticide chemicals should not be overused has found expression within the concept of integrated pest management, supported to some extent by the chemical producers themselves. The realization by agrochemical companies that promoting optimal rather than maximum pesticide use was in their interest in combating pest resistance and improving the image of their product, was the critical factor in the development of the norm. The establishment of avoiding pesticide overuse as a global norm was confirmed by the appearance of a recommendation for IPM at the 1992 UN Conference on Environment and Development.

> *Governments at the appropriate level and, where necessary, with the assistance of international and regional organizations, the private sector, non-governmental organizations and academic and scientific institutions should: . . . Promote the use of integrated pest management based on the judicious use of bio-control agents.*[29]

There has been some response to the norm in developed countries. In the developing world, however, it seems to be in the interests of neither the farmer nor the industry to promote alternatives to chemical control, and it is far less evident that a norm of minimizing chemical use is behaviourally significant.

Avoiding the overuse of chemicals in pest control as an international issue would appear, therefore, to be unregulated. No international bodies can be shown to be a source of authoritative allocations of the norm and respected by most actors in the issue system. The previous chapter outlined how the FAO Code of Conduct provisions concerning the trade in pesticides have taken on the form of a legal framework and undoubtedly affected actor behaviour. The Code of Conduct also contains provisions on integrated pest management. Article 3.8 states: 'Governments and the pesticide industry should develop and promote integrated pest management.'[30] It is difficult to comprehend FAO performing the role of a regime with concern for promoting IPM however. Support for limiting the role of chemicals within pest control seems to come from the pesticide industry only when it serves their interests to do so. David Bull refers to a chairman of the British Agrochemicals Association who confirms this point.

> *There is no getting away from the fact that companies will promote what they have to sell through the medium of advertizing. Good agricultural practice, integrated methods of pest control are unlikely to feature in advertisements unless they help to promote the product in question.*[31]

In the developing world, pure chemical control is promoted as avidly as ever and it is clear that IPM has not been legitimized as a rule to be observed by salient actors to the same extent as seen in the issue of pesticide trading.

Equally, environmental groups often appear only to promote IPM as a public compromise or front behind moves to try and eliminate all uses of chemicals in pest control. This is evident in the subtle change in emphasis seen when basically anti-pesticide lobbyists define integrated pest management. A report by the World Commission on Environment and Development seems to envisage IPM as a transitional phase towards the complete replacement of chemical control by alternative methods:

> *... an optimal combination of biological and chemical control technologies with the gradual phasing out of the latter to rely on natural controls.*[32]

Similarly, PAN have stated that 'IPM means non-chemical methods of pest control should be implemented first and foremost'.[33]

Support for IPM by both industry and environmentalists, then, seems to some extent to be forthcoming only when serving their principal interests, namely either promoting or eliminating chemicals. This would seem to prove that a regime does not exist for the issue of avoiding pesticide overuse, because in general the salient actors have not been persuaded to adopt different forms of behaviour. The result of this has been to make the concept of IPM highly ambiguous and, consequently, frequently misunderstood.

FAO/UNEP Panel of Experts on IPC

The task of clarifying such ambiguity usually lies with an epistemic community, and in this case this role falls principally on the shoulders of the FAO/UNEP Panel of Experts on IPC (integrated pest control). An FAO Panel of Experts first met in 1967, and in 1974 collaborated with UNEP experts to establish a global programme with regular biennial sessions. The panel has described its role to be that of: 'enhancing awareness and adoption of IPM practices, particularly in the developing world'.[34] The panels contain a regular quota of 12 experts from FAO and UNEP, plus a varied assortment of speakers from international organizations and universities, who present papers advocating specific recommendations for action concerning the implementation of IPM. Sub-panel working groups provide technical information on specific areas of interest such as biotechnology, IPM training programmes, IPM for vegetables, pesticide resistance, the biological control of plant pathogens, biodiversity, and pesticide subsidies. A number of IPM programmes have been initiated by the panel, one of the most influential being the Inter-Country Programme for the Development and Application of IPC in Rice Growing in South and South-East Asia, involving nine states.

However, as outlined earlier, IPM is a process requiring training, expertise and certain levels of technology, and this has been a constraining factor in its widespread adoption in the developing world. The FAO/UNEP Panel of Experts has explicitly recognized a lack of resources as hampering their progress. The 1979 session reported that the 'Near East Inter-Country Programme for IPM in Cotton' would have to be limited in scope because 'the training/ liaison officer post could not be established for lack of funds'.[35] Bull concludes that the dissemination of information on IPM is 'appallingly limited'.[36]

Global IPM Facility

As a response to the financial restrictions under which the Expert Panel have had to operate, a multi-institutional project was initiated in 1995 to assist in the cause of providing support and expertise for governments wishing to introduce IPM schemes. IPM Expert Panel advocacy and NGO pressure prompted the FAO to secure UNEP, UN Development Programme (UNDP) and World Bank support for a global IPM facility, charged with the task of financing pest control schemes which reduce chemical use. Over US$1 million a year has been pledged by the four institutions, initially centred on a series of pilot IPM projects in developing countries. The first three projects dealt with vegetable production in Kenya, Zimbabwean cotton and the control of the *striga* pest in West Africa. Significantly, in response to NGO pressure, it has been agreed by the four institutions that the agrochemical industry will play no role in the facility. This was a major setback for the industry whose work in this area now carries less weight than it used to. FAO act as the secretariat for the facility, which is anticipated to widen its scope over time.[37]

The Impact of International IPM Promotion

Even when the IPM proponents succeed in providing information for the governments of the developing world, the willingness to act upon it is not always there. For a start, any governments adopting a national IPM promotion campaign will be competing with huge multinational corporations promoting chemical control, in the battle to win the minds of the farmers.

Thailand, for instance, hosted the first South-East Asian Pesticide Management and IPM Workshop in 1987 which recommended governmental backing for IPM schemes and the ending of state subsidies on pesticides.[38] Thailand has enacted domestic legislation in line with the FAO Code in its registration procedure requiring permits for all people using 'poisonous articles' and guidelines for the storage and disposal of pesticide containers, but has not acted to advance IPM and alternatives to chemical pest control. Thailand has a very large and labour intensive agricultural sector, which uses a lot of pesticides, most of which are imported by multinational companies. The drive to increase food exports is at the heart of the Thai government's aim to expand its economy, and, whilst they are sensitive to the hazards associated with pesticide misuse, they seem reluctant to impose restrictions on the multinationals when they appear to have aided Thailand's growth in food exports.

A similar situation seems to exist in Brazil, where the need to service an enormous national debt led to a blinkered drive to increase the production of cash crops, such as sugar cane and coffee, for export. Between 1964 and 1979 pesticide use increased by 421 per cent, although agricultural productivity rose by only 4.9 per cent.[39] The Brazilian government has taken steps to provide for the safety of workers using pesticides and generally complied with the FAO labelling standards, but continues to effectively discourage alternative pest control measures by subsidizing pesticides. Tax rebates exist on pesticides, whilst general reductions on the importing of raw materials and finished products provide further incentives for farmers and plantation owners to maintain chemical based control strategies.

Not all developing country governments have remained immune to the arguments of the IPM epistemic community, centred on the FAO/UNEP Panel of Experts and the Global IPM Facility. The Minister of National Development for Indonesia proudly exclaimed in a January 1987 press conference that 'Indonesia is the first nation in the world to . . . put into effect as national policy what is known as integrated pest management'.[40] This move was accompanied by the banning of 57 of the more hazardous pesticides, representing a dramatic shift in government policy for a country which had actively promoted pesticides through government subsidies for many years.

The cause of this U-turn appears to have been a combination of increased pest resistance and secondary resurgence in the face of pesticide applications, along with the coming to light of pesticide related tragedies, in particular the case of the DDT plant at Cicadas, Java (outlined in Chapter 4). Some five years earlier than the Indonesian policy change, the government of Nicaragua set up a National Committee on Integrated Control and implemented IPM techniques. This followed a dramatic dip in the yields of Nicaragua's principal cash crop, cotton, due to widespread pest resistance.[41] A conclusion from these cases seems to be that some situation of crisis has to occur before the adoption of new strategies in line with the opinions of the epistemic community takes place. Bull's research points him towards this hypothesis also:

> *Where IPM programmes do exist they are usually applied to the protection of plantation and cash crops, and to large holdings, often as a response to a pesticide crisis.*[42]

Mansbach and Vasquez's issue cycle, described in the opening chapter, concurs with this hypothesis with its assertion that issues need to pass through a 'crisis stage' before entering the political agenda. The Indonesian example could also suggest that maybe an international regime does in fact exist for the issue of introducing IPM, but is reliant on domestic crises for its implementation. Young and Osherenko included as factors inducing regime formation, 'knowledge' in the particular form of epistemic communities, and as a subset of 'interest' factors, 'exogenous shocks or crises'.[43] Environmental regimes undoubtedly are very influenced by the emergence of crises, be they a tragic catastrophe such as at Cicadas, or 'manufactured crises', as Young and Osherenko describe the instances of long running problems suddenly brought to the agenda by media or NGO interest.[44] Examples can be found to bear out this theory. The discovery of the hole in the ozone layer above Antarctica was the trigger which prompted governments to heed the advice of various scientific bodies, who had been warning of the dangers of chlorofluorocarbon emissions for years. Haas, writing on the role of epistemic communities, also supports the hypothesis. 'Regimes are created following widely publicized environmental disasters which mobilize public (and epistemic) demands for governmental action'.[45]

It is difficult, however, to demonstrate conclusively that governments require dramatic evidence of the shortcomings of chemical pest control, before they act to encourage their national farmers to begin adopting IPM schemes. Indonesia represents a rare instance of a state government actively promoting alternative modes of plant protection, in association with the expert advice of FAO and other organizations. The governments of Denmark, Sweden and the Netherlands introduced radical pesticide reduction programmes without the spur of any great national emergencies. India, shaken by the Bhopal disaster, would appear to be a likely source of interest for pesticide alternatives, but its government, whilst responsive to the need for pesticide legislation, has not adopted any crusade to transform crop protection in the way seen in Indonesia. A number of IPM schemes have been put into operation around the world, but they have tended to be isolated examples, backed by groups within the epistemic community rather than national schemes with government backing. The FAO Programme for Integrated Pest Management in Rice, of which Indonesia is part, embraces countries responsible for 82 per cent of the world's supply. However, out of the 120 million farmers working on rice plantations in the countries included in the programme, only an estimated 500,000 have actually been affected by it. This, according to Peter Kenmore, the coordinator of the programme, can only represent a 'drop in the bucket'.[46]

CONCLUSIONS

It would appear, therefore, that the norm of minimizing pesticide applications in line with the concept of integrated pest management is an issue supported by an international epistemic community but which cannot be said to be regulated by an international regime. As we have seen, the epistemic community, made up of the FAO/UNEP Panel of Experts, the IPM Global Facility and other bodies such as the University of California/USAID Pest Management and Related Environmental Protection Project and the British Centre for Overseas Pest Research, has influenced individual farmers and occasionally governments to adopt IPM in favour of traditional techniques of pest control. However, no political mechanisms have developed alongside this knowledge-based system. Although IPM has widespread support from both environmental and industrial actors in pesticides politics, it is still not sufficiently established as the correct practice for farmers to follow and governments to support, that non-compliance with the norm invokes any sort of sanction. In short, there is no authoritative allocation of the norm. According to Haas, under an epistemic consensus regime 'both leaders and laggards will have to modify their policies in light of the new regime.'[47] Whereas some evidence of this can be seen in the issues of trading pesticides and pesticide residues in food, IPM has not had this level of widespread influence.

The question remains as to why the epistemic community proposing IPM adoption throughout the world has not been the catalyst for regime formation of the sorts seen in the pesticide trade and pesticide food contamination issues. Three partial explanations have been touched upon in this section. Firstly, the epistemic community lacks the resources to make its knowledge available to all potential benefactors. Secondly, the epistemic community's knowledge has to compete with contrary bodies of opinion still advocating traditional pesticide use, which possess greater resources and influence. Thirdly, as a corollary of the first two points and the fact that the knowledge espoused by the epistemic community is complex, serious flaws in the existing knowledge of potential recipients seem to be required before the alternative option is chosen. This is compounded by the fact that IPM is a difficult concept to implement. It is a straightforward task for a farmer or government to comply with standards of acceptable labelling on pesticide containers or permissible levels of pesticides in foods, but less so to know how not to use too much of a pesticide. An ambiguous norm will always be prone to ambiguous implementation.

9 From Value Systems to Regulatory Systems: Reflections on the Seven Issues of Pesticide Politics

PESTICIDE NORMS AND THE GLOBAL AGENDA

It is apparent that the international regulation of pesticide production and use derives from a complex amalgam of organizations, rules and informal norm-guided patterns of behaviour. This book has attempted to clarify this complexity by disaggregating the whole area of international pesticide politics into seven particular issues. The seven issues have been isolated by considering which global norms are responsible for guiding actor behaviour in relation to pesticide use and production questions and then discerning where this has led to the formation of distinct systems of actors in contention over related questions.

The seven issue systems that are isolated for analysis clearly overlap, both in terms of the actors to whom the issues are salient and, in some cases, the policy questions. Governments and specific pressure and interest groups such as the Pesticides Action Network (PAN) and the Global Crop Protection Federation (GCPF), have an interest in all pesticide issues. Equally, some policy questions may have a bearing on two or more issues. The question of labelling standards for pesticide containers, for example, cross-cuts the issues of human poisoning and the international trade in pesticides. Similarly, whilst the problem of drinking water contamination can be seen as a facet of general food contamination, it cannot be divorced from the issue of environmental pollution.

However, for many of the actors involved in pesticide politics, only one of the seven issues may be salient. The International Agency for Research on Cancer has made a notable input into pesticide questions, but solely those concerning the issue of human health. Likewise the involvement of the World Wide Fund for Nature and the Parents for Safe Food campaign in pesticide politics is almost exclusively confined to the issues of environmental pollution and food contamination respectively. Thus, the group of actors for whom a particular issue is salient varies across the seven issues considered here.

The clearest means of contrasting political behaviour on the issues comes from considering the extent to which the norms are endorsed by actors. In particular, this leads us to contrast the formation of epistemic groupings and decision-making bodies within the issue systems. It is clear from this study that pesticide use and production is unevenly regulated, with some issues featuring a far greater patterning of actor behaviour than others. In six of the seven issues considered, international bodies have been established to deal at least partly with the issue, either in a regulatory or in a purely epistemic capacity. The exceptional issue is that of increasing crop yields through pesticide use. This issue system does not contain any specific epistemic or regulatory bodies' operating through economic market processes. The continuation of the market is supported by GCPF and the chemical industry, as it sustains their desire to maximize profits from pesticide production and use, countering the five proscriptive norms advocated by other actors. All seven cases meet the Mansbach and Vasquez criteria for an issue as featuring 'contention among actors over proposals for the disposition of stakes among them'.[1]

Global Norms

Chapter 1 introduced the idea of norms as applied in this book, and stated the seven norms around which the issues of pesticide production and use are focused. Chapter 1 also described the ways in which the seven norms are linked to each other, either by a common underlying value, or through the fact that an issue represents an area of contention over competing norms. The norm upon which the issue of avoiding the overuse of pesticides is based, for instance, is shown in fact to be derivative of five of the more general norms of pesticide politics (see Figure 8.1).

It has become clear through the course of this book that the levels of adherence of actors to the seven norms vary considerably. An actor's adherence to a global norm is determined, firstly, by how salient they perceive the norm to be to them in allocating stakes to satisfy a particular value by which they are guided. Secondly, an actor may be influenced by other actors into adhering to a particular norm. This political process can come either in the form of coercion, whereby an actor is persuaded into compliance against its own instinctive self-interest, or as a result of education, by which actors are made to see that a norm is salient to them by reason.

Salience

The perceived salience of a norm to an actor is, of course, relative to the perceived salience of other norms. The process of influence through education, previously described, amounts to the act of convincing others that a particular norm is more salient to them than a competing norm. Mansbach and Vasquez summarize this aspect of agenda setting as 'a struggle over salience rankings'.[3]

This 'struggle over salience rankings' is the central dynamic of pesticide politics. All seven norms considered in this book are salient to the central actors on both sides of the fence in pesticide politics (ie the agrochemical industry and the consumer/environmental lobby). The political stance of those actors emerges from how they choose to prioritize those norms. Basically this amounts to a contest between the prescriptive norms of optimizing crop yields and limiting pest transmitted damage and disease, and the proscriptive norms of avoiding human poisoning, limiting environmental pollut- ion, limiting food contamination, regulating trade and avoiding the overuse of pesticides. Most environmental pressure groups accept the importance of pesticide use as an aid to improving crop yields, but in their eyes this norm should not be satisfied at the expense of considerations of environmental quality. Equally, the chemical industry is not oblivious to the potential dangers inherent in pesticide production and use, but serves to promote the positive side of it to potential recipients.

For those more peripheral actors for whom only certain norms of pesticide use and production are salient, the struggle over salience rankings is clearly less influential in determining their political stance. These actors, however, still contribute to this process of agenda formation through the advocacy of particular norms, intended to highlight the salience of them to other actors. The International Agency for Research on Cancer is only concerned with pesticide questions in so far as they overlap with the issue of cancer prevention. Thus, the IARC can pursue goals which may impinge on other pesticides issues, but they are not influenced by norms other than those of avoiding human poisoning by pesticides and limiting food contamination by pesticides. In this way, issue specific actors can still serve to influence the overall prioritizing of norms in pesticide politics, as determined by the central actors, governments and regimes.

Values

The obvious contrasts in the political stances of different actors are in the nature of the values that they are aiming to satisfy in prioritizing the norms in the way they do. The fact that the agrochemical industry should promote the use of agrochemicals is, of course, wholly predictable as it is in its self-interest to do so. However, this self-interest can still be understood as value guided behaviour, a fact commonly overlooked in the traditional realist approach to international politics. The chemical industry promotes chemical crop protection and chemical-based public health campaigns, because they represent stakes for the value of maximizing economic returns. The environmentalist and consumer groups' political position, however, derives from more abstract values, such as the desire to avoid human suffering and the protection of the environment as a common good.

Mansbach and Vasquez recognize this difference in making a distinction between 'concrete' and 'transcendental' stakes. Stakes represent the basic gains or losses that stand to be incurred by actors in contention over a norm. Concrete stakes represent a means of directly satisfying a value, whereas transcendental stakes are 'entirely abstract and non-specific, and which concern beliefs, prescriptions, or norms about how people should live or behave'.[4] Clearly the prescriptive norms of pesticide use and production, in the eyes of the chemical industry, involve concrete stakes. Conversely, the prioritizing of the proscriptive norms by environmental and consumer groups represents a case of acting on transcendental stakes for the achievement of more abstract values.

Similarly, Rolston has distinguished between instrumental and intrinsic values: 'Instrumental value uses something as a means to an end; intrinsic value is worthwhile in itself'.[5] Rolston introduces this distinction to appeal for environmental protection to become considered as an intrinsic value and respected for its own sake, rather than respecting it merely when it invokes other values such as security or wealth maximization. The evidence gathered in this study, concerning the issue of environmental pollution by pesticides, suggests that, internationally, stakes in environmental questions are generally perceived to be instrumental. The international agreement on curbing methyl bromide use and production came about because of the fact that the chemical represents a threat to global security, as it is an agent of ozone depletion. The existence of regional environmental regimes, regulating common stretches of seas or rivers, can be understood as rational, utilitarian acts of cross border cooperation in order to reduce the costs of ensuring clean drinking water and fish stocks.

Fish and clean drinking water represent 'concrete' stakes as opposed to the 'transcendental' stake of having a clean river for its own sake. Hence, the ideas of concrete and transcendental stakes and intrinsic and instrumental values share much common ground. Corporate groups will invariably find concrete stakes most salient, whilst actors guided by ideology, such as environmental pressure groups, will place greater emphasis on transcendental stakes, which they perceive as having intrinsic value. Nevertheless, the distinction between concrete and transcendental stakes is not clear cut ultimately. It is possible to conceptualize a clean river as a concrete stake, salient to environmentalists because it is instrumental in satisfying the abstract value of environmental quality.

Nevertheless, it is clear that the salience of an issue to an actor can be due either to its direct or indirect potential for value satisfaction. A clear example of actor support for reasons of indirect value satisfaction is seen in the issue of food contamination by pesticides. The chemical industry has come to support the global norm of avoiding human suffering through the establishment of international standards, because this is seen as a means to the end of increasing the trade in pesticides. The norm emerged as a specific interpretation of the value of avoiding human suffering, but has come to be salient to the chemical industry for its role in realizing the very different value of maximizing economic returns. Hence, 'actors may seek the same stake in the name of different values'.[6]

A similar case in point is seen in the agrochemical industry's compliance with the norm of regulating the international trade in pesticides. As was demonstrated, GIFAP/GCPF have come to adhere to the prior informed consent (PIC) rule to which they had previously been vehemently opposed, because this was seen to be the best means of safeguarding the trading of pesticides. As was stated in the conclusions to Chapter 7, the industry tactically retreated in the battle over PIC, in order not to risk losing the war over free trade. Had they not responded to demands to introduce the PIC procedure, the possibility of greater restrictions on trade in the form of prohibitions on the trade in certain chemicals would have loomed. The guiding ethos of free trade, derived from the value of maximizing economic gains, in this instance had persuaded the industry to acquiesce to a norm derived from a contrasting value and to accept a rule that actually was designed to restrain their capacity to trade in pesticides. As commentators have been frequently prompted to pronounce, politics can make strange bedfellows.

We have seen that pesticide politics, in common with many areas of political contention, revolves around a struggle for salience rankings amongst competing norms for the formation of an international agenda. The struggle between the prescriptive and proscriptive norms of pesticide use and production has led to a situation whereby the same prescriptive norms have acquired different rankings for different issues. For example, we have seen that pesticide use is generally more proscribed in agriculture, when the aim is to satisfy the norm of optimizing crop yields, than it is for purposes of pest control in public health programmes. This has been demonstrated by the government decisions given under the PIC rule, whereby they are required to indicate whether or not they wish to permit the future import of particular pesticides. A number of governments are shown to have given consent to the future importation of the insecticides aldrin, dieldrin and DDT, but for public health operations only.[7] The World Health Organization (WHO) still advocates the use of DDT in certain situations, despite recognizing the dangers inherent in its use by categorizing it 1 in their Classification by Hazard scheme (see Chapter 4). A scientific officer at the WHO's malaria unit is reported to have recommended DDT for malaria control, stating that it was 'the first choice for indoor . . . spraying'.[8]

Hence, different sorts of political decisions concerning pesticide use and production have been made in each of the different issue systems. Ultimately, this is reflected in the fact that international regimes have been formed within the two issue systems of pesticide trading and food contamination by pesticides, but not within any of the other issue systems.

Political decisions concerning pesticide use and production cannot, however, be made solely within the issue system of one of the seven issues. The issues clearly are functionally linked. Increasing pesticide use in the face of a crop shortage or on the outbreak of a pest transmitted disease may well rectify such problems, but may do so at the expense of environmental quality, human safety or food purity. As a result, governments to some extent will make decisions on questions of pesticide use and production from the broader perspective of the whole policy system, rather than solely within a particular issue system. A large section of pesticides politics is invariably affected by a government decision on any pesticide question. The decision of The Netherlands government to reduce greatly their dependence on pesticides, and in particular soil fumigants, was made because of concerns over worker safety and environmental pollution but has had ramifications for the Dutch flower industry in the form of reduced yields. A government spokesperson when asked the reasons for taking a decision which could undermine one of the country's major industries explained: 'The plan will cause the growers some financial problems, but environmental protection is a priority'.[9]

Thus it can be seen that decisions on questions of pesticide use and production are very often considered in terms of a costs versus benefits assessment, which incorporates a number of issues. Whereas pressure groups and corporate representatives will have clearly defined spheres of interest, a government has to be concerned with all issues that its country has a stake in and order its priorities in the way it feels is most appropriate. Pimentel, relating this situation to the US, announced: 'The dilemma that society faces is how to protect the nation's food resources from pests while protecting the environment and public health'.[10]

Pimentel attempts to quantify the US's costs and benefits accrued through the use and production of pesticides, whilst acknowledging the difficulty of setting figures for environmental and health 'losses'. The US is estimated to spend around US$4 billion per year on pesticides, from which it gains US$16 billion in improved crop yields.[11] Added to the costs of pest control are the 'indirect costs' due to environmental and health damage resulting from pesticides. Pimentel has calculated that this amounts to a figure of around $1 billion, summarized in Table 9.1.

Whilst these figures on the face of it seem to provide a clear vindication for current rates of pesticide use in the US, Pimentel uses them as a basis for arguing for substantial cuts in their use. Pimentel proposes that although a 50 per cent reduction in pesticide use, achieved by implementing non-chemical control methods, would increase costs by about US$1 billion, it would be desirable in that it would reduce environmental and health costs.[13]

Clearly, of course, such a cost-benefit analysis of the whole pesticide policy area would produce very different conclusions if applied to countries less economically developed than the US. As we have seen, developing country governments faced with famine and tropical diseases have more acute problems to remedy than their

Table 9.1 *Estimated costs of US pesticide use*[12]

	Cost (millions $)
Human poisonings	250
Animal poisonings & contaminated livestock products	15
Reduced natural enemies	150
Pesticide resistance	150
Honeybee poisonings & reduced pollination	150
Losses of crops & trees	75
Fishery & wildlife losses	15
Government regulations concerning pesticide pollution	150
TOTAL	955

developed world counterparts. At the same time, such governments lack the resources to solve such problems with non-chemical control methods, which may be environmentally favourable and safer to use, but are more expensive. Hence the dilemma central to international pesticides politics: the prescriptive norms are most salient to those same countries where the proscriptive norms are also most salient. The cost-benefit analysis for many African, Asian and Latin American countries amounts to a choice between higher rates of pesticide pollution and poisoning and higher rates of malnutrition and malaria. The proscriptive norms can only take priority on a national agenda when that government is able to continue satisfying the prescriptive norms. As Algerian President Boumédienne is reported to have stated in the run-up to the creation of the Mediterranean Action Plan in the 1970s: 'If improving the environment means less bread for the Algerians then I am against it'.[14]

There are seven distinct issue systems making up the political arena of pesticides, invoking different values and involving different sets of actors, but at the same time they are clearly interdependent. The prioritizing of one norm will inevitably lead to the relegation of another one on the political agenda. We have seen how such acts of prioritizing one norm over another will vary from country to country, according to circumstances and how governments perceive their responsibilities. This delicate balancing act becomes all the more difficult when the system of interest is widened, as it is in the devising of global regulations.

Internationally, we have seen that priority appears to be given to limiting food contamination and regulating pesticide trade above the other proscriptive norms of pesticide politics. The issue systems based on these two norms have developed global regimes, phenomena not present in the other issue systems (although regional environmental regimes do exist as does the global ozone depletion regime, which overlaps pesticides politics through its provisions on methyl bromide). The following section aims to offer some explanations as to why the apparent prioritizing of norms in this way has occurred internationally and whether this alone accounts for the process of regime formation seen in two of the issue systems. At the same time it will be considered whether, in addition, factors within the issue system are influential in fostering or inhibiting regime creation.

EXPLANATORY FACTORS FOR REGIME CREATION

Hegemony

The belief that regime creation results from the desire to prioritize those global norms that are considered to enhance international order rests on the theory of hegemonic stability. According to this theory, the dominant international actor is the catalyst for regime formation, seeking to enforce norms and rules that will ultimately serve to maintain its hegemony, and with it international security. Thus, according to this approach, regime creation can be accounted for structurally in line with the balance of international capabilities. This hypothesis, in its strictest sense, therefore implies that political behaviour within individual issue systems is irrelevant in accounting for the development of international regimes.

> *Order in world politics is typically created by a single dominant power. Since regimes constitute elements of an international order, this implies that the formation of regimes normally depends on hegemony.*[15]

The theory of hegemonic stability incorporates the central realist axiom, of states rationally aiming to secure themselves through maximizing their power, in the face of growing interdependence between countries. The chief exponents of this view, including Kindleberger,[16] Keohane,[17] Krasner[18] and Gilpin[19], are principally concerned with the politics of the world economy, for which the theory does appear to have some descriptive utility. The US undoubtedly found itself in a position of hegemony in the international system in the years after the Second World War until the 1970s, having a preponderance of economic resources and military capabilities. Consequently, much of the post-war international economic and military order was moulded to suit their interests. Institutions such as the North Atlantic Treaty Organization (NATO), South East Asia Treaty Organization (SEATO) and the security treaty between Australia, New Zealand and the US (ANZUS) coopted much of the non-communist world to a US view of security, whilst the Bretton Woods system of financial agreements tied most developed capitalist countries monetarily and through trade to the US economy. The other classic example of hegemonic stability advanced by the realists is the international trade system of the mid-to late-19th Century, which was dominated by the UK by virtue of its vast empire and naval strength.

Without doubt, the UK and the US were able to utilize their capabilities to order international cooperative arrangements to suit their needs in the 19th and 20th Centuries respectively. However, critics of hegemonic stability theory point out that many international institutions and regimes have either survived the decline of a hegemon or been created in the absence of one. Although the decline of US hegemony in the 1970s was accompanied by the cessation of the Bretton Woods fixed exchange rates system, most other international arrangements including the General Agreement on Tariffs and Trade (GATT), the World Bank and the regional banks continued to function according to the same guiding norms as before.

In addition to this, many examples of regimes created in the last 20 years, when US hegemony has receded, have been offered by writers seeking to prove the deficiencies of hegemonic stability theory. A range of environmental and conservation regimes have been established in the last two decades, which seemingly owe little to the balance of capabilities in the state system. A regime aiming to conserve polar bears in the Arctic was set up in 1973 including both major Cold War protagonists, the US and USSR, and a number of smaller powers, because it represented a common (non-security) concern which transcended ideological differences, without apparently advancing the economic or military interests of any of the participating governments.[20]

A number of explanations have been offered for the failure of many international institutions and regimes to collapse in the absence of continued US hegemony. One response is to argue that, although US power relative to the rest of the world has declined, it still maintains a sufficiently preponderant position to continue directing international arrangements in a way which favours its interests.[21]

An alternative view is the argument that a hegemony still exists within the international system in the form of a trilateral power structure formed by the US, Japan and the EU. This view accepts that US hegemony has declined and that in terms of economic power it is rivalled by Japan and the EU. However, as this group shares a general ideology in favour of capitalism and liberal democracy, it can be reasoned that they jointly have assumed the role previously enjoyed alone by the US, of expressing their values in the form of international institutions and regimes.

A third explanation comes from the idea of a time-lag existing between the rise and fall of regimes and underlying changes in the structure of power. The assumption here is that regimes formed during eras of hegemonic stability assume a life of their own,[22] and so are liable to continue despite subsequent realignments of power in international society. Krasner explains the phenomenon of time-lags as being a result of custom, uncertainty and cognitive failing.[23] States party to a regime may continue to adhere to its rules and principles through habit, being reluctant to defect in order to maximize short-term interests through the fear of incurring long-term costs. Equally, although states may not be entirely satisfied with the regime to which they are party, they may be unwilling to bear the costs of constructing an alternative system. It is through these sorts of feedback mechanisms,[24] Krasner argues, a regime can survive the decline of the hegemon whose preponderant position in the international system had created the conditions for its creation.

These explanations can be offered as reasons for the maintenance of regimes set up during the age of US hegemony. However, they do not account satisfactorily for the setting up of regimes such as that described for polar bear conservation, or indeed for the regime regulating the trading of pesticides, outlined in Chapter 7. Polar bear conservation cannot be seen as serving the interests of any hegemonic power structure, be it unilateral, trilateral or otherwise. Equally, the forces behind the instigation of a regime for the trade in pesticides were, if anything, counter hegemonic. The PIC rule was established against the wishes of the governments of the US and UK and in the interests of developing countries, rather than any of the powerful states.

The regime dealing with the issue of pesticide residues in food, however, could be argued to represent an attempt to legitimize the interests of a hegemonic group. As was argued in Chapter 6, moves to empower the Codex Alimentarius Commission with the right to have its residue tolerance levels made legally binding in international trade over those set nationally, have come from the big chemical corporations in North America and Western Europe. In this instance, as we have seen, hegemonic power was not a significant factor in the regime's establishment. It could be argued, however, that it has assisted in its maintenance and remains a potentially significant variable for regime change.

The conclusion that can be drawn from the evidence of regimes in pesticide politics and elsewhere, is that while hegemony may be a factor in regime creation, maintenance and change, it is not the single overriding variable that the hegemonic stability theorists would have us believe. Hegemony is not a necessary condition for regime creation, rather it is one of a number of variables which can explain the phenomenon.

Issue Specific Power

The hegemonic group referred to earlier as that aiming to change the normative nature of the food residues regime, does not meet the criteria of a hegemon in the classical sense. The agrochemical industry, which is the driving force behind moves to empower the Codex Alimentarius Commission with supranational authority in pesticide residue legislation, is not a hegemon in terms of the international system as a whole. They are an influential lobby to the governments of North America and Western Europe, but they do not wield much influence in issues outside chemical politics. Thus, the power possessed by the agrochemical industry is *issue specific* and infungible, unlike that purported to be wielded by the US government in the post-World War Two years. However, issue specific power has invariably been conceptualized in terms of coherent state actors, rather than non-state hegemons such as the agrochemical industry.

Neo-realist theorists were made aware of the low fungibility of state power by the US's inability to utilize its military capabilities in the economic sphere, where it had become rivalled by Japan and the EU, and adopted an 'issue-differentiated theory of hegemonic stability'.[25] According to this modification of hegemonic stability theory, an actor with a preponderant share of resources within a particular issue system is able to foster the creation of a regime in that issue system which serves its interests.

Jonsson adopts an issue specific power framework to try to explain the attempt by the US government, in the late 1970s, to change the international aviation regime by increasing deregulation and so improving the US's commercial share of international flights.

> *Although the regime challenge came at a time when there were cumulative signs of declining overall American power, there was no corresponding change of the issue specific power structure in international air transport. The United States remained by far the strongest aviation nation and did not hesitate to exploit its issue specific power.*[26]

This US challenge failed to change the nature of the aviation regime, despite its advantage over its competitors in terms of aeronautical technological development and vehicle manufacturing and the fact that it represented by far the biggest market in world air commerce. Jonsson accounts for the failure of the US challenge by the fact that its actions had the effect of mobilizing a coalition of opponents, who were able to derive their influence from the fact that they essentially were supporting the status quo and had the backing of the existing regime, the International Air Transport Association (IATA).

An additional factor identified by Jonsson is the fact that the US itself was split on the issue, a situation IATA was able to exploit. This is a key point and one which has been inadequately addressed by power based theorists. The development of complex interdependence in the international system has increased the number of instances whereby the state actor is an unusable concept. This is most clearly so for states with highly pluralistic political systems, such as the US. Chapter 8 highlights the divergence of opinion between the US cabinet and the Environmental Protection Agency over the issue of pesticide residues in food. Here we see one part of the government, informed by chemical industry representatives, campaigning for international standards that are opposed by another part of the government that currently commands most legal authority on such questions.

We have already seen that national authorities deal with a wide range of political issues, which forces them to prioritize some over others. In some instances this inevitably leads to issues where different sections of a state's apparatus seek to advocate positions which are in some way contradictory. This clearly presents another problem for the theory of hegemonic stability, even in its issue specific form. The US's capabilities, even when considered purely within the confines of individual issues such as international aviation and food contamination by pesticides, may still represent an inaccurate guide to its level of influence. Firstly, the capabilities of a state may be divided between competing forces and, secondly, a government may not be able to translate an advantage in capabilities into preferred outcomes. As the aviation regime case shows, actors resisting change can utilize factors that compensate for any disadvantage in resources. Issue-specific knowledge and the facility to use existing political arrangements to form blocking coalitions are prominent amongst such factors.

Leadership

Young accepts the premise that state power is of only limited utility in explaining cases of regime formation.

> *The role of power in international society is not limited to structural power exercised by states. Individuals may also become leaders by acting to translate the structural power of states into bargaining leverage applicable to specific instances of regime formation.*[27]

This form of power utilization is described by Young as 'structural leadership'[28] and can be seen as a modified version of hegemonic stability theory, omitting the underlying assumption of that theory that an actor's resources can and will always be mobilized. Hence, Young ascribes the role of Henry Morgenthau, the US representative at the 1944 Bretton Woods Conference, as that of a structural leader able to draw upon his country's predominant resources in negotiating the post-war international monetary regime.[29]

Young goes further in arguing that individual leadership can still be an important factor in regime creation even when the actor being represented does not possess significant structural power. Individuals negotiating on behalf of parties not in command of any advantage in resources may still help fashion international arrangements by acting as either 'entrepreneurial' or 'intellectual' leaders. Young's 'entrepreneurial leader' shares some similarity to Keohane's 'political entrepreneur',[30] referred to in Chapter 1. For both, the entrepreneur's chief contribution to regime formation is to facilitate cooperation between actors where the potential for mutual benefits exists, but a spur is needed to induce collaboration. This is achieved by the individual acting as an innovator for the popularization of an issue. Where Young and Keohane differ is over the latter's proviso that the entrepreneur needs to be 'large relative to the whole set of potential beneficiaries'.[31] Young accepts that structural power can augment the bargaining leverage of an entrepreneurial leader, but reasons that it is not essential to the cause. He rightly cites the numerous examples of influential individuals in intergovernmental organizations who actually derive their influence from being the representatives of small states, which gives them credibility in the eyes of others as agents of the common good, rather than that of national interest.[32]

The intellectual leader, according to Young, is an individual who shapes the comprehension of an issue and how to deal with it, through reasoning and innovative thinking. The role of Monnet in inspiring European integration in the 1950s is used as an example of such an individual. Young considers the presence of a leader, in one of the three guises, to be an essential criterion for regime creation. He goes further in arguing that: 'The establishment of effective international institutions ordinarily requires the interplay of at least two forms of leadership'.[33]

Individual leadership is not a striking feature of pesticide politics, but the development of the PIC rule, upon which the international pesticide trade regime is based, was aided by some displays of leadership. David Bull of Oxfam first coined the phrase 'prior informed consent', which was adopted by PAN as the prescribed means of regulating the trade in pesticides. He was also responsible for producing the first draft of the FAO International Code of Conduct on the Distribution and Use of Pesticides, in which PIC was included as a provision. PAN's European region coordinator in the 1980s, Marianne Werning, was a focal point for the lobbying of FAO national delegates to support the pesticides code as a whole, and the PIC procedure in particular. At the FAO conferences, certain delegates took the lead in organizing support for PIC. Delegates from The Netherlands, which was the first country to introduce PIC into domestic law in 1985, continually acted as proponents of the procedure being included in the FAO Code of Conduct. The leaders of the Southern coalition which built up in favour of PIC were the delegates of Ecuador and The Philippines, whose speeches at the 1985 FAO Conference have been seen as a significant stage in its legitimization.[34] The failure to obtain an endorsement of PIC in 1985 might be interpreted by some analysts as a result of a hegemonic influence wielded by the chemical industry and the governments of the US and UK. However, the mobilization of delegates in 1985 and 1987 in favour of PIC ultimately led to its incorporation into the FAO Code in 1989. PAN delegates helped instigate PIC as an issue of Southern solidarity at the 1987 UNEP Governing Council by circulating amended versions of UNEP's London Guidelines for the Exchange of Information on Chemicals in International Trade, featuring PIC, to all delegates who belonged to the Group of 77.[35] If Young's threefold classification is applied to the pesticides trade issue, Bull and a number of PAN representatives, led by Werning, can be seen as intellectual leaders, whilst the delegates of Ecuador and The Philippines played the role of the entrepreneurs.

Epistemic Communities

The utilization of the 'power of ideas'[36] by individual leaders represents an attempt to reshape the knowledge that actors possess on an issue. This knowledge will be reflected in the principles of any regime set up to regulate the issue. Whereas the norms of a regime will emerge from consensus within the whole issue system, an epistemic consensus on technical questions will tend to be arrived at by a subset of that issue system, establishing principles which serve as yardsticks in understanding the nature of the problems faced and the consequent emergence of norms. This sub-set of actors has been termed an 'epistemic community'.[37]

Haas considers epistemic communities to be an explanatory variable for regime creation, alongside power and interest based explanations. His most extensive research has been on the development of the Mediterranean Action Plan (MAP), a regional regime regulating marine pollution in that sea.[38] The crucial factor in the creation of MAP was the decision of the North African countries to take part in the regime after initially showing hostility to it as being counter to their interests. Haas' research found that this redefinition of interests was not the result of any 'arm twisting' by the region's hegemonic power, France, over countries heavily dependent on her trade. Conversely, Algerian compliance with the rules of MAP came at a time when their trade with France had dropped considerably.[39]

Instead, Haas proposes that the MAP's creation was chiefly instigated by a grouping of like-minded ecologists and marine scientists who gained access to national administrations and the UNEP secretariat. This epistemic community established the principles that were gradually accepted by the Mediterranean state governments in formulating the norms and rules of the regime.

The principles are that Mediterranean currents and wind patterns transmit pollutants across national borders and that these pollutants interfere with other uses of the sea (such as recreation, tourism, fishing and navigation) thereby necessitating coordinated national control policies'.[40]

Haas considers epistemic communities to be most influential in environmental issue systems, where the principles being established are of a highly technical, scientific nature. In such cases, the epistemic community gains empowerment from the fact that they provide an understanding of areas that are unfamiliar to decision makers. Hence, the discovery of a hole in the ozone layer over Antarctica in 1985 and the consensus of scientific opinion as to the causal role of chlorofluorocarbons in this process led to the formation of an international regime curbing CFC use and production within two years. The principle that 'CFCs are eroding the ozone layer' was established by a small group of atmospheric physicists and chemists from a variety of national and international organizations, including UNEP and the British Antarctic Survey.[41] The expertise of this group in relation to the issue was accepted by most governments and the principle became the catalyst for political action.

The issue of ozone depletion clearly represents a case whereby the establishment of an epistemic consensus was the starting point for international political cooperation and regime formation. In such cases, a united voice of recognized experts on an issue serves to provide a clear understanding of a problem requiring a political response. In effect they create a new 'fact', of which political actors must be aware and respond to in some way. This cognitive process of establishing a fact may occur some time after its physical establishment. The hole in the ozone layer is actually believed to have emerged in 1975 and the pollution of the Mediterranean had been going on for many years prior to the signing of the MAP. The key factors in regime creation appear to be, firstly, for the political actors to be persuaded that a principle espoused by an epistemic community is indeed a fact and, secondly, for them to accept that a new fact is significant enough to warrant a re-prioritization of the norms that guide them on a particular issue.

Epistemic consensus is a powerful force for political action, but scientists and intellectual groupings do not always reach harmonious conclusions. For instance, there is not the same level of scientific convergence on the causes of the global problem of rainforest depletion as there is for ozone depletion, which is reflected in the absence of any effective international regime for rainforest conservation. We have seen that an epistemic consensus is lacking in some of the areas of pesticide politics, particularly in the issues of human poisoning and pesticide residues in food. Estimates of human deaths and illnesses attributable to pesticides vary considerably and proponents of proscriptive and prescriptive norms both use scientific opinion to bolster their positions. The competition between different bodies of scientific opinion, or 'scientific politicking',[42] is a recurrent theme in pesticide politics issues and tends to inhibit the establishment of principles as facts in the minds of political actors.

A crucial point here is that scientific opinion can be a product of the political process as well as an input into it. It is too simplistic and idealistic to think that an epistemic consensus will always emerge independently and proceed to unite all actors within an issue system. Favourable scientific opinions can be seized upon by particular actors and then magnified by their power and/or leadership skills. The controversial opinions of cancer scientist Bruce Ames, who feels that the carcinogenic threat posed by pesticides is exaggerated, have been utilized extensively by the chemical industry in countering the claims of the anti-pesticide lobby (see Chapter 6). Furthermore, scientists may be employed by a political actor to produce data which serve their cause. GCPF and the American Chemical Society regularly publish scientific research on pesticide toxicity which ultimately serves to promote its production and use, albeit in a responsible manner.

At the ultimate level, scientific opinion may be politically manipulated or even corrupted. In Chapter 6 we saw how the Reagan administration in the USA attempted to dilute the regulatory standards governing the issue of pesticide residues in food. The government appointed scientists sympathetic to its cause to the key regulatory and epistemic body, the Environmental Protection Agency, and attempted to alter the rules by which the EPA came to calculate its safe tolerance levels.[43] Also in the US, we have seen the occurrence of fraudulent testing by scientists, in order to gain political approval for particular pesticide products.

Internationally, environmental and consumer pressure groups have expressed concern over the level of influence wielded by the chemical industry over UN bodies dealing with pesticide issues. FAO has long been criticized for being too cosy with industry in general.[44] In particular, the level of corporate influence at Codex Alimentarius Commission (CAC) meetings is cited as a reason for the establishment of pesticide residue limits far less strict than those of North America and Europe.[45]

In this instance, however, it is not the epistemic community that is being manipulated, but governments. The Joint Meeting on Pesticide Residues (JMPR), the scientific body responsible for FAO/WHO testing and data on residue questions, is not composed of any corporate representatives, but government delegations to CAC committees are heavily weighted in favour of the food and chemical industries. This represents an instance of a powerful actor using its capabilities and leadership skills to use the output of an epistemic community in a way which furthers its interests. The industry has accepted the validity of JMPR research but succeeded in reinterpreting its output as serving to establish maximum rather than minimum global standards. Hence an epistemic consensus which originally helped uphold the norm that residue levels in food should be limited, because of the principle that residues can harm human health, is being utilized to uphold the very different value of promoting free trade. Similarly, the chemical industry has reinterpreted the meaning of the PIC rule in pesticide trading.[46] A rule formulated to control pesticide trade has been reconceptualized as a means of delegitimizing any attempt by governments to outlaw completely the export of particular pesticides.

For the issues of pesticide residues in food and pesticide trading, the industry has been forced to acknowledge the legitimacy of a rule and respond to it politically. In both cases they have had the capacity and adroitness to respond in a way which minimizes their losses. In the case of food residues, the industry could actually be seen to increase their gains, since the enforcement of the current global regulations would represent a lowering of most current national standards.

Scientific politicking is a feature of all seven issues in international pesticide politics. The issues of human poisoning, environmental pollution and food contamination are all conspicuous for a lack of epistemic consensus. The issue of avoiding pesticide overuse by implementing a policy of integrated pest management owes its existence to an epistemic consensus on the desirability of the concept, but this has not led to the formation of an international regime. Part of the reason for this is that the epistemic group upholding the desirability of IPM has to contend with the existing, still well-established body of opinion on the merits of conventional chemical pest control.

An epistemic consensus is clearly an important factor in the establishment of an issue on the international agenda, but for a regime to evolve from the issue system it is necessary for the epistemic consensus to overturn the existing knowledge of actors concerning that issue and any other issues to which it may be linked by value or function. This can happen in two ways. Firstly, the epistemic consensus may be augmented by the structural power and/ or leadership skills of actors who can then persuade others of a norm's salience to them. Thus, the chemical industry's support for the international regulation of pesticide residues in traded food products has been important in the creation of the regime based on the Codex Alimentarius Commission. Similarly, their eventual support for the PIC rule was the crucial factor in the creation of an international regime governing pesticide trade. The second way in which epistemic consensus on an issue may lead to the overturning of existing knowledge and the creation of a regime is when the principle espoused by an epistemic community is conceived by actors to be superior to their present knowledge. This inducing of salience through enlightenment is usually the result of a discovery by an epistemic community, which is significant enough to alter immediately the actors' established knowledge and alter their prioritizing of norms and issues. The discovery of a hole in the ozone layer above Antarctica represents such a case, as does the subsequent discovery that the soil fumigant, methyl-bromide, is an agent of ozone depletion. Ozone depletion since 1985 has been universally conceived of as a threat to security and, hence, political responses have followed. This leads us to another partial explanatory factor for regime creation, the onset of a crisis.

Crises

The clearest way by which an actor can be convinced of the need to place a particular issue higher up its political agenda and move towards international cooperation is when that issue becomes conceived of as a threat to its security. Hence, the discovery of a hole in the ozone layer, coupled with the understanding that this posed a major health threat, prompted a quick international response. Similarly, the Chernobyl nuclear accident in 1986 dramatically highlighted the need for international safety standards, which were formulated in agreements the following year.[47] In such circumstances the role of epistemic communities becomes crucial, as governments seek expert advice to try to establish the principles upon which to base cooperation.

Decision makers do not always recognize that their understanding of complex issues and linkages is limited and it often takes a crisis or shock to overcome institutionalized inertia and habit and spur them to seek help from an epistemic community.[48]

The sudden emergence of such threats to global security is obviously not common, but cooperation may be ignited by crises of a lesser sort in which public opinion is mobilized sufficiently strongly for governments or international organizations to act. Young refers to a 'manufactured crisis', consisting of media and NGO pressure, as being partially responsible for the formation of the regime aiming to conserve polar bears.[49]

Clearly any crisis, even in a lesser form in which no threat to security is apparent, needs to have international ramifications for it to act as a catalyst for international cooperation. The erosion of the ozone layer potentially threatens everybody, whilst spills of nuclear radiation can travel thousands of miles and threaten the livelihoods of people outside the country where the accident occurred. However, as we saw in Chapter 5, environmental pollution by pesticides rarely becomes an international problem and as such tends to remain regulated at the national level. The international agreement to freeze methyl bromide use and production arose because this represented a global threat, whilst the various marine pollution regimes dealing with the issue have remained localized to countries sharing common stretches of water. Pesticide politics' greatest ever crisis must surely have been the Bhopal disaster of 1984, in which thousands of people died and world media attention highlighted the culpability of lax safety standards for the tragedy. Despite the attempts of pressure groups and activists to try to utilize the crisis' impact for the development of safety guidelines,[50] Bhopal was not a catalyst for international action in the way that Chernobyl was. This was basically because the chemical industry was able to show satisfactorily that safety standards prevented any possibility of such an accident occurring in the North.

A crisis is very likely to induce governments and other actors into creating an international regime based on principles that are upheld by a consensus of experts, when that crisis is sufficiently salient to them. The level of salience need not necessarily be of the order of a threat to security, as is evidenced by the polar bear and other conservation regimes, but if the crisis is seen to hold little significance outside its country of origin then significant cooperation is unlikely.

Utilitarian Explanations

According to the liberal/idealist school of thought, against which realism initially emerged as a response,[51] international cooperation was inherently desirable as a means of reaping joint gains for all, as opposed to relying on the actions of governments who tend only to maximize their own short-sighted interests. This approach, which can be seen as a forerunner of the modern pluralist paradigm of international relations, represented an adaptation of the classic economic liberalism of Adam Smith and his contemporaries. The maximization of economic utility, it was argued, could only be achieved by minimizing governmental control of the world economy and promoting free trade. Hence, GATT and other forms of international economic cooperation were encouraged in the years since the Second World War.

Utilitarian arguments in favour of international cooperation have been applied outside the economic sphere, as responses to international problems where only a collective response can facilitate an optimal outcome for all. The theories of public goods and the prisoners dilemma, outlined in Chapter 1, describe how norms which do not maximize short-term utility calculations can nevertheless serve as beneficial guides to behaviour. Hence, an international regime to control CFC emissions can be conceptualized as a rational response to the problem, even for those governments for whom curbing CFC production incurs most costs.

The adaptation of utilitarian arguments for regime creation from the economic sphere to the public goods sphere can, however, produce contradictions. That fundamental expression of economic liberalism, free trade, is diametrically opposed to many forms of utilitarian cooperation over the allocation of public goods. Any international regime that proscribes the use, production and trade of a particular item, on the grounds that it is likely to be depleted to levels that are disadvantageous to all, runs counter to economic utilitarianism.

The inability to provide public goods, and other areas exogenous to economic production in which cooperation is necessary, have been termed 'political market failures'.[51] When such cases arise, cooperation will still be in the interests of all but may require a 'political entrepreneur' to bear the short-term costs of initiating the process. Keohane considers that regime creation partly represents the rational maximizing of utilities by actors. He is at pains to point out that such a functional analysis is 'not a substitute for the analysis of power',[52] but rather should supplement hegemonic stability as an explanatory theory of regime formation. The basic assumption behind the utilitarian/functionalist theory of regime creation is that actors will cooperate in order to reap joint gains.

This returns us to the debate, opened up in Chapter 1, over the nature of norms, the consensual guides to behaviour from which issue systems derive and regimes may subsequently form. The utilitarian approach clearly assumes norms to be 'artificial virtues'[53] which merely reflect the interests of actors. If this approach is supplemented by hegemonic stability theory, as in Keohane's work, the norms will be seen as reflecting the interests of actors but in a way weighted in favour of the more powerful actors. Hence Donelan defines a norm as 'a record of the methods and results of power politics'.[54]

Certainly, examples can be offered of norms that serve to satisfy the interests of all participating actors. As was argued in Chapter 1, much of customary international law can be understood in this light. The development of the norms that maritime states are entitled to claim jurisdiction over bays and continental shelves adjacent to their territories or declare a 200 mile exclusive economic zone in the surrounding seas bears testimony to this. However, many international regimes have succeeded in legitimizing norms and rules, and gaining compliance from actors, for reasons other than self-interest or the interests of a dominant actor.

An interesting illustration of this is provided by Harald Muller, from the realist preserve of security politics.[55] Muller shows how the Anti-Ballistic Missile (ABM) Treaty, which had formed the centrepiece of a strategic nuclear arms regime since 1972, managed to survive with its norms, rules and principles intact despite a move by the US government in the early 1980s to abandon it for reasons of national interest. The Reagan administration announced its desire to implement a strategic defence initiative policy, which would achieve national security through exploiting the US's advantage in capabilities, rather than putting their faith in a bilateral treaty based on trust. This policy proposal was abandoned after a concerted campaign, both domestic and international, which sought to uphold the norms of the ABM Treaty. The US State Department valued the confidence provided by maintaining a security regime; the US's allies feared that a unilateral US approach to security would ignore their security needs; and the body of experts (epistemic community) responsible for negotiating and implementing the ABM Treaty added their opposition.

> *... the rules of the regime were used throughout the debate as the standard of measurement for permitted and prohibited behaviour. Despite great efforts by the SDI proponents, they were not able to overcome the barrier the regime had created to their preferred projects. Opponents were able to mobilize around the ABM Treaty rules as a 'system of reference', and also to rally opposition around the regime norms against which SDI was basically directed.*[56]

In pesticide politics, we have seen that the UK and US governments and the chemical industry finally came to accept the legitimacy of PIC as a rule governing the trade in pesticides, despite having previously blocked its incorporation and possessing the capabilities to do so again. Earlier in this chapter it was shown how the US government attempted to create a new international aviation regime to suit the interests of US airlines but were prevented from doing so. As with the ABM case, this attempt by the US administration to utilize its capabilities in order to maximize its interests floundered on both domestic and international opposition which rallied around the existing regime structure.

Positing that international regimes are created rationally as a means of reaping mutual gains for actors is too simplistic. Norms can emerge from values other than those of maximizing economic returns or wielding power. PIC was legitimized as an international rule because those proposing it were able to claim the higher moral ground. The norm of regulating the trade in pesticides was derived from the value of minimizing human suffering, which was evidenced by the casualties of pesticide misuse in developing countries. Against this, arguments based on maintaining free trade were eventually overcome and moral reason was able to triumph over *raison d'etat*.

Cognitive Theories

A further challenge to the rationality of the utilitarian approach comes from cognitive theory, which stresses the ambiguous nature of reality and the subsequent importance of ideology and perception in determining behaviour. Jonsson has argued that the concept of an international regime is inherently cognitive and subjective.[57] Krasner's widely accepted definition of an international regime adds to the four components – principles, norms, rules and decision making procedures – the qualifying phrase, 'around which actors' expectations converge in a given issue area'. As the linking of issues into issue areas is also essentially a mental construction, Jonsson reasons that cognitive considerations must play a part in the process of cooperation and regime building.

The importance of psychological factors in decision making has been stressed by foreign policy analysts since the 1950s. The Sprouts in 1956 first elaborated the concept of separate operational and psychological environments in decision making. Decisions may be implemented in the 'operational world' but they are decided in the 'psychological world' of the decision makers' mental constructions.[58] Jonsson seeks to apply such an approach to regime theory, as an accompaniment to the utilitarian explanation. 'Cognitive theory does not assume irrationality but explores the *limits* of human rationality'.[59]

Ernst Haas, probably the leading exponent of cognitive theory in international relations, concurs in the belief that the approach should only be considered as a partial explanation for regime creation. In his opinion, a theory of regime creation or change must accept:

> . . . *the existence of power differentials and the importance of hierarchy among states – without sacrificing to such a view the possibility of choice based on perception and cognition inspired by additional calculations.*[60]

Haas stresses the importance of actors sharing a common perception of a problem as requiring cooperation before any fruitful bargaining process can be initiated. The idea of consensual knowledge as a prerequisite for cooperation clearly echoes the work on epistemic communities and their role in the establishment of principles, in response to which regimes may be created. However, cognitive theory can also offer insights into the nature of the bargaining process itself and the determinants of its success or failure.

A key factor in the successful fostering of cooperation must be a sense of trust between the parties concerned. An actor needs to have some assurance that their partners in cooperation will abide by the norms and rules of a regime before they too will accept them. Thus the perceptions that cooperating parties hold of each other are significant in the bargaining process which precedes regime formation.

The level of trust one actor will have in another will be gauged according to the previous behaviour of that actor in similar cooperating situations. In other words, the reputation of an actor is integral to successful bargaining and regime creation. 'International regimes depend on reputational mechanisms to get norms started'.[61] Reputation will aid regime formation in two ways. Firstly, as we have seen, an actor must have a trustworthy reputation for others to agree to cooperate and formulate concessional agreements. Secondly, an actor may be induced into acquiescing to norms and rules that are against its immediate interests for fear of developing an untrust-worthy reputation which could hinder future cooperation on political questions more salient to them. This idea points up a fundamental flaw in the utilitarian approach to regime formation. An actor cannot afford to maximize utility on a particular issue if it means that they will be shunned in future and be unable to cooperate in areas that do further their interests or values.

Thus, moral pressure can induce an actor into acquiescing in a global norm and abiding by the rules of a regime, through fear of the effects on its reputation of not doing so. This was surely a factor in the decision of the chemical industry to back down to pressure and accept the legitimacy of the PIC rule in regulating the inter-national trade in pesticides. The potential loss in trade through having its exports to developing countries more closely monitored, was offset by the prospect of acquiring a poor reputation which would damage its public image and ability to negotiate with pressure groups in future. The industry thus took the decision to bow to pressure and act against its direct interests in order to strengthen its position in countering the greater potential threat to its interests of the outright prohibition of exporting certain pesticides. Compromise is the art of bargaining, and bargaining, to a large extent, is the art of international politics.

Implementation

A final, and essential, criterion for regime formation is the qualif-ication that, before it can be accepted as a phenomenon, actor behaviour must be affected by the regime's norms, rules and decision making procedures. As pointed out in the conclusions to Chapter 7, List and Rittberger have added the appendage of 'minimal effect-iveness' to Krasner's standard definition of an international regime.[62] As List and Rittberger point out, this qualification enables us to distinguish between regimes and treaties, since a regime's rules may be informal. It also enables a distinction to be made between rules that are actually observed and rules which exist in writing but have no discernible influence on actor behaviour.

Hence, Mendler's research into the issue of the working conditions of foreign journalists concludes that there is no regime in operation, despite the existence of norms, rules and a principle.[63] Rittberger states of this case:

Norm observance and rule compliance varied so greatly over time and across countries, especially in Eastern Europe and the Soviet Union, that – using effectiveness as a criterion – it did not seem warranted to acknowledge the existence of an international regime.[64]

Similarly, despite the fact that there is a norm declaring that human poisoning by pesticides should be minimized and there are various global safety standards for working with pesticides and for selling them, there is no regime in existence for the issue of human poisoning by pesticides. In contrast, the PIC rule is part of the same FAO Code of Conduct as the provisions for safety, advertising and labelling, but it can be seen as having formed the basis for a regime. This is because it has been implemented and had some effect on the behaviour of the actors within the issue system.

A regime's behavioural effects may be sub-optimal, when compared to the initial goal of the norm from which it emerged, but if it can still be seen to have influenced political behaviour then its existence can be confirmed. Not adopting this criterion for the existence of an international regime serves to make the phenomenon indistinguishable from that of an issue system. An issue-system is an area of contention around a norm or number of norms, which represent specific interpretations of more general values applied to a set of political questions. For a regime to be seen to have emerged from an issue system there needs to be evidence of political behaviour, an authoritative allocation of the norms and values being contended. This can be said to have occurred if a set of rules and decision-making procedures have been laid down by a would-be regulatory body, and the rules and decisions are also acted upon by the actors within the issue system.

CONCLUSIONS

The seven issues of pesticide politics, we have seen, each represent an area of consensus around a particular norm of behaviour concerning pesticide use and production. Actors in pesticides politics will need to prioritize some of these norms over others in determining their behaviour in relation to pesticides policy questions. At the most fundamental level, this choice will be between one of the two norms prescribing pesticide production and use and one or more of the five proscriptive norms (Table 9.2). In addition, however, actors will also tend to prioritize between the proscriptive norms in that some of them will be deemed to override the prescriptive norms more often than others. As a result of this process of ranking norms, the seven issue systems feature different levels of contention over their constituent policy-questions.

Table 9.2 *Summary table of the seven norms of pesticide politics and their derivative issue-systems*

Norms	Structure of Issue System
Prescriptive	
1) *We should strive to attain optimum food yields*	UNREGULATED. Wide consensus on the use of pesticides. Norm competes with all proscriptive norms
2) *Disease and damage due to pests should be limited*	UNREGULATED. Wide consensus on the use of pesticides has begun to erode
Proscriptive	
3) *The misuse of pesticides leading to human poisoning should be prevented*	UNREGULATED. Global guidelines in FAO Code of Conduct but not widely adhered to
4) *Environmental pollution by pesticides should be limited*	UNREGULATED. Regional regimes and global controls on ozone depleting pesticides, but no system-wide global regulation
5) *The contamination of food by pesticides should be limited*	REGULATED. Codex Committee on Pesticide Residues sets global standards which have behavioural effect
6) *The international trade in pesticides should be controlled*	REGULATED. Rotterdam Convention has made Prior Informed Consent rule part of International Law
7) *Pesticides should not be overused*	UNREGULATED. Some national and local implementation of IPM measures, but no real global implementation.

Where an issue system features a high degree of consensus over its central norm and a high rate of actor compliance with rules and decisions designed to uphold that norm, then an international regime can be seen to have emerged, regulating the issue. The regulation of an issue at the global level is a complex process requiring a combination of favourable circumstances for its accomplishment. This chapter has examined a number of factors which influence the development of international regimes. The lack of a world legislature, executive or judiciary comparable to those found in most domestic political systems makes any authoritative allocation of values internationally difficult to achieve. Authoritative allocations of global norms and values do occur, however, and they do not necessarily represent the imposition of rules favouring a dominant actor or coalition of actors.

Values inform political stances and decisions and are promoted internationally by pressure groups, by international institutions and even by governments. Moral pressure can induce powerful actors to compromise and come to the bargaining table more often than traditional power politics theory would have us believe. International institutions, in particular those contained within the United Nations system, may fall well short of the 'embryonic world government' vision of utopian internationalists, but they have attained sufficient credibility to help foster cooperation amongst divergent interests and make the international system something less than anarchic. International regimes are able to emerge from this international system of mixed actors (governments, international institutions, transnational corporations and non-governmental organizations) in which values compete alongside power and interests in shaping the norms and rules by which actor behaviour is guided.

Appendix
International Code of Conduct on the Distribution and Use of Pesticides

(Amended to include Prior Informed Consent in Article 9 as adopted by the 25th Session of the FAO Conference in November 1989)

The Food and Agriculture Organization of the United Nations wishes to encourage the dissemination of the material contained in this publication and welcomes applications for its reproduction and use. Such applications, with a statement of the purpose and extent of the reproduction, should be addressed to the Director, Publications Division, Food and Agriculture Organization of the United Nations, Via delle Terme di Caracalla, 00100 Rome, Italy.

FOOD AND AGRICULTURE ORGANIZATION OF THE UNITED NATIONS
Rome, 1990

CONTENTS

Preface 175

Text of the Code 177

    Article 1   Objectives of the Code 177

    Article 2   Definitions 178

    Article 3   Pesticide management 181

    Article 4   Testing of pesticides 183

    Article 5   Reducing health hazards 184

    Article 6   Regulatory and technical requirements 186

    Article 7   Availability and use 187

    Article 8   Distribution and trade 187

    Article 9   Information exchange and prior informed consent 189

    Article 10   Labelling, packaging, storage and disposal 191

    Article 11   Advertising 192

    Article 12   Monitoring the observance of the Code 194

Annex: FAO Conference Resolution 10/85 195

References 196

Additional technical guidelines 197

PREFACE

The action by FAO to develop, in consultation with appropriate United Nations agencies and other organizations, an International Code of Conduct on the Distribution and Use of Pesticides follows and accompanies many other events, some going back 25 years. All these events were designed to benefit the international community and to serve to increase international confidence in the availability, regulation, marketing and use of pesticides for the improvement of agriculture, public health and personal comfort.

One of the basic functions of the Code, which is voluntary in nature, is to serve as a point of reference, particularly until such time as countries have established adequate regulatory infrastructures for pesticides.

The Director-General of FAO in 1981 suggested that such a Code could help to overcome a number of difficulties associated with pesticides. The FAO Panel of Experts on Pesticide Specifications, Registration Requirements and Application Standards, at its meeting in 1982, agreed that activities involving the export and import of pesticides, and thereby their safe use, might be best dealt with through the adoption of a Code of Conduct. To that end a working paper was prepared for the FAO Second Government Consultation on International Harmonization of Pesticide Registration Requirements, Rome, 1–5 October 1982. The formal decision to develop the Code was taken at that Consultation, which recommended that FAO, in consultation with the appropriate United Nations organizations and bodies and international organizations outside the United Nations system, should draft a Code (1).

The Code itself was adopted by the FAO Conference at its Twenty-third Session in 1985 by way of Resolution 10/85, which appears as an Annex to the present publication.

A number of governments and organizations have expressed concern about the propriety of supplying pesticides to countries which do not have infrastructures to register pesticides and thereby to ensure their safe and effective use. It should be noted that the development of national regulatory programmes is the first priority of FAO activities in this field. There has also been concern over the possibility that residues of certain pesticides, not needed or not permitted in particular countries, are present in imported agricultural commodities produced in other countries where the use of such pesticides is not restricted. While recognizing that it is impossible to eliminate all such occurrences, because of diverging pest control needs, it is none the less essential that every effort be made to apply pesticides only in accordance with good and recognized practices. It is at the same time important for industrially developed countries to recognize, in their regulatory activities concerning residues, the pest control needs of developing countries, particularly the needs of countries in tropical regions.

In the absence of an effective pesticide registration process and of a governmental infrastructure for controlling the availability of pesticides, some countries importing pesticides must heavily rely on the pesticide industry to promote the safe and proper distribution and use of pesticides. In these circumstances foreign manufacturers, exporters and importers, as well as local formulators, distributors, repackers, advisers and users, must accept a share of the responsibility for safety and efficiency in distribution and use.

The role of the exporting country needs to be considered. Much emphasis has been given recently to the desirability of regulating the export of pesticides from producing countries. It is generally accepted that no company should trade in pesticides without a proper and thorough evaluation of the pesticide, including any risks. However, the fact that a product is not used or registered in a particular exporting country is not necessarily a valid reason for prohibiting the export of that pesticide. Developing countries are mostly situated in tropical and semitropical regions. Their climatic, ecological, agronomic, social, economic and environmental conditions and therefore their pest problems are usually quite different from those prevailing in countries in which pesticides are manufactured and exported. The government of the exporting country, therefore, is in no position to judge the suitability, efficacy, safety or fate of the pesticide under the conditions in the country where it may ultimately be used. Such a judgement must, therefore, be made by the responsible authority in the importing country in consultation with industry and other government authorities in the light of the scientific evaluation that has been made and a detailed knowledge of the conditions prevailing in the country of proposed use.

The export to developing countries of pesticides which have been banned in one or more other countries or whose use has been severely restricted in some industrialized countries has been a subject of public concern which has led to intensive discussions. In addressing this issue, the FAO Conference at its Twenty-fifth Session in 1989 agreed to introduce provisions for Prior Informed Consent (PIC) procedures. These procedures are described in the revised Article 9 on Information exchange and Prior Informed Consent.

While a Code of Conduct may not solve all problems, nevertheless it should go a long way toward defining and clarifying the responsibilities of the various parties involved in the development, distribution and use of pesticides, and it should be of particular value in countries which do not yet have control procedures. Where there is a pesticide regulatory process in a country, the need for a Code of Conduct will obviously be less than where there is no such scheme in operation.

The Code of Conduct is not a short or simple document, mainly because the nature, properties, uses and effects of pesticides are diverse and therefore require comprehensive consideration. Furthermore, the strong public pressure for banning or restricting the use of some effective and much needed pesticides often stems from a lack of understanding of the many important issues involved. This document is designed, therefore, also to provide the general public with some basic guidance on these issues.

EDOUARD SAOUMA
Director-General

TEXT OF THE CODE

Article I Objectives of the Code

1.1 The objectives of this Code are to set forth responsibilities and establish voluntary standards of conduct for all public and private entities engaged in or affecting the distribution and use of pesticides, particularly where there is no or an inadequate national law to regulate pesticides.

1.2 The Code describes the shared responsibility of many segments of society, including governments, individually or in regional groupings, industry, trade and international institutions, to work together so that the benefits to be derived from the necessary and acceptable use of pesticides are achieved without significant adverse effects on people or the environment. To this end, all references in this Code to a government or governments shall be deemed to apply equally to regional groupings of governments for matters falling within their areas of competence.

1.3 The Code addresses the need for a cooperative effort between governments of exporting and importing countries to promote practices which ensure efficient and safe use while minimizing health and environmental concerns due to improper handling or use.

1.4 The entities which are addressed by this Code include international organizations; governments of exporting and importing countries; industry, including manufacturers, trade associations, formulators and distributors; users; and public-sector organizations such as environmental groups, consumer groups and trade unions.

1.5 The standards of conduct set forth by this Code:

    1.5.1 encourage responsible and generally accepted trade practices;

    1.5.2 assist countries which have not yet established controls designed to regulate the quality and suitability of pesticide products needed in that country and to address the safe handling and use of such products;

    1.5.3 promote practices which encourage the safe and efficient use of pesticides, including minimizing adverse effects on humans and the environment and preventing accidental poisoning from improper handling;

    1.5.4 ensure that pesticides are used effectively for the improvement of agricultural production and of human, animal and plant health.

1.6 The Code is designed to be used, within the context of national law, as a basis whereby government authorities, pesticide manufacturers, those engaged in trade and any citizens concerned may judge whether their proposed actions and the actions of others constitute acceptable practices.

Article 2 Definitions

For the purpose of this Code:

Active ingredient means the biologically active part of the pesticide present in a formulation.

Advertising means the promotion of the sale and use of pesticides by print and electronic media, signs, displays, gift, demonstration or word of mouth.

Banned means a pesticide for which all registered uses have been prohibited by final government regulatory action, or for which all requests for registration or equivalent action for all uses have, for health or environmental reasons, not been granted.

Common name means the name assigned to a pesticide active ingredient by the International Standards Organization or adopted by national standards authorities to be used as a generic or non proprietary name for that particular active ingredient only.

Distinguishing name means the name under which the pesticide is labelled, registered and promoted by the manufacturer and which, if protected under national legislation, can be used exclusively by the manufacturer to distinguish the product from other pesticides containing the same active ingredient.

Distribution means the process by which pesticides are supplied through trade channels on local or international markets.

Environment means surroundings, including water, air, soil and their inter-relationship as well as all relationships between them and any living organisms.

Extension service means those entities in the country concerned responsible for the transfer of information and advice to farmers regarding the improvement of agricultural practices, including production, handling, storage and marketing.

Formulation means the combination of various ingredients designed to render the product useful and effective for the purpose claimed; the form of the pesticide as purchased by users.

Hazard means the likelihood that a pesticide will cause an adverse effect (injury) under the conditions in which it is used.

Integrated pest management means a pest management system that, in the context of the associated environment and the population dynamics of the pest species, utilizes all suitable techniques and methods in as compatible a manner as possible and maintains the pest populations at levels below those causing economically unacceptable damage or loss.

Label means the written, printed or graphic matter on, or attached to, the pesticide; or the immediate container thereof and the outside container or wrapper of the retail package of the pesticide.

Manufacturer means a corporation or other entity in the public or private sector or any individual engaged in the business or function (whether directly or through an agent or through an entity controlled by or under contract with it) of manufacturing a pesticide active ingredient or preparing its formulation or product.

Marketing means the overall process of product promotion, including advertising, product public relations and information services as well as distribution and selling on local or international markets:

Maximum residue limit (MRL) means the maximum concentration of a residue that is legally permitted or recognized as acceptable in or on a food, agricultural commodity or animal feedstuff.

Packaging means the container together with the protective wrapping used to carry pesticide products via wholesale or retail distribution to users.

Pesticide means any substance or mixture of substances intended for preventing, destroying or controlling any pest, including vectors of human or animal disease, unwanted species of plants or animals causing harm during or otherwise interfering with the production, processing, storage, transport, or marketing of food, agricultural commodities, wood and wood products or animal feedstuffs, or which may be administered to animals for the control of insects, arachnids or other pests in or on their bodies. The term includes substances intended for use as a plant growth regulator, defoliant, desiccant, or agent for thinning fruit or preventing the premature fall of fruit, and substances applied to crops either before or after harvest to protect the commodity from deterioration during storage and transport.

Pesticide industry means all those organizations and individuals engaged in manufacturing, formulating or marketing pesticides and pesticide products.

Pesticide legislation means any laws or regulations introduced to regulate the manufacture, marketing, storage, labelling, packaging and use of pesticides in their qualitative, quantitative and environmental aspects.

Poison means a substance that can cause disturbance of structure or function, leading to injury or death when absorbed in relatively small amounts by human beings, plants or animals.

Poisoning means occurrence of damage or disturbance caused by a poison, and includes intoxication.

Prior Informed Consent (PIC) refers to the principle that international shipment of a pesticide that is banned or severely restricted in order to protect human health or the environment should not proceed without the agreement, where such agreement exists, or contrary to the decision of the designated national authority in the participating importing country.

Prior Informed Consent Procedure (PIC procedure) means the procedure for formally obtaining and disseminating the decisions of importing countries as to whether they wish to receive future shipments of pesticides that have been banned or severely restricted. A specific procedure was established for selecting pesticides for initial implementation of the PIC procedures. These include pesticides that have been previously banned or severely restricted as well as certain pesticide formulations that are acutely toxic. This procedure is described in the Guidelines on the Operation of Prior Informed Consent. (15).

Product means the pesticide in the form in which it is packaged and sold; it usually contains an active ingredient plus adjuvants and may require dilution prior to use.

Protective clothing means any clothes, materials or devices that are designed to provide protection from pesticides when they are handled or applied.

Public sector groups means (but is not limited to) scientific associations; farmer groups; citizens' organizations; environmental, consumer and health organizations; and labour unions.

Registration means the process whereby the responsible national government authority approves the sale and use of a pesticide following the evaluation of comprehensive scientific data demonstrating that the product is effective for the purposes intended and not unduly hazardous to human or animal health or the environment.

Repackaging means the transfer of pesticide from any commercial package into any other, usually smaller, container for subsequent sale.

Residue means any specified substances in food, agricultural commodities, or animal feed resulting from the use of a pesticide. The term includes any derivatives of a pesticide, such as conversion products, metabolites, reaction products, and impurities considered to be of toxicological significance. The term 'pesticide residue' includes residues from unknown or unavoidable sources (e.g. environmental) as well as known uses of the chemical.

Responsible authority means the government agency or agencies responsible for regulating the manufacture, distribution or use of pesticides and more generally for implementing pesticide legislation.

Risk means the expected frequency of undesirable effects of exposure to the pesticide.

Severely restricted – a limited ban – means a pesticide for which virtually all registered uses have been prohibited by final government regulatory action but certain specific registered use or uses remain authorized.

Toxicity means a physiological or biological property which determines the capacity of a chemical to do harm or produce injury to a living organism by other than mechanical means.

Trader means anyone engaged in trade, including export, import, formulation and domestic distribution.

Use pattern embodies the combination of all factors involved in the use of a pesticide, including the concentration of active ingredient in the preparation being applied, rate of application, time of treatment, number of treatments, use of adjuvants and methods and sites of application which determine the quantity applied, timing of treatment and interval before harvest, etc.

Article 3 Pesticide management

3.1 Governments have the overall responsibility and should take the specific powers to regulate the distribution and use of pesticides in their countries.

3.2 The pesticide industry should adhere to the provisions of this Code as a standard for the manufacture, distribution and advertising of pesticides, particularly in countries lacking appropriate legislation and advisory services.

3.3 Governments of exporting countries should help to the extent possible, directly or through their pesticide industries, to:

> 3.3.1 provide technical assistance to other countries, especially those with shortages of technical expertise, in the assessment of the relevant data on pesticides, including those provided by industry (see also Article 4);
>
> 3.3.2 ensure that good trading practices are followed in the export of pesticides, especially to those countries with no or limited regulatory schemes (see also Articles 8 and 9).

3.4 Manufacturers and traders should observe the following practices in pesticide management, especially in countries without legislation or means of implementing regulations:

3.4.1 supply only pesticides of adequate quality, packaged and labelled as appropriate for each specific market;

3.4.2 pay special attention to formulations, presentation, packaging and labelling in order to reduce hazard to users, to the maximum extent possible consistent with the effective functioning of the pesticide in the particular circumstances in which it is to be used;

3.4.3 provide, with each package of pesticide, information and instructions in a form and language adequate to ensure safe and effective use;

3.4.4 retain an active interest in following their products to the ultimate consumer, keeping track of major uses and the occurrence of any problems arising in the actual use of their products as a basis for determining the need for changes in labelling, directions for use, packaging, formulation or product availability.

3.5 Pesticides whose handling and application require the use of uncomfortable and expensive protective clothing and equipment should be avoided, especially in the case of small scale users in tropical climates.

3.6 National and international organizations, governments, and pesticide industries should take action in coordinated efforts to disseminate educational materials of all types to pesticide users, farmers, farmers' organizations, agricultural workers, unions and other interested parties. Similarly, affected parties should seek and understand educational materials before using pesticides and should follow proper procedures.

3.7 Governments should allocate high priority and adequate resources to the task of effectively managing the availability, distribution and use of pesticides in their countries.

3.8 Concerted efforts should be made by governments and pesticide industries to develop and promote integrated pest management systems and the use of safe, efficient, cost-effective application methods. Public-sector groups and international organizations should actively support such activities.

3.9 International organizations should provide information on specific pesticides and give guidance on methods of analysis through the provision of criteria documents, fact sheets, training sessions, etc.

3.10 It is recognized that the development of resistance of pests to pesticides can be a major problem. Therefore, governments, industry, national institutions, international organizations and public sector groups should collaborate in developing strategies which will prolong the useful life of valuable pesticides and reduce the adverse effects of the development of resistant species.

Article 4 Testing of Pesticides

4.1 Pesticide manufacturers are expected to:

4.1.1 ensure that each pesticide and pesticide product is adequately and effectively tested by well recognized procedures and test methods so as to fully evaluate its safety, efficacy (2) and fate (3) with regard to the various anticipated conditions in regions or countries of use;

4.1.2. ensure that such tests are conducted in accordance with sound scientific procedures and good laboratory practice (4) – the data produced by such tests, when evaluated by competent experts, must be capable of showing whether the product can be handled and used safely without unacceptable hazard to human health, plants, animals, wildlife and the environment (3);

4.1.3 make available copies or summaries of the original reports of such tests for assessment by responsible government authorities in all countries where the pesticide is to be offered for sale. Evaluation of the data should be referred to qualified experts;

4.1.4 take care to see that the proposed use pattern, label claims and directions, packages, technical literature and advertising truly reflect the outcome of these scientific tests and assessments;

4.1.5 provide, at the request of a country, advice on methods for the analysis of any active ingredient of formulation that they manufacture, and provide the necessary analytical standards;

4.1.6 provide advice and assistance for training technical staff in relevant analytical work. Formulators should actively support this effort;

4.1.7 conduct residue trials prior to marketing in accordance with FAO guidelines on good analytical practice (S) and on crop residue data (6, 7) in order to provide a basis for establishing appropriate maximum residue limits (MRLs).

4.2 Each country should possess or have access to facilities to verify and exercise control over the quality of pesticides offered for sale, to establish the quantity of the active ingredient or ingredients and the suitability of their formulation (8).

4.3 International organizations and other interested bodies should, within available resources, consider assisting in the establishment of analytical laboratories in pesticide importing countries, either on a country or on a multilateral regional basis; these laboratories should be capable of carrying out product and residue analysis and should have adequate supplies of analytical standards, solvents and reagents.

4.4 Exporting governments and international organizations must play an active role in assisting developing countries in training personnel in the interpretation and evaluation of test data.

4.5 Industry and governments should collaborate in conducting post-registration surveillance or monitoring studies to determine the fate and environmental effect of pesticides under field conditions (3).

Article 5 Reducing Health Hazards

5.1 Governments which have not already done so should:

5.1.1   implement a pesticide registration and control scheme along the lines set out in Article 6;

5.1.2   decide, and from time to time review, the pesticides to be marketed in their country, their acceptable uses and their availability to each segment of the public;

5.1.3   provide guidance and instructions for the treatment of suspected pesticide poisoning for their basic health workers, physicians and hospital staff;

5.1.4   establish national or regional poisoning information and control centres at strategic locations to provide immediate guidance on first aid and medical treatment, accessible at all times by telephone or radio. Governments should collect reliable information about the health aspects of pesticides. Suitably trained people with adequate resources must be made available to ensure that accurate information is collected;

5.1.5   keep extension and advisory services, as well as farmers' organizations, adequately informed about the range of pesticide products available for use in each area;

5.1.6   ensure, with the cooperation of industry, that where pesticides are available through outlets which also deal in food, medicines, other products for internal consumption or topical application, or clothing, they are physically segregated from other merchandise, so as to avoid any possibility of contamination or of mistaken identity. Where appropriate, they should be clearly marked as hazardous materials. Every effort should be made to publicize the dangers of storing foodstuffs and pesticides together.

5.2 Even where a control scheme is in operation, industry should:

5.2.1 cooperate in the periodic reassessment of the pesticides which are marketed and in providing the poison control centres and other medical practitioners with information about hazards;

5.2.2 make every reasonable effort to reduce hazard by:

5.2.2.1 making less toxic formulations available;

5.2.2.2 introducing products in ready-to-use packages and otherwise developing safer and more efficient methods of application;

5.2.2.3 using containers that are not attractive for subsequent reuse and promoting programmes to discourage their reuse;

5.2.2.4 using containers that are safe (e.g. not attractive to or easily opened by children), particularly for the more toxic home use products;

5.2.2.5 using clear and concise labelling;

5.2.3 halt sale, and recall products, when safe use does not seem possible under any use, directions or restrictions.

5.3 Government and industry should further reduce hazards by making provision for safe storage and disposal of pesticides and containers at both warehouse and farm level, and through proper siting and control of wastes from formulating plants.

5.4 To avoid unjustified confusion and alarm among the public, public-sector groups should consider all available facts and try to distinguish between major differences in levels of risk among pesticides and uses.

5.5 In establishing production facilities in developing countries, manufacturers and governments should cooperate to:

5.5.1 adopt engineering standards and safe operating practices appropriate to the nature of the manufacturing operations and the hazards involved;

5.5.2 take all necessary precautions to protect the health and safety of operatives, bystanders and the environment;

5.5.3 maintain quality-assurance procedures to ensure that the products manufactured comply to the relevant standards of purity, performance, stability and safety.

Article 6 Regulatory and Technical Requirements

6.1 Governments should:

6.1.1 take action to introduce the necessary legislation for the regulation, including registration, of pesticides and make provisions for its effective enforcement, including the establishment of appropriate educational, advisory, extension and health-care services; the FAO guidelines for the registration and control of pesticides (9) should be followed, as far as possible, taking full account of local needs, social and economic conditions, levels of literacy, climatic conditions and availability of pesticide application equipment;

6.1.2 strive to establish pesticide registration schemes and infrastructures under which products can be registered prior to domestic use and, accordingly, ensure that each pesticide product is registered under the laws or regulations of the country of use before it can be made available there:

6.1.3 protect the proprietary rights to use of data;

6.1.4 collect and record data on the actual import, formulation and use of pesticides in each country in order to assess the extent of any possible effects on human health or the environment, and to follow trends in use levels for economic and other purposes.

6.2 The pesticides industry should:

6.2.1 provide an objective appraisal together with the necessary supporting data on each product;

6.2.2 ensure that the active ingredient and other ingredients of pesticide preparations marketed correspond in identity, quality, purity and composition to the substances tested, evaluated and cleared for toxicological and environmental acceptability;

6.2.3 ensure that active ingredients and formulated products for pesticides for which international specifications have been developed conform with the specifications of FAO (8), where intended for use in agriculture; and with WHO pesticide specifications (10), where intended for use in public health;

6.2.4 verify the quality and purity of the pesticides offered for sale;

6.2.5 when problems occur, voluntarily take corrective action, and when requested by governments, help find solutions to difficulties.

Article 7 Availability and Use

7.1 Responsible authorities should give special attention to drafting rules and regulations on the availability of pesticides. These should be compatible with existing levels of training and expertise in handling pesticides on the part of the intended users. The parameters on which such decisions are based vary widely and must be left to the discretion of each government, bearing in mind the situation prevailing in the country.

7.2 In addition, governments should take note of and, where appropriate, follow the WHO classifications of pesticides by hazard (11) and associate the hazard class with well-recognized hazard symbols as the basis for their own regulatory measures. In any event, the type of formulation and method of application should be taken into account in determining the risk and degree of restriction appropriate to the product.

7.3 Two methods of restricting availability can be exercised by the responsible authority: not registering a product; or, as a condition of registration, restricting the availability to certain groups of users in accordance with national assessments of hazards involved in the use of the product in the particular country.

7.4 All pesticides made available to the general public should be packaged and labelled in a manner which is consistent with the FAO guidelines on packaging (12) and labelling (13) and with appropriate national regulations.

7.5 Prohibition of the importation, sale and purchase of an extremely toxic product may be desirable if control measures or good marketing practices are insufficient to ensure that the product can be used safely. However, this is a matter for decision in the light of national circumstances.

Article 8 Distribution and Trade

8.1 Industry should:

8.1.1 test all pesticide products to evaluate safety with regard to human health and the environment prior to marketing, as provided for in Article 4, and ensure that all pesticide products are likewise adequately tested for efficacy and stability and crop tolerance, under procedures that will predict performance under the conditions prevailing in the region where the product is to be used, before they are offered there for sale;

8.1.2 submit the results of all such tests to the local responsible authority for independent evaluation and approval before the products enter trade channels in that country;

8.1.3 take all necessary steps to ensure that pesticides entering international trade conform to relevant FAO (8) WHO (10) or equivalent specifications for composition and quality (where such specifications have been developed) and to the principles embodied in pertinent FAO guidelines, and in rules and regulations on classification and packaging, marketing, labelling and documentation laid down by international organizations concerned with modes of transport (ICAO, IMO, RID and IATA in particular);[1]

8.1.4 undertake to see that pesticides which are manufactured for export are subject to the same quality requirements and standards as those applied by the manufacturer to comparable domestic products;

8.1.5 ensure that pesticides manufactured or formulated by a subsidiary company meet appropriate quality requirements and standards which should be consistent with the requirements of the host country and of the parent company;

8.1.6 encourage importing agencies, national or regional formulators and their respective trade organizations to cooperate in order to achieve fair practices and safe marketing and distribution practices and to collaborate with authorities in stamping out any malpractices within the industry;

8.1.7 recognize that the recall of a pesticide by a manufacturer and distributor may be desirable when faced with a pesticide which represents an unacceptable hazard to human and animal health and the environment when used as recommended, and cooperate accordingly;

8.1.8 endeavour to ensure that pesticides are traded by and purchased from reputable traders, who should preferably be members of a recognized trade organization;

---

1 ICAO: International Civil Aviation Organization
   IMO: International Maritime Organization
   RID: International regulations concerning the carriage of dangerous goods by rail
   IATA: International Air Transport Association

8.1.9　see that persons involved in the sale of any pesticide are trained adequately to ensure that they are capable of providing the buyer with advice on safe and efficient use;

8.1.10　provide a range of pack sizes and types which are appropriate for the needs of small-scale farmers and other local users to avoid handling hazards and the risk that resellers will repackage products into unlabelled or inappropriate containers.

8.2 Governments and responsible authorities should take the necessary regulatory measures to prohibit the repackaging, decanting or dispensing of any pesticide in food or beverage containers and should rigidly enforce punitive measures that effectively deter such practices.

8.3 Governments of countries importing food and agricultural commodities should recognize good agricultural practices in countries with which they trade and, in accordance with recommendations of the Codex Alimentarius Commission, should establish a legal basis for the acceptance of pesticide residues resulting from such good agricultural practices (7, 14).

Article 9 Information Exchange and Prior Informed Consent

9.1 The government of any country that takes action to ban or severely restrict the use or handling of a pesticide in order to protect health or the environment should notify FAO as soon as possible of the action it has taken. FAO will notify the designated national authorities in other countries of the action of the notifying government (15).

9.2 The purpose of notification regarding control action is to give competent authorities in other countries the opportunity to assess the risks associated with the pesticides, and to make timely and informed decisions as to the importation and use of the pesticides concerned, after taking into account local, public health, economic, environmental and administrative conditions. The minimum information to be provided for this purpose should be:

9.2.1　the identity (common name, distinguishing name and chemical name);

9.2.2　a summary of the control action taken and of the reasons for it − if the control action bans or restricts certain uses but allows other uses, such information should be included:

9.2.3　an indication of the additional information that is available, and the name and address of the contact point in the country to which a request for further information should be addressed.

Information Exchange Among Countries

9.3 If export of a pesticide banned or severely restricted in the country of export occurs, the country of export should ensure that necessary steps are taken to provide the designated national authority of the country of import with relevant information.

9.4 The purpose of information regarding exports is to remind the country of import of the original notification regarding control action and to alert it to the fact that an export is expected or is about to occur. The minimum information to be provided for this purpose should be:

> 9.4.1 a copy of, or reference to, the information provided at the time of the notification of control action;

> 9.4.2 indication that an export of the chemical concerned is expected or is about to occur.

9.5 Provision of information regarding exports should take place at the time of the first export following the control action, and should recur in the case of any significant development of new information or condition surrounding the control action. It is the intention that the information should be provided prior to export.

9.6 The provision to individual countries of any additional information on the reasons for control actions taken by any country must take into account protection of any proprietary data from unauthorized use.

Prior Informed Consent

9.7 Pesticides that are banned or severely restricted for reasons of health or the environment are subject to the Prior Informed Consent procedure. No pesticide in these categories should be exported to an importing country participating in the PIC procedure contrary to that country's decision made in accordance with the FAO operational procedures for PIC.

9.8 FAO will:

> 9.8.1 review notifications of control actions to ensure conformity with definitions in Article 2 of the Code, and will develop the relevant guidance documents;

> 9.8.2 in cooperation with UNEP, develop and maintain a data base of control actions and decisions taken by all Member Governments;

> 9.8.3 inform all designated national authorities and relevant international organizations of, and publicize in such form as may be appropriate, notifications received under Article 9.1 and decisions communicated

to it regarding the use and importation of a pesticide that has been included in the PIC procedure;

9.8.4 FAO will seek advice at regular intervals and review the criteria for inclusion of pesticides in the Prior Informed Consent procedure and the operation of the Prior Informed Consent scheme and will report to Member Governments on its findings.

9.9 Governments of importing countries should establish internal procedures and designate the appropriate authority for the receipt and handling of information.

9.10 Governments of importing countries participating in the PIC procedure, when advised by FAO of control action within this procedure, should:

9.10.1 decide on future acceptability of that pesticide in their country and advise FAO as soon as that decision has been made;

9.10.2 ensure that governmental measures or actions taken with regard to an imported pesticide for which information has been received are not more restrictive than those applied to the same pesticide produced domestically or imported from a country other than the one that supplied the information;

9.10.3 ensure that such a decision is not used inconsistently with the provisions of the General Agreement on Tariffs and Trade (GATT).

9.11 Governments of pesticide exporting countries should:

9.11.1 advise their pesticide exporters and industry of the decisions of participating importing countries;

9.11.2 take appropriate measures, within their authority and legislative competence, designed to ensure that exports do not occur contrary to the decision of participating importing countries.

Article 10 Labelling, Packaging, Storage and Disposal

10.1 All pesticide containers should be clearly labelled in accordance with applicable international guidelines, such as the FAO guidelines on good labelling practice (13).

10.2 Industry should use labels that:

10.2.1 include recommendations consistent with those of the recognized research and advisory agencies in the country of sale;

10.2.2 include appropriate symbols and pictograms whenever possible, in addition to written instructions, warnings and precautions;

10.2.3 in international trade, clearly show appropriate WHO hazard classification of the contents (11) or, if this is inappropriate or inconsistent with national regulations, use the relevant classification;

10.2.4 include, in the appropriate language or languages, a warning against the reuse of containers, and instructions for the safe disposal or decontamination of empty containers;

10.2.5 identify each lot or batch of the product in numbers or letters that can be read, transcribed and communicated by anyone without the need for codes or other means of deciphering;

10.2.6 are marked with the date (month and year) of formulation of the lot or batch and with relevant information on the storage stability of the product.

10.3 Industry should ensure that:

10.3.1 packaging, storage and disposal of pesticides conform in principle to the FAO guidelines for packaging and storage (12), the FAO guidelines for the disposal of waste pesticides and containers (16), and WHO specifications for pesticides used in public health (10);

10.3.2 in cooperation with governments, packaging or repackaging is carried out only on licensed premises where the responsible authority is convinced that staff are adequately protected against toxic hazards, that the resulting product will be properly packaged and labelled, and that the content will conform to the relevant quality standards.

10.4 Governments should take the necessary regulatory measures to prohibit the repacking, decanting or dispensing of any pesticide into food or beverage containers in trade channels and rigidly enforce punitive measures that effectively deter such practices.

Article 11 Advertising

11.1 Industry should ensure that:

11.1.1 all statements used in advertising are capable of technical substantiation;

11.1.2 advertisements do not contain any statement or visual presentation which, directly or by implication, omission, ambiguity or exaggerated claim, is likely to mislead the buyer, in particular with regard to the safety of the product, its nature, composition, or suitability for use, or official recognition or approval;

11.1.3 pesticides which are legally restricted to use by trained or registered operators are not publicly advertised through journals other than those catering for such operations, unless the restricted availability is clearly and prominently shown;

11.1.4 no firm or individual in any one country simultaneously markets different pesticide active ingredients or combinations of ingredients under a single distinguishing name;

11.1.5 advertising does not encourage uses other than those specified on the approval label;

11.1.6 promotional material does not include use recommendations at variance with those of the recognized research and advisory agencies;

11.1.7 advertisements do not misuse research results or quotations from technical and scientific literature; and scientific jargon and irrelevances are not used to make claims appear to have a scientific basis they do not possess;

11.1.8 claims as to safety, including statements such as 'safe', 'nonpoisonous', 'harmless', 'non-toxic', are not made, with or without a qualifying phrase such as 'when used as directed';

11.1.9 statements comparing the safety of different products are not made;

11.1.10 misleading statements are not made concerning the effectiveness of the product;

11.1.11 no guarantees or implied guarantees e.g. 'more profits with. . .', 'guarantees high yields' etc are given unless definite evidence to substantiate such claims is available;

11.1.12 advertisements do not contain any visual representation of potentially dangerous practices, such as mixing or application without sufficient protective clothing, use near food, or use by or near children;

11.1.13 advertising or promotional material draws attention to the appropriate warning phrases and symbols as laid down in the labelling guidelines (13);

11.1.14 technical literature provides adequate information on correct practices, including the observance of recommended rates, frequency of applications, and safe pre-harvest intervals;

11.1.15 false or misleading comparisons with other pesticides are not made;

11.1.16 all staff involved in sales promotion are adequately trained and possess sufficient technical knowledge to present complete, accurate and valid information on the products sold;

11.1.17 advertisements encourage purchasers and users to read the label carefully, or have the label read to them if they cannot read.

11.2 International organizations and public-sector groups should call attention to departures from this Article.

11.3 Governments are encouraged to work with manufacturers to take advantage of their marketing skills and infrastructure, in order to provide public-service advertising regarding the safe and effective use of pesticides. This advertising could focus on such factors as proper maintenance and use of equipment, special precautions for children and pregnant women, the danger of reusing containers, and the importance of following label directions.

Article 12 Monitoring the Observance of the Code

12.1 The Code should be published and should be observed through collaborative action on the part of governments, individually or in regional groupings, appropriate organizations and bodies of the United Nations system, international governmental organizations and the pesticide industry.

12.2 The Code should be brought to the attention of all concerned in the manufacture, marketing and use of pesticides and in the control of such activities, so that governments, individually or in regional groupings, industry and international institutions understand their shared responsibilities in working together to ensure that the objectives of the Code are achieved.

12.3 All parties addressed by this Code should observe this Code and should promote the principles and ethics expressed by the Code, irrespective of other parties' ability to observe the Code. The pesticide industry should cooperate fully in the observance of the Code and promote the principles and ethics expressed by the Code, irrespective of a government's ability to observe the Code.

12.4 Independently of any measures taken with respect to the observance of this Code, all relevant legal rules, whether legislative, administrative, judicial or customary, dealing with liability, consumer protection, conservation, pollution control and other related subjects should be strictly applied.

12.5 FAO and other competent international organizations should give full support to the observance of the Code, as adopted.

12.6 Governments should monitor the observance of the Code and report on progress made to the Director-General of FAO.

12.7 Governing Bodies should periodically review the relevance and effectiveness of the Code. The Code should be considered a dynamic text which must be brought up to date as required, taking into account technical, economic and social progress.

ANNEX

FAO Conference Resolution 10/85:
International Code of Conduct
on the Distribution and Use of Pesticides

THE CONFERENCE,

Recognizing that increased food production is a high priority need in many parts of the world and that this need cannot be met without the use of indispensable agricultural inputs such as pesticides,

Noting that FAO's study entitled Agriculture: toward 2000 foresees a steady increase in the worldwide use of pesticides,

Convinced that such growth in pesticide use is likely to take place in spite of necessary intensive parallel efforts to introduce biological and integrated pest control systems,

Acknowledging that pesticides can be hazardous to humans and the environment and that immediate action must be taken by all concerned, including governments, manufactures, traders and users, to eliminate, as far as possible and within the scope of their responsibility, unreasonable risks, not only in the country of origin but also in the countries to which pesticides may be exported,

Being aware that the requirements for the safe and proper use of pesticides in some developed countries have led to the adoption of complex systems of regulations and of enforcement mechanisms, but that many other countries have neither such mechanisms nor the necessary legislation, regulations or infrastructures to control the import, availability, sale or use of pesticides,

Convinced that additional efforts are needed to enable such countries to control pesticides more effectively and to assess the hazards which could result from their use or misuse,

Recognizing that a voluntary International Code of Conduct, based on internationally agreed technical guidelines, would provide a practical framework for the control of pesticides, especially in countries that do not have adequate pesticide registration and control schemes,

Noting that such a draft Code was reviewed by the Committee on Agriculture at its Eighth Session, and endorsed by the Council at its Eighty-eighth Session,

Having further noted the conclusions and recommendations of these bodies,

1 *Hereby adopts* a voluntary International Code of Conduct on the Distribution and Use of Pesticides as given in the annex to this Resolution;

2 *Recommends* that all FAO Member Nations promote the use of this Code in the interests of safer and more efficient use of pesticides and of increased food production;

3 *Requests* governments to monitor the observance of the Code in collaboration with the Director-General who will report periodically to the Committee on Agriculture;

4 *Invites* other United Nations agencies and other international organizations to collaborate in this endeavour within their respective spheres of competence.

(Adopted 28 November 1985)

REFERENCES

1 *Report of Second Government Consultation on International Harmonization of Pesticide Registration Requirements*, FAO, Rome, 11–15 October 1982.

2 *Guidelines on efficacy data for the registration of pesticides for plant protection.* Rome, FAO. 1985.

3 *Guidelines on environmental criteria for the registration of pesticides.* Rome, FAO. 1985.

4 *Good laboratory practice.* Paris, Organisation for Economic Co-operation and Development. 1981.

5 *Codex guidelines on good practice in pesticide residue analysis.* Rome, FAO. 1984.

6 *Guidelines on crop residue data.* Rome, FAO. 1985.

7 *Codex recommended national regulatory practices to facilitate acceptance and use of Codex maximum limits for pesticide residues in foods.* Rome, FAO. 1985.

8 *The use of FAO specifications for plant protection products.* Rome, 1986. FAO Plant Production and Protection Paper.

9 *Guidelines for the registration and control of pesticides (including a model scheme for the establishment of national organizations).* Rome, FAO. 1985.

10 *Specifications for pesticides used in the public health,* 6th ed. Geneva, World Health Organization. 1985.

11 *The WHO recommended classification of pesticides by hazard and guidelines to classification 1986–87.* Geneva, World Health Organization. 1986.

12 *Guidelines for the packaging and storage of pesticides.* Rome, FAO. 1985.

13 *Guidelines on good labelling practice for pesticides.* Rome, FAO. 1985.

14 *Guidelines on good agricultural practice in the use of pesticides: guide to Codex recommendations concerning pesticide residues.* Rome, FAO. 1984.

15 *Guidelines on the operation or Prior Informed Consent (PIC).* Rome, FAO. 1990.

16 *Guidelines for the disposal of waste pesticides and pesticide containers on the farm.* Rome, FAO. 1985.

ADDITIONAL TECHNICAL GUIDELINES ADOPTED AFTER THE FAO CONFERENCE OF 1985 AND PUBLISHED UP TO MAY 1990

Pictograrms for pesticide labels. Rome, FAO.

Guidelines on pesticide residue trials to provide data for the registration of pesticides and the establishment of maximum residue limits. Rome, FAO. 1986.

Addenda to the guidelines for the registration and control of pesticides. Rome, FAO. 1988.

Guidelines on post-registration surveillance and other activities In the field of pesticides. Rome, FAO. 1988.

Guidelines on the registration of biological pest control agents. Rome, FAO. 1988.

Guidelines for retail distribution of pesticides with particular reference to storage and handling at the point of supply to users in developing countries. Rome, FAO. 1988.

Guidelines for legislation on the control of pesticides. Rome, FAO. 1989.

Guidelines on personal protection when using pesticides in hot climates. Rome, FAO. 1990.

References and Notes

CHAPTER 1

1 Carson, R (1965) *Silent Spring*, Penguin, Harmondsworth (first published 1962)
2 Ordish, G (1976) *The Constant Pest. A Short History of Pests and their Control*, Peter Davies Ltd, London pp43–46
3 Ibid p160
4 Easton, D (1965) *A Framework for Political Analysis*, Prentice Hall, Englewood Cliffs NJ
5 Reynolds, P (1986) *An Introduction to International Relations*, Second Edition, Longman, London & New York p9
6 Bosso, J (1987) *Pesticides and Politics. The Life Cycle of a Public Issue*, University of Pittsburgh Press, Pittsburgh p59
7 Morgenthau, H (1972) *Politics Among Nations*, Fifth Edition, A Knopf, New York p324
8 Rosenau, J (1971) *The Scientific Study of Foreign Policy*, Free Press, New York p161
9 Williams R (1960) *American Society*, Second Edition, A Knopf, New York p24
10 Kratochvil, F (1989) *Rules, Norms and Decisions. On the Conditions of Practical and Legal Reasoning in International and Domestic Affairs*, Cambridge University Press, Cambridge p64
11 Hobbes, T (1651) *Leviathan*, Andrew Crooke, London
12 Durkheim, E (1964) *The Rules of Sociological Method*, Free Press, New York
13 Hume, D (1964) *The Philosophical Works* vol 2 (eds T Green & T Groze) Scientica, Aalen p105
14 Smart, J (1961) *An Outline of a System of Utilitarian Ethics*, Melbourne University Press, Melbourne p30
15 Rosencrance, R (1973) *International Relations. Peace or War?*, McGraw-Hill, New York p25
16 Kratochvil (1989) op cit p63
17 Ibid p64
18 Keohane, R (1984) *After Hegemony*, Princeton University Press, Princeton p99
19 Ibid pp110–132
20 Sartorius, R (1975) *Individual Conduct and Social Norms*, Encino & Belmont, California p66
21 Keohane, R (1983) 'The Demand for International Regimes' in Krasner (ed) *International Regimes*, Cornell University Press, Ithaca & London p155
22 Sartorius (1975) op cit p77
23 Young, O (1989) *International Cooperation. Building Regimes for Natural Resources and the Environment*, Cornell University Press, Ithaca & London

24 Krasner, S (1982) 'Structural Causes and Regime Consequences: Regimes as Intervening Variables', *International Organization* 36, p185

CHAPTER 2

1 Davies, Smith, & Freed (1978)'Agromedical Approach to Pesticide Management', *Annual Review of Entomology* p353
2 Pimentel, D (1986) 'Agroecology and Economics', in Kogan, M (ed), *Ecological Theory and Integrated Pest Management Practice*, John Wiley & Sons, New York 1986 pp299–319
3 Pimentel, D (1983) 'Environmental aspects of Pest Management' in Schemilt, L (ed), *Chemistry and World Food Supplies : The New Frontiers. CHEMRAWN II.* Pergamon Press, Oxford p185
4 Green, M (1976) *Pesticides, Boon or Bane?*, Elektra Books, London p17
5 Table from WHO (1990), *Public Health Impact of Pesticides Used in Agriculture*, WHO Geneva 1990 p22. This table was adapted from Edwards, C 'Agrochemicals as Environmental Pollutants', in Hofsten, B & Ekstrom, G (1986) *Control of Pesticide Applications and Residues in Food.* Swedish Science Press p2
6 Norris, R (ed) (1982), *Pills, Pesticides and Profits – The International Trade in Toxic Substances*, North River Press, Croton on Hudson NY p23
7 Swezey, Murray, & Daxl (1986), 'Nicaragua's Revolution In Pesticide Policy', *Environment* vol 28 no 1 p9
8 Pimentel, D (1991) 'The Dimensions of the Pesticide Question' in Bormann, F & Kellert, S (eds), *Ecology, Economics, Ethics – The Broken Circle*, Yale University Press, New Haven & London p63
9 Swezey, Murray & Daxl (1986) op cit p9
10 Chart based on WHO (1990) op cit p26. This chart in turn was adapted from; Green, M et al (1977), *Chemicals for Crop Protection and Control*, Pergamon Press, Oxford
11 Graph derived from 'Pesticide Use in Europe', *Pesticides News – The Journal of the Pesticides Trust* no 39, March 1998 p18. Figures based on European Crop Protection Association Annual Report 1996–7
12 Shemilt, L (ed) (1983), *Chemistry and World Food Supplies: The New Frontiers. CHEMRAWN II.* Pergamon Press, Oxford pxi
13 Ibid
14 GCPF, (1997) *The Benefits of Using Crop Protection Products with Specific Reference to Habitat Preservation and Biodiversity GCPF Internet site* http://www.gcpf.org/positions/biodiver.html
15 See for example: *The Ecologist* vol 21, no 2 March/April 1991, special edition entitled, 'FAO- Promoting World Hunger'
16 List, M & Rittberger, V (1992) 'Regime Theory and International Environmental Management', in Hurrell, A & Kingsbury, B *The International Politics of the Environment*, Clarendon Press, Oxford p104

CHAPTER 3

1 McEwen, F & Stephenson, G (1979) *The Use and Significance of Pesticides in the Environment*, John Wiley & Sons, New York, Chichester, Brisbane, Toronto, p11
2 Pampana, E & Russell, P (1955) 'Malaria. A World Problem', *Chronicle of the WHO 9*, WHO, Geneva 1955 p31
3 McEwen & Stephenson (1979) op cit p23
4 Hicks, J (1992) 'DDT – Friend or Foe?', *Pesticides News, Journal of the The Pesticides Trust*, no 17 September p14
5 Ibid
6 Connor, S (1991) 'Control of Malaria Breaks Down as Drugs Prove Ineffective', *The Independent* 9 October
7 WHO Internet site, *http://www.who.ch/ctd/act/malact.htm#further,* WHO 1997
8 *Everymans Encyclopedia*, J.M. Dent & Sons, London, Melbourne, Toronto, 1978
9 WHO Internet site, *http://www.who.ch/programmes/ctd/act/onchact.htm*, WHO 1997
10 *Lymphatic Filariasis: The Disease and its Control*, Fifth Report of the WHO Expert Committee on Filariasis, Technical Report Series no 821, WHO Geneva 1992.
11 Edwards, C (1986) 'Agrochemicals as Environmental Pollutants', in Hofsten, B & Ekstrom, G (eds) *Control of Pesticide Applications and Residues in Food*, Swedish Science Press p6
12 WHO Internet site, *http://www.who.ch/programmes/ctd/leisacfr.htm*, WHO 1995
13 Bull, D (1982) *A Growing Problem – Pesticides and the Third World Poor,* Oxfam, Oxford p36
14 Ibid
15 NB, The government of Thailand has permitted the import of aldrin and DDT. The government of Zaire has permitted the import of aldrin. The governments of Kenya, Bolivia, Republic of Guinea and Mexico have permitted DDT Imports. 'Import Decisions for Aldrin, DDT, Dieldrin, Dinoseb & Dinoseb Salts, Fluoroacetamide and HCH (mixed isomers) as of February 1993', UNEP/FAO Joint Programme for the Operation of Prior Informed Consent (PIC), Geneva & Rome 1993
16 Bull (1982) op cit pp35–36
17 *Safe Use of Pesticides*, Fourteenth Report of the WHO Expert Committee on Vector Biology and Control, WHO Technical Report Series 813, Geneva 1991 p12–13
18 Ibid p1
19 *Biological Control of Vectors of Disease*, Sixth Report of the WHO Expert Committee on Vector Biology and Control, WHO Technical Report Series 679, Geneva 1982
20 *Safe Use of Pesticides*, Ninth Report of the WHO Expert Committee on Vector Biology and Control, WHO Technical Report Series 720, Geneva 1985
21 WHO (1976) Introducing the WHO, Geneva pp61–62
22 *Safe Use of Pesticides*, 14th Report, op cit p21
23 Ibid p5
24 WHO (1985) *Specifications for Pesticides Used in Public Health*, 6th Edition, WHO, Geneva
25 World Development Report 1993, *Investing in Health*, Oxford University Press, New York p19

26 *Fifth Report of the WHO Expert Committee on Filariasis*, op cit
27 See for example: Cherfas, J (1992) 'Poison Lingers in the System', *The Independent* 22 June

CHAPTER 4

1   WHO (1973) *Safe Use of Pesticides, 20th Report of the WHO Expert Committee on Insecticides*, Technical Report Series no 513, Geneva
2   Copplestone, J (1977) 'A Global View of Pesticide Safety' in Watson, D & Brown, W (eds), *Pesticide Management and Insect Resistance*, Academic Press, New York pp147–155
3   WHO, *Informal Consultation on Planning Strategy for the Prevention of Pesticide Poisoning*, Unpublished WHO document WHO/VBC/86.926. Available on request from: Division of Environmental Health, WHO, Geneva
4   From *Pesticides in Perspective – The Safety Factor* BAA Pamphlet 1985
5   K Mellamby, taken from, N Hildyard in *The Ecologist* March 1980
6   Hildyard, N (1980) report in *The Ecologist* March 1980
7   Jeyaratnam, DeAlwis, & Copplestone (1982) 'Survey of Pesticide Poisoning in Sri Lanka' *Bulletin of WHO*, 60 (4)
8   Jeyaratnam, J (1987) 'Survey of Acute Pesticide Poisoning Among Agricultural Workers in Four Asian Countries' *Toxicology Letters* 33 pp195–201
9   WHO (1990) *Public Health Impact of Pesticides Used in Agriculture*, WHO, Geneva pp83–84
10 Wong, K & Ng, T (1982) 'Paraquat Poisoning', *The Family Practitioner* vol 5, no 3 December
11 Jeyaratnam et al (1982) op cit
12 Copplestone, J (1985) 'Pesticides and Health in Developing Countries', in Turnbull, G (ed), *Occupational Hazards of Pesticide Use*, Taylor & Francis, London, p75
13 Baker, E et al (1978) 'Epidemic Malathion Poisoning in Pakistan Malaria Workers, *The Lancet* vol 1 pp31–4
14 Turnbull, G (1985) *Occupational Hazards of Pesticide Use*, Taylor & Francis, London p99
15 The term 'acute' usually refers to cases where symptoms develop within up to a few days of exposure
16 Wilkinson, C (1987) 'The Science and Politics of Pesticides', in Marco, G (ed), *Silent Spring Revisited*, American Chemical Society, Washington DC p39
17 Mabuchi, Lillingfield & Snell (1980), *Preventative Medicine* 9 pp51–77
18 Davies, J & Doon, R (1987)'Human Health Effects of Pesticides', in Marco, G (ed) *Silent Spring Revisited*, American Chemical Society, Washington DC p39
19 Mackinnon, I & Sage, A (1982) 'Pesticide Worker Gets £90,000 For Cancer', *The Independent* 18 July 1982
20 Taylor, R et al (1976), 'Neurological Disorder Induced by Kepone', preliminary report in, *Neurology* 26 pp358–363
21 See for example Wharton, D et al (1977) 'Infertility in Male Pesticide Workers, *The Lancet* 2 p1259
22 Pesticides Trust (1998) '£80,000 for Dip Exposure' *Pesticides News – Journal of the Pesticides Trust* no 39 March p23

23 *The Guardian* (1982) 'Chemical Spray Blamed for 'Gassing' Villagers' 17 May

24 This represents 53 per cent of all spray drift complaints and 29 per cent of all pesticide related complaints. Figures from, Rose, C (1985) *Pesticides: The First Incidents Report*, Friends of The Earth, London p171

25 Booker, C (1997) Letter, *Sunday Telegraph* 3 August p26

26 Dudley, N (1987) *This Poisoned Earth – The Truth About Pesticides*, Piatkus Books, London, p75

27 *Dow Jones Magazine*, New York, 25 March 1991

28 Ibid

29 *Garden News* 6 March 1982. Quoted by: Friends of the Earth (1983) *Pesticides. The Case of an Industry Out of Control*, FoE, London

30 Honigsbaum, M (1991) 'Is One Man's Preservative Another's Poison?', *The Independent* 12 December 1991

31 Ibid

32 Weir, D (1987) *The Bhopal Syndrome – Pesticides, Environment and Health*, Earthscan, London p40

33 Dudley (1987) op cit p146–7

34 Weir (1987) op cit p16

35 Dudley (1987) op cit px

36 Weir (1987) op cit pix

37 Dudley (1987) op cit p107

38 Weir (1987) op cit p65

39 Connor, S & Thomas, A (1984) 'How Britain Sprayed Malaya With Dioxin', in, Sahabat Alam Malaysia *Pesticide Dilemma in the Third World. A Case Study of Malaysia*

40 Ibid

41 Hay, A (1982) *The Chemical Scythe – Lessons of 2,4,5,T and Dioxin*, Plenum Press, New York, p147. Figures from National Academy of Sciences(1974) *The Effects of Herbicides in South Vietnam*, Part A Summary and Conclusions. Washington DC pp5–6

42 Murphy, Hay, & Rose (1984) *No Fire No Thunder*, Pluto Press, London and Sydney p23 (Figure based on National Academy of Sciences (1974) op cit ppvii–9

43 See for example, Cook, J & Kaufman, C (1982) *Portrait of a Poison*, Pluto Press, London and Sydney

44 Westling, A (1984) *Herbicides in War – The Long Term Ecological and Human Consequences*, Taylor & Francis, London p143

45 Do Thuc Trinh, 'Long Term Morbid Effects Following Herbicidal Attack', in Westling ibid p166

46 Stevens, K (1981) 'Agent Orange Toxicity: a Quantitative Perspective', *Human Toxicology* vol 1 p31

47 Hay (1982) op cit p151

48 Environmental Liaison Centre (1987) *Monitoring and Reporting the Implementation of the International Code of Conduct on the Use and Distribution of Pesticides*, Final Report ELC Nairobi p12

49 Exceptions to this generalization include Indonesia and Nicaragua who have relatively stringent domestic laws. See Chapter 8.

50 IUCN (1957) Proclamation of the 5th General Assembly, pp31–85

51 Bull, D (1983) *A Growing Problem – Pesticides and the Third World Poor*, Oxfam, Oxford p160

52 PAN (1987) *Summary Position Paper for the 24th FAO Conference*, Rome 7–26th November 1987

53 *The WHO Recommended Classification of Pesticides by Hazard and Guidelines to Classifications*, Pesticide Development and Safe Use Unit, Division of Vector Biology and Control, WHO, Geneva 1986–7 p19

54 WHO (1990) op cit p43

55 See Turnbull (1985) op cit p44

56 IPCS Booklet, available on request, WHO, Geneva p3

57 Ibid p6

58 Ibid

59 Preparatory Committee for the United Nations Conference on Environment and Development, *Recommendations of the Meeting of Experts to Discuss Draft Proposals for an Intergovernmental Mechanism for Chemical Risk Assessment and Management*, A/CONF.151/PC/115, UN General Assembly, New York, March 11th 1992

60 UNEP (1997) UNEP Internet page (http://www.unep/partners/global/ifcs/home.htm)

61 FAO (1986) *International Code of Conduct on the Distribution and Use of Pesticides*, Article 1.6 FAO Rome

62 Paarlberg, P (1993) 'Managing Pesticide Use in Developing Countries', in: P Haas, R Keohane & M Levy, *Institutions for the Earth: Sources of Effective Environmental Protection*, MIT Press, Cambridge MA p321

63 FAO (1986) op cit

64 Outlined in, *Good Agricultural Practice*, OECD, Paris 1981, c (81) 30, annex II

65 *The Role of GIFAP*, available on request, GIFAP, Brussels p9

66 Metzger, H (1977) 'Will Harmonization be Achieved in Rome?' *Farm Chemicals*, Vol 141, No9, pp14–16

67 Council of Europe, Committee of Ministers, *Resolution (59) 23*, 16 November 1959. Taken from R Boardman (1986) *Pesticides in World Agriculture. The Politics of International Regulation*, MacMillan, Basingstoke p90

68 *Directive 91/414/EC on the Placing of Plant Protection Products on the Market*, European Commission, Brussels 1991

69 *Council Directive 94/43 of July 27 1994 Establishing Annex VI of Directive 91/414 Concerning the Placing of Plant Protection Products on the Market*, Official Journal of the European Communities, no L 227 1 Sept 1994 p31

70 ELC (1987) op cit p30

71 Ibid p28

72 *GIFAP Annual Report 1991*, GIFAP, Brussels p10

73 US Environmental Protection Agency (1997) internet page (http://www.epa.gov/oppfead1/international/qandasht.htm)

Chapter 5

1 McEwen, F & Stephenson, G (1979) *The Use and Significance of Pesticides in the Environment*, John Wiley & Sons New York, Chichester, Brisbane, Toronto, p231

2 From Pimentel, D & Levitan, L 'Pesticides: Amounts Applied and Amounts Reaching Pests', *Bioscience* vol 36 no2

3 Ibid p89

4 GIFAP (1987) *The Persistence of Pesticide Residues in Soil,* Technical Monograph no 11, GIFAP, Brussels

5 Bull, D (1982) *A Growing Problem. Pesticides and the Third World Poor,* Oxfam, Oxford p54 (Extract from letter from development agency to USAID 2 December 1979)

6 *The Independent* (1991) 18 July p10

7 Society for the Conservation of Nature and the Environment (SCONE) (1981) *SCONE Bulletin* no 3 September, Editorial, Oxfam Oxford

8 Edwards, C (ed) (1973) *Environmental Pollution by Pesticides,* Plenum Press, New York & London p4

9 Sahabat Alam Malaysia (1984) *Pesticide Dilemma in the Third World – a Case Study of Malaysia,* Sahahat Alam Malaysia Report, Penang p33

10 McEwen & Stephenson (1979) op cit pp326–332

11 Marquardt, S (1989) *Exporting Banned Pesticides: Fuelling the Circle of Poison,* Greenpeace USA Washington, DC

12 Maybank, Yoshida & Grover (1978) 'Spray Drift from Agricultural Pesticide Applications', *Journal of the Air Pollution Control Association* no 28

13 McEwen & Stephenson (1979) op cit pp349–364

14 Wheatley, G (1973) 'Pesticides in the Atmosphere', in Edwards, C (ed) op cit pp365–408

15 UNEP (1992) *Synthesis Report on the Methyl Bromide Interim Scientific Assessment,* UNEP, Nairobi

16 Martin, G (1981) *New Scientist* 30 April

17 Friends of the Earth (1983) *Pesticides – the Case of an Industry out of Control,* an FoE report for PAN, London

18 Mallis, A (1969) *Handbook of Pest Control,* MacNair-Dorland, New York p1158

19 Newton, Willie, & Asher, (1992) 'Mortality from the Pesticides Aldrin and Dieldrin in British Sparrowhawks and Kestrels' *Ecotoxicology* vol 1, no 1 September p31

20 Ibid

21 Moore, T (1984) 'Report Slams the Pesticide Plague', *Sunday Times* April 22nd

22 Douthwaite, R (1992) 'Effects of DDT Treatments Applied for Tsetse Fly Control in White-Headed Black Chat (the Minolea Amoli) Populations in Zimbabwe, Part 1: Population Changes', *Ecotoxicology* vol 1, no 1, September p17

23 McEwen & Stephenson (1979) op cit pp418–9

24 Ibid p451

25 Ghazi, P (1991) 'Herbicide Giant is Accused of Ruining Farmers Beet Crop', *Observer* 31 March

26 Raver, A (1992) 'Farmers Worried as a Chemical Friend Turns Foe', *New York Times* 24 February

27 Pimentel, D et al (1980), *Oikos* no 34 pp127–140

28 McEwen & Stephenson (1979) op cit p15

29 National Research Council (1980) *Regulating Pesticides,* a report prepared by the Committee on Prototype Explicit Analyses for Pesticides, National Academy of Sciences, Washington, DC p22

30 Boardman, P (1986) *Pesticides in World Agriculture: The Politics of International Regulation,* Macmillan Press, Basingstoke pp107–108

31 For an elaboration of this concept see: Groom, A & Taylor, P (eds) (1975) *Functionalism: Theory and Practice in International Relations*, London University Press, London

32 From the *Final Declaration of the Third International Conference on the Protection of the North Sea*, The Hague 1990

33 Caldwell, L (1990) *International Environmental Policy – Emergence and Dimensions*, Duke University Press, Durham & London pp145–146

34 International Joint Commission For The Great Lakes (1992) *Sixth Biennial Report on Great Lakes Water Quality* April

35 Ando, N (1981) 'The Law of Pollution Prevention in International Rivers and Lakes', in Zacklin, R & Caflisch, L (eds) *The Legal Regimes of International Rivers and Lakes*, Nijhoff Publishers, The Hague, London, & Boston

36 *Pesticide News – Journal of the Pesticides Trust* no 17, September 1992, London p22

37 For a detailed study see Johnson, S & Corcelle, G (1989) *The Environmental Policy of the European Communities*, Graham and Trotman, London

38 An organohalogen is a chemical with molecules composed of both carbon and atoms from the halogen group of elements. Hence, it is a wider category than organochlorine, but they possess similar properties (long persistence)

39 Buffin, D (1997) 'End for methyl bromide', *Pesticide News – Journal of the Pesticides Trust* no 38 December p9

40 Williams, F (1997) 'Regional Pact to Curb Toxic Pesticides', *Financial Times – International Edition* 25 January p3

41 World Wide Fund for Nature (1992) *Pesticide Reduction Programmes in Denmark, The Netherlands, and Sweden*, WWF International, Gland, Switzerland

42 IUCN (1967) Proclamatiom of the 9th General Assembly, IUCN, Gland, Switzerland pp199–200

43 IUCN, UNEP & WWF (1980) *World Conservation Strategy: Living Resource Conservation for Sustainable Development*, Sections 2–5, IUCN, Gland, Switzerland

44 Chapman, E (1993) 'Problems of Pesticide Exposure', speech presented at the PEGS/Pesticides Trust Conference, *Pesticides: The Way Ahead*, Friends House, London 14 June

45 Gosovic, B (1992) *The Quest for World Environmental Cooperation – The Case of the UN Global Environmental Monitoring System*, Routledge, London & New York p35

46 Ibid p52

47 Ibid

48 UNEP/ WHO (1988) *GEMS Assessment of Freshwater Quality* unpublished document, available on request from Division of Environmental Health, WHO, Geneva

49 WHO (1984) *Guidelines for Drinking Water Quality: Vol 1 Recommendations*, WHO, Geneva

50 UNEP (1985) *Annual Report of the Executive-Director 1984*, UNEP, Nairobi p40

51 See for example UK Ministry of Agriculture, Pesticide Usage Survey Group 1992

CHAPTER 6

1 Al Tikriti, K & Al Mufti, A (1976) 'An Outbreak of Organomercury Poisoning Among Iraqi Farmers', *Bulletin of the WHO* vol 53, Geneva pp15–21
2 See for example Consumers Association of Penang (1985) *Pesticide Problems, Legislation and Consumer Action in the Third World – The Malaysian Experience,* Malaysia p31; Dinham, B (1993) *The Pesticides Hazard – A Global and Environmental Audit,* Zed Books, London & New Jersey pp137,146
3 *Daily Telegraph* 16 January 1992
4 Diggery, Landrigan, Latimer, Elmington, Kinbrough, Liddle, Cline & Surek (1977) 'Fatal Parathion Poisoning Caused by Contamination of Flour in International Commerce', *American Journal of Epidemiology* vol 106(2), August pp145–153
5 *Annual Report of the Working Party on Pesticide Residues: 1991,* HMSO London 1992
6 GIFAP (1986) 'Pesticide Residues in Food- is There a Real Problem?', in BV Hofsten & G Ekstrom (eds), *Control of Pesticide Applications and Residues in Food,* Swedish Scientific Press p31
7 Ibid
8 The Pesticides Trust (1992) 'Irish Cucumber Poisoning', *Pesticides News – Journal of the Pesticides Trust* no 17, p16
9 Dudley, N (1987) *This Poisoned Earth – The Truth About Pesticides,* Piatkus, London p61
10 The Pesticides Trust (1992), *Pesticides News – Journal of the Pesticides Trust* no 17, p16
11 The Pesticides Trust (1992) 'US Pesticide Testers Indicted', *Pesticides News – Journal of the Pesticides Trust* no 18, December p21
12 Erlichman, J (1991) 'US Inquiry Raises Doubts', *The Guardian* 14 October
13 Wheelwright, E (1984) *Consumers, Transnational Corporations and the Developing World in the 1980s. II: The Pesticide Industry,* Australian Consumer Association. Paper presented at 11th World Congress of The International Organization of Consumer Unions, Bangkok
14 Fishlock, D (1990) 'One's Meat is Another's Poison', *Financial Times,* 9 October
15 Charles, D (1991) 'California's War on Pesticides', *New Scientist* 2 March p43
16 Lang, T & Clutterbuck, C (1991) *P is For Pesticides,* Ebury Press, London p128
17 See for example Kearney, P (1980) 'Nitrosamines and Pesticides. A Special Report on the Occurrence of Nitrosamines as a Terminal Residue Resulting From the Agricultural Use of Certain Pesticides', *Pure and Applied Chemistry* 53, pp499–526
18 'Residues in Food', *Which? Magazine,* October 1992 p177
19 Lang & Clutterbuck (1991) op cit p65
20 Schoon, N (1992) 'City's Water Polluted by Pesticides', *The Independent* 13 February
21 Lang & Clutterbuck (1991) op cit p49
22 GIFAP (1984) *Pesticide Residues in Food,* GIFAP Document, Brussels p2

23 Wilson, M (1992) International Institute of Entomology, letter to *The Independent*, 27 June
24 Abraham, M & Mott, L (1985) *Your Daily Dose of Pesticide Residues*, Pesticides Action Network
25 Ibid
26 Codex Alimentarius Commission (1989) *Procedural Manual, Seventh Edition*, FAO Rome, p31
27 WHO (1984) *Guidelines for Drinking Water Quality*. Volume 1 – Recommendations, WHO, Geneva
28 Quoted by Pearce, F (1992) 'Counting the Cost of Cleaner Water', *Independent on Sunday* 20 September
29 Ibid
30 Codex Alimentarius Commission (1989) op cit p1
31 Ibid p42
32 Figure derived from Codex chart, ibid p117
33 GIFAP (1984) p2
34 Ladomey, L (1984) 'Methods of Assessing Consumer Exposure to Pesticide Residues', *Pesticide Chemistry and Biotechnology*
35 The full title is the Joint Meeting of the FAO Panel of Experts in Food and the Environment and the WHO Expert Group on Pesticide Residues
36 Codex Alimentarius Commission (1989) pp28–29
37 Ibid pp29–30
38 Boardman, R (1986) *Pesticides in World Agriculture- The Politics of International Regulation*, Macmillan Press, Basingstoke p74
39 Personal communication with Pearson, G (1991) Pesticides Safety Division, Ministry for Agriculture, Fisheries and Food UK, March
40 Ibid
41 Commission of the EC, *Single European Act*, Luxembourg 1986
42 Commission of the EC, *The Residues in Fruit and Vegetables Directive, (*90/642/EEC)
43 Commission of the EC, *The Residues Directive*, (76/895/EEC)
44 Commission of the EC, *The Cereals Directive*, (86/362/EEC)
45 Commission of the EC, *The Animal Origins Directive*, (86/363/EEC)
46 Global Environmental Monitoring System, *Chemical Contaminants in Food: 1980–1983*, unpublished WHO Document WHO/EHE/FOS/86.5. Available on request from Division of Environmental Health, WHO, Geneva
47 GIFAP (1984) op cit p17
48 Hathaway, D (1991) *Production in Brazil,* unpublished report produced for Greenpeace Brazil
49 Ritchie, M (1990) 'GATT, Agriculture and the Environment: the US Double Zero Plan', *The Ecologist* vol 20, no 6 November/December p216
50 Millstone, E quoted by Avery, N 'Fears Over Food Quality Standards – Pesticide Residue Levels Harmonized to Promote Trade', *Pesticide News – Journal of the Pesticides Trust* vol 20, p4
51 Avery, Drake, & Lang (1993) *Cracking the Codex – An Analysis of Who Sets World Food Standards*, National Food Alliance, London
52 Ritchie (1990) op cit p216
53 See Hoberg, G (Jr) (1990) 'Reaganism, Pluralism and the Politics of Pesticide Regulation', *Policy Sciences* vol 23, pp257–280

54 J Longfield of the National Food Alliance (UK), quoted by Avery, N (1993)'Fears Over Food Quality Standards – *Pesticide Residue Levels Harmonized to Promote Trade, Pesticide News – Journal of the Pesticides Trust* vol 20, 1993 p5

55 Estimates taken from Lang, T & Hines, C (1993) 'Free Trade? We all Need Protection', *The Independent* 12 July 1993

56 Harrison, K (1991) 'Between Science and Politics: Assessing the Risks of Dioxins in Canada and the USA', *Policy Sciences* vol 24 p385

CHAPTER 7

1 Erlichman, J (1990) 'The Deadly Cocktails', in *The Guardian* 2nd March 1990

2 Norris, R (ed) (1982) *Pills, Pesticides & Profits – The International Trade in Toxic Substances*, North River Press, Croton-on-Hudson US (taken from, Weir, D & Schapiro, M (1981) *Circle of Poison*, San Francisco Institute for Food and Development Policy

3 Norris (1982) op cit p15

4 Dudley, N (1987) *This Poisoned Earth – The Truth About Pesticides*, Piatkus, London p121. (taken from, Weir & Schapiro (1981) op cit

5 Lappé, F & Collins, J (1979) *Food First: Beyond the Myth of Scarcity*, Ballantive, New York p145

6 Weir & Schapiro (1981) op cit

7 Swezey, Murray & Daxl, (1986) 'Nicaragua's Revolution in Pesticide Policy', *Environment* vol 28 no 1 p29

8 Peterson, E & Harris, R (1981) *Background Report on the Executive Order on Federal Policy Regarding the Export of Banned or Severely Restricted Substances*, White House, Washington DC, January p10 (as used by Bull, D (1983) *A Growing Problem – Pesticides and the Third World Poor*, Oxfam, Oxford p60)

9 Goldeman, G & Rengam, S (1987) *Problem Pesticides, Pesticide Problems – A Citizens' Action Guide to the International Code of Conduct on the Distribution and Use of Pesticides*, International Organization of Consumers Unions, Penang Malaysia p6

10 Personal communication with JW Huismans (1992) director of the International Register for Potentially Toxic Chemicals, UNEP/IRPTC, Geneva, 14th August

11 UN General Assembly (1984) *Consolidated List of Products Whose Consumption and/or Sale Have Been Banned, Withdrawn, or Not Approved by Governments, 2nd Edition* Available from Assistant Secretary General, DIESA, UN, New York

12 FAO (1986) *International Code of Conduct on the Distribution and Use of Pesticides*, FAO, Rome

13 Environmental Liaison Centre (1987) *Monitoring and Reporting the International Code of Conduct on the Use and Distribution of Pesticides (The FAO Code) – Final Report*, ELC, Nairobi p37

14 Ibid

15 Johnson, E (1991) 'Pesticide Regulation in Developing Countries of the Asia-Pacific Region', in Marco, Hollingworth & Plimmer (eds), *Regulation of Agro-chemicals – A Driving Force in Their Evaluation*, American Chemical Society, Washington, DC p62

16 Pesticides Action Network (1987) *The International Code of Conduct on the Distribution and Use of Pesticides and Prior Informed Consent*, Discussion Paper for FAO Conference, Rome 7–2 November p1
17 Ibid
18 OECD (1984) *Guiding Principles on Information Exchange Related to Export of Banned or Severely Restricted Chemicals*, OECD, Paris
19 UNEP (1984) *Provisional Notification Scheme for Banned and Severely Restricted Chemicals*, UNEP, Nairobi
20 Erlichman, J (1985) 'Poisons Sold Without Consent', *The Guardian* 2 November (NB: the UK withdrew from UNESCO the day after this report was made)
21 Official minutes of FAO Conference March 1985, taken from PAN, (1987) op cit p2
22 Lord Belstead, UK Agriculture Minister 1985. (taken from Erlichman (1985) op cit)
23 EC Directive EEC2455/92
24 IRPTC/UNEP (1987) *London Guidelines for the Exchange of Information on Chemicals in International Trade*, IRPTC, Geneva
25 Paarlberg, R (1993) 'Managing Pesticide Use in Developing Countries', in Keohane, Haas & Levy, *Institutions for the Earth: Sources of Environmental Protection*, MIT Press, Cambridge MA p324
26 FAO Resolution 5/87, FAO Biennial Conference, November 1987
27 Personal communication with A Sunden, Officer in Charge UNEP/IRPTC, Geneva, 19 April 1993
28 FAO/UNEP Secretariat (1993) *Guidance for Governments on the Operation of the Prior Informed Consent Procedure*, Distributed to the designated national authorities of all participating countries
29 *GIFAP Annual Report 1991*, available on request GIFAP, Brussels p13
30 Ibid p11
31 Ivers, Krueger, Mead & Prather (1998) Report on the Fifth Session of the INC for an International Legally Binding Instrument for the Application of the Prior Informed Consent Procedure for Certain Hazardous Chemicals and Pesticides in International Trade, *Earth Negotiations Bulletin* vol 15 no 4, 16 March p1
32 Ibid
33 Dinham, B 'A Toothless PIC? Convention negotiations move slowly' *Pesticide News – Journal of the Pesticides Trust*, no 38 December 1997 p15
34 Ivers et al (1998) op cit
35 Krasner, S (1982) 'Structural Causes and Regime Consequences: Regimes as Intervening Variables', *International Organization* 36, p185
36 Finlayson, J & Zacher, M (1983) 'The GATT and the Regulation of Trade Barriers: Regime Dynamics and Functions', in Krasner, S (ed) *International Regimes*, Cornell University Press, Ithaca and London p277
37 List, M & Rittberger, V (1992) 'Regime Theory and International Environmental Management', in Hurrell, A & Kingsbury, B (eds) *The International Politics of the Environment*, Clarendon Press, Oxford p89
38 Personal communication with FJ Cedar, Plant Industry Directorate, Ministry of Agriculture, Ottawa, 28 June 1993
39 Ibid
40 Personal communication with G Ekstrom, Swedish National Chemicals Inspectorate, Solna, 27 March 1993
41 IRPTC (1993) op cit p3

CHAPTER 8

1 World Wide Fund For Nature (1992) *Pesticide Reduction Programmes in Denmark, The Netherlands and Sweden*, WWF International, Gland, Switzerland

2 FAO (1986) *International Code of Conduct on the Use and Distribution of Pesticides*, FAO Rome

3 Shell Chemicals (1983) *The Agrochemical Business*, ShellReprographics, London

4 Georghiou, G & Taylor, C (1976) 'Pesticide Resistance as an Evolutionary Phenonemenon', in *Proceedings of the XVth International Congress of Entomology*, Washington, DC p760

5 Sahahat Alam Malaysia (1984) *Pesticide Dilemma in the Third World – a Case Study of Malaysia*, Sahahat Alam Malaysia Report p35

6 Ibid

7 Ibid

8 Ibid p40

9 *African Farmer*, November 1990 p33

10 Hocchberg, M & Waage, J (1991) 'Biopesticide Control Engineering' *Nature: International Weekly Journal of Science* 4 July

11 Rose, C (ed), *Pesticides. The Case of an Industry Out of Control*, An FoE Report for PAN(UK)

12 Kelly, M (1992) 'Thanks to the Test Tube Banana', *The Independent*, 2nd March

13 Gates, P (1990) 'The Chemical Warfare of Natural Enemies', *Independent on Sunday Magazine* 27 May p42–43

14 Food and Agricultural Organization (1980) *Fighting World Hunger*, FAO, Rome

15 Cremlyn, R (1978) *Pesticides: Preparation and Mode of Action*, Wiley, Chichester

16 *New York Times* 23 August 1987

17 *African Farmer* November 1990 p32

18 Hawkes, N (1992) 'Anti-Pest Grass' *The Times* 25 February

19 Ibid

20 PAN (1987) *Sustainability: The Case for Reducing the Use of Chemical Pesticides*, PAN discussion paper for the FAO Conference 2–26 November

21 Sattaur, O (1988) 'A New Crop of Pest Controls', *New Scientist* 14 July

22 Lacewell, R & Masud (1989) N 'Economic Analysis of Cotton IPM Programs' in Frisbie, R & El Zik, K (eds) *Integrated Pest Management Systems and Cotton Production*, Wiley, Chichester pp361–388

23 Sahahat Alam Malaysia (1984) op cit p40

24 Hochberg & Waage (1991) op cit

25 Ibid

26 Ibid

27 Gates (1990) op cit

28 *FAO Plant Protection Bulletin* vol 38 no 2 1990

29 UN General Assembly, *Environmentally Sound Management of Biotechnology*, Section II, Chapter 8, of Agenda 21. A/CONF.151/PC/WG. I/L.45., 30 March 1992 (p11)

30 FAO (1986) *International Code of Conduct on the Distribution and Use of Pesticides*, FAO, Rome

31 Quotation by Chris Major, former Chairman of the British Agricultural Association on Nay 27 1981 in Bull, D (1982) *A Growing Problem. Pesticides and the Third World*, Oxfam, Oxford p142

32 World Commission on Environment and Development (1987) *Food 2000. Global Policies for Sustainable Agriculture*, Zed Books, London & New Jersey p43

33 PAN (1987) op cit

34 *FAO Plant Protection Bulletin* vol 38, no 2, 1990

35 *Report of the 9th Session of the FAO/UNEP Panel of Experts*, Sudan 9–15 December 1979, Rome 1980, p6

36 Bull (1982) op cit p130

37 PAN North America (1995) 'IPM Facility Announced', *PANUPS Updates Service* 12 May

38 Environmental Liaison Centre (1987) *Monitoring and Reporting the Implementation of the International Code of Conduct on the Use and Distribution of Pesticides*, ELC, Nairobi p29

39 Ibid p3

40 Hansen, M and Rengan, S (1987) *Violating the Pesticide Code*, IOCU, Penang pp18–19

41 Swezey, Murray & Daxl (1986) 'Nicaragua's Revolution in Pesticide Policy', *Environment* vol 28 no 1, 1986 pp6–35

42 Bull (1982) op cit p30

43 Young, O and Osherenko, G (1993) 'Testing Theories of Regime Formation: Findings, Research Priorities and Applications', in Rittberger, V (ed) *Regime Theory and International Relations*, Clarendon Press, Oxford pp223–251

44 Ibid

45 Haas, P (1993) 'Epistemic Communities and the Dynamics of International Environmental Cooperation', in Rittberger (ed) op cit p188

46 Blackwell, P (1991) 'FAO Puts Pest Management to the Fore, *Financial Times* 18 October

47 Haas (1993) op cit p15

Chapter 9

1 Mansbach R & Vasquez J (1981), *In Search of Theory. A New Paradigm for Global Politics*, Columbia University Press, New York p59

2 Young, O (1989) *International Cooperation, Natural Resources and the Environment*, Cornell University Press, Ithaca & London, p13

3 Mansbach & Vasquez (1981) op cit p110

4 Ibid p62

5 Rolston, H (1991) 'Environmental Ethics: Values in and Duties to the Natural World', in Bormann, F & Kellert, S (eds), *Ecology, Economics, Ethics: The Broken Circle*, Yale University Press, New Haven p91

6 Mansbach & Vasquez (1981) op cit p56

7 UNEP/FAO (1993) *Import Decisions for Aldrin, DDT, Dieldrin, Dinoseb and Dinoseb Salts, Fluoroacetamide and HCH (mixed isomers) as of February 1993*, UNEP/FAO Joint Programme for the Operation of Prior Informed Consent(PIC), Geneva & Rome

8 Pushba Herath, WHO Scientific Officer. Quoted by: Cherfas, J (1992) 'Poison Lingers in the System' *The Independent* 22 June

9 Fuller, M (1992)'Pesticide Ban Will Hit Tulips', *The Times* 3 April

10 Pimentel, D (1991) 'The Dimensions of the Pesticide Question', in Bormann & Kellert (1991) op cit p60

11 Pimentel, McLoughlin, Zepp, Lakitan, Kraus, Kleinman, Vancini, Roach, Selig, Keeton & Graap (1991) 'Environmental and Economic Benefits of Reducing US Agricultural Pesticide Use', in Pimentel, D (ed) *Handbook of Pest Management in Agriculture* vol 1, second edition, Chemical Rubber Co Press, Boca Raton, Florida

12 Pimentel (1991) op cit p68

13 Ibid

14 NOVA, 'Mediterranean Prospect'. WGBH Transcripts, Boston Mass, 1980 p13 quoted in Haas, P (1989) 'Do Regimes Matter? Epistemic Communities and Mediterranean Pollution Control', *International Organization 43*, Summer p379

15 Keohane, R (1984) *After Hegemony. Cooperation and Discord in the World Political Economy*, Princeton University Press, New Jersey p31

16 Kindleberger, C (1973) *The World in Depression 1929–1939*, University of California Press, Berkeley

17 Keohane (1984) op cit

18 Krasner, S (1976) 'State Power and the Structure of International Trade' *World Politics* 28 (3) April pp317–343

19 Gilpin, R (1975) *US Power and the Multinational Corporation*, Basic Books, New York

20 See Fikkan, Osherenko & Arikainen, 'Polar Bears: The Importance of Simplicity, in Young, O & Osherenko, G (eds) (1993) *Polar Politics. Creating International Environmental Regimes*, Cornell University Press, Ithaca & London pp96–152

21 See for example, Russett, B (1985) 'The Mysterious Case of Vanishing Hegemony; or is Mark Twain Really Dead?' *International Organization* vol 39 no 2, Spring pp207–231

22 Krasner, S (1983) (ed), *International Regimes*, Cornell University Press, Ithaca & London p358

23 Ibid pp359–360

24 Ibid

25 Keohane, (1984) op cit p202

26 Jonsson, C (1987) *International Aviation and the Politics of Regime Change*, Francis Pinter, London p158

27 Young & Osherenko (1993) op cit p11

28 Young, O (1991) 'Political Leadership and Regime Formation: on the Development of Institutions in International Society', *International Organization* vol 45 no 3 Summer p288

29 Ibid (p290)

30 Keohane, R 'The Demand for International Regimes' in Krasner, S (1983) op cit p155

31 Ibid

32 Young (1991) op cit pp295–296

33 Ibid p302

34 Pesticides Action Network International (1985), 'Pesticide Control Code Set for Approval at FAO Rome', Unpublished Document, PAN, November

35 Paarlberg, S (1993) 'Managing Pesticide Use in Developing Countries', in Haas, Keohane & Levy, *Institutions for the Earth: Sources of Effective Environmental Protection*, MIT Press, Cambridge MA p323

36 Young & Osherenko (1993) op cit p18
37 Haas, P (1990) 'Obtaining International Environmental Protection Through Epistemic Consensus' *Millenium* vol 19 no 3 Winter p349
38 Haas, P 'Do Regimes Matter? Epistemic Communities and Mediterranean Pollution' *International Organization*, vol 43 no 3, Summer 1989 pp377–403
39 Ibid p399
40 Ibid pp381–382
41 Haas, P (1993) 'Stratospheric Ozone: Regime Formation in Stages', in Young & Osherenko op cit p176–177
42 List, M & Rittberger, V (1992) 'Regime Theory and International Environmental Management', in Hurrell, A & Kingsbury, B *The International Politics of the Environment*, Clarendon Press, Oxford p104
43 Hoberg, G (Jr) (1990) 'Reaganism, Pluralism and the Politics of Pesticide Regulation', *Policy Sciences* 23 pp257–280
44 See for example *The Ecologist* vol 21, no 2 March–April 1991, special edition entitled, 'FAO – Promoting World Hunger'
45 See for example Avery, Drake & Lang, (1993) *Cracking the Codex – An Analysis of Who Sets World Food Standards*, National Food Alliance, London
46 Although this is not a scientific principle, it fulfills the same function in that it is a legal concept devized and supported by an epistemic community
47 i) Convention on Early Notification of a Nuclear Accident 1986. ii) Convention on Assistance in the Case of a Nuclear Accident or Radiological Emergency 1986
48 Haas, P (1992) 'Introduction: Epistemic Communities an International Policy Coordination', *International Organization* 46 1 Winter p14
49 Young, O & Osherenko, G (1993)'Testing Theories of Regime Formation-Findings From a Large Collaborative Research Project', in Rittberger, V (ed), *Regime Theory and International Relations*, Clarendon Press, Oxford p234
50 The 'No More Bhopals Network' set up by the Environmental Liaison Centre and International Coalition for Development Action is the clearest example of this
51 Keohane (1984) op cit p85
52 Keohane, R 'The Analysis of International Regimes', in Rittberger (ed) (1993) p37
53 Hume, D (1964) *The Philosophical Works* (eds Green, T & Grose, T) vol 2, Scientica, Aalen p105
54 Donelan, M (1990) *Elements of International Political Theory*, Allen & Unwin, Oxford p36
55 Muller, H (1993) 'The Internalization of Principles, Norms and Rules by Governments', in Rittberger (ed) (1993) op cit pp361–388
56 Ibid pp382–383
57 Jonsson, C (1993) 'Cognitive Factors in Explaining Regime Dynamics', in V Rittberger (ed) op cit p202
58 Sprout, H & Sprout, M (1956) *Man-Milieu Relationship Hypotheses in the Context of International Politics*, Princeton University Press, Princeton
59 Jonsson (1993) op cit p203
60 Haas, E (1980) 'Why Collaborate? Issue-Linkage and International Regimes', *World Politics* 32 p360

61 Axelrod, R (1980) 'An Evolutionary Approach to Norms', *American Political Science Review* 80

62 List & Rittberger (1992) op cit. See also Rittberger, V (ed) (1990) *International Regimes in East-West Politics*, Pinter, London & New York

63 Mendler, M (1993) 'Working Conditions of Foreign Journalists in East-West Relations: Regulating a Conflict About Values Without A Regime', in Rittberger (1993) op cit pp216–249

64 Rittberger (1993) op cit p10

Index

AAAS *see* American Association for the Advancement of Science

ABM *see* Anti-Ballistic Missile Treaty

acceptable daily intakes (ADIs) 95, 99

accidental poisoning by pesticides 39–48

active ingredient 11, 178

ADIs *see* acceptable daily intakes

advertising 63, 64, 178, 192–4

Aedes aegypti mosquito 126

aerial crop spraying 42–3, 68, 71

Africa
  biological control 127
  Environment Liaison Centre (ELC) (Nairobi), human poisoning 63
  pesticide use/crop yields 18, 19
  pesticide-resistant plant strains 128
  trypanosomiasis 29, 34, 74

Agent Orange 47, 49, 50

'agromedicine', definition 17

air contamination 71

aldicarb 90

aldrin 4, 73, 148

American Association for the Advancement of Science (AAAS), Operation Ranch Hand 53

American trypanosomiasis 30

Ames, Bruce 91–2, 94, 160

Anopholes spp 26–7, 31

Anti-Ballistic Missile (ABM) Treaty 165–6

ANZUS *see* Australia, New Zealand and US security treaty

aquatic organisms, mortality 70

arsenical, definition 11

atmospheric pollution 71

Australia, war veterans compensation 50

Australia, New Zealand and US security treaty (ANZUS) 152

availability of pesticides, FAO Code of Conduct 187

Bacillus sphaericus 29, 33, 35

Bacillus thuringiensis 5, 28, 33, 127, 128, 134

bananas, Black Sigatoka resistant 129

banned, FAO Code of Conduct definition 178

bees, pesticide residues 72

behaviour, regime effects 168–9

benzene hexachloride (BHC), discovery 4

BHC *see* benzene hexachloride

Bhopal disaster 2, 45–8

bilharziasis *see* schistosomiasis

biological vector control 5, 32–6, 127–8, 130

biomagnification, definition 73

biopesticides 127–8, 133

birds 72, 73, 85, 87

birth defects 48, 49, 50

Black Sigatoka 129

body fat, organochlorine residues 41–2

Bosso, J, norms/values 6

Brazil, Integrated Pest Management 139

Bull, David 31, 32, 60, 136, 157

Canada, PIC scheme 122

cancer 41, 49, 54, 91, 160
  see also International Agency for Research on Cancer

carbamates, definition 11

carcinogenic, definition 11

Carson, Rachel 1, 6, 53, 76

CCPR *see* Codex Alimentarius Commission, Committee on Pesticide Residues

CFCs *see* chlorofluorocarbons

Chaga's disease 30
Chemical Research Applied to World
    Needs (CHEMRAWN)
    1983 Conference, Pimentel, D. 17
    IUPAC-sponsored conferences 22
Chemical Review Council (CRC) 118,
    119–20
chemistry of pesticides 4–5
CHEMRAWN *see* Chemical Research
    Applied to World Needs
chlorofluorocarbons (CFCs) 83, 159
Classification by Hazard Scheme
    (WHO) 44–5, 55–7, 60
*Classification, Packaging, and Labelling of
    Dangerous Preparations (Pesticides)
    Directive* (EC) 56
Code of Conduct on the Use and
    Distribution of Pesticides (FAO)
    see International Code of Conduct
    on the Distribution and Use of
    Pesticides
Codex Alimentarius Commission
    (CAC)
    bias 160
    Committee on Pesticide Residues
        (CCPR)
        Codex activities 106
        drinking water contamination 96
        GIFAP activities 94
        structure/activities 99–101
    future of 103–5
    hegemony 154
    MRLs 99–103
    organizational structure 98
    regime nature 106–7
cognitive theories 166–8
collateral poisoning, aerial pesticide
    spraying 42–3
common name, FAO Code of Conduct
    definition 178
contamination *see* environmental
    pollution; food, contamination
Copplestone, J 37, 38
cosmetic effects, pesticides 92
cotton crops 19, 133
crises, regimes formation 162–3
crop residue destruction 130
crop rotation 130
crop yields

see also aerial crop spraying
    countries 18–19
    developing countries 18
    politics of 21–4
    increases 17–25
    Integrated Pest Management 132
    losses through environmental
        pesticide pollution 75
    norms 6–7, 10
cultural controls, pest habitats 130–1

DDT *see* dichlorodiphenyltrichloro-
    ethane
deaths *see* mortality
decisionmaking
    cognitive theories 167
    pesticide use 148–9
definition of pesticides 4–5
definitions, FAO Code of Conduct
    terms 178–1
defoliant, definition 11
degradation of pesticides, soil
    pollution 68–9
dengue fever 29
Denmark 125, 135, 141
developing countries
    crop yields 18, 21–4
    FAO code 63
    importation of pesticides 110
    Integrated Pest Management 137–9
    occupational pesticide poisoning 40
    regulation of pesticides 52
    suicide 38
    water pollution 69
diazinon 43
dichlorodiphenyltrichloroethane
    (DDT)
    air pollution 71
    birds 73, 74
    discovery 4
    Indian cotton yields 19
    international trade in 109
    malaria eradication programme 26–7
    political aspects 148
    public health programmes 30–1
    residues health risk 41–2
    success 1
    WHO reliance on 36
dieldrin 4, 72, 73, 148

dioxin 47–8, 49
Dirty Dozen campaign 95
disease transmission, pesticides role
    26–36
disposal, FAO Code of Conduct 191–2
distinguishing name, FAO Code of
    Conduct definition 178
distribution
    FAO Code of Conduct 187–9
    FAO Code of Conduct definition
        178
domestically-used pesticides 43–5
drinking water 93, 96
Dudley, N, domestic pesticide use 44

ecology *see* environmental pollution
ELC *see* Environment Liaison Centre
    (Nairobi)
elephantiasis 28
entomology, definition 11
environment, FAO Code of Conduct
    definition 178
Environment Liaison Centre (ELC)
    (Nairobi), FAO code 63
environmental pollution
    air contamination 71
    crop losses 75
    food and drink 88–108
    political aspects 76–87
    soil contamination 67–9
    water contamination 69–70
    wildlife 71–4
Environmental Protection Agency
    (EPA) 52, 105
enzyme, definition 11
EPA *see* Environmental Protection
    Agency
epidemiology, definition 11
Epidocrasis lopezi 127
epistemic communities
    consensus 106–7, 160
    Integrated Pest Management 141–2
    IUPAC's role 22
    regime creation 158–62
    WHO Expert Committee on Vector
        Biology and Control 32–4
ethics *see* values
European Community
    Classification, Packaging, and Labelling

*of Dangerous Preparations
    (Pesticides) Directive* 56
Directive on Residues in Fruit and
    Vegetables (1990) 101
drinking water contamination 96
environmental pollution 80–1
pesticide registration 61–2
pesticide use/crop yields 18
residues regulation 101
Uniform Principles Directive 62,
    80–1
European Union (EU) 19–20, 153
exportation *see* importation
extension, FAO Code of Conduct
    definition 178

falcons, DDT 74
FAO *see* Food and Agriculture
    Organization
FAO Code of Conduct *see* International
    Code of Conduct on the
    Distribution and Use of Pesticides
Federal Environmental Pesticide
    Control Act (FEPCA) 77
Federal Insecticide, Fungicide and
    Rodenticide Act of 1947 (FIFRA)
    77
Fennah, Dr Ronald 94
FIFRA *see* Federal Insecticide,
    Fungicide and Rodenticide Act of
    1947
filariasis 28–9, 34
fish 70, 147
FoE *see* Friends of the Earth
food
    see also Food and Agriculture
        Organization; residues
    contamination 88–108
        drinking water 93
        extent of problem 88–92
        political aspects 93–108
        pressure groups 95
        toxicity testing 90–4
    crop yield increases 17–25
    industry 104–5
Food and Agriculture Organization
    (FAO)
    see also Codex Alimentarius
        Commission; International Code

of Comduct on the Use and
Distribution of Pesticides; Prior
Informed Consent
GIFAP liaison 24
*Guidelines for the Registration and
Control of Pesticides* 60
Integrated Pest Management 131,
137–8
IUPAC activities 22
Prior Informed Consent 117, 119,
123, 157–8
WHO Expert Committee on Vector
Biology and Control 33
formulated products, definition 11
formulation, FAO Code of Conduct
definition 178
free trade, regimes 25
Friends of the Earth (FoE) 53, 75, 96
fruit, cosmetic use of pesticides 92, 101
fumigants, definition 11
fungicide, definition 11

garden pesticides, poisoning from 43–4
GCPF *see* Global Crop Protection
Federation
GEMS *see* Global Environmental
Monitoring System
genetic engineering, biopesticides 133
genetically-modified organisms
(GMOs) *see* *Bacillus sphaericus*,
Bacillus thuringiensis
GHS *see* Globally Harmonized Scheme
GIFAP *see* Groupement International
des Associations de fabricants de
Produits Agrochemiques
Global Crop Protection Federation
(GCPF) 21, 22–5, 60, 111
Global Environmental Monitoring
System (GEMS) 85–6, 102
Global Malaria Control Strategy 27–8
Globally Harmonized Scheme (GHS)
64–5
GMOs *see* genetically-modified
organisms
Groupement International des
Associations de fabricants de
Produits Agrochemiques (GIFAP)
Codex MRLs international impact
102

FAO relationship 24
GCPF relationship 22
harmonised pesticide control 60, 61
health/safety issues 54
Prior Informed Consent 116–17
Residue Working Group 94–5
soil pollution 68
*Guidelines for the Registration and Control
of Pesticides* (FAO) 60
Gulf War Syndrome 51

Haas, Ernst 167
Haas, Peter 158–9
haemorrhagic fever 29
hazard
see also risk
Classification by Hazard Scheme
(WHO) 55–7
FAO Code of Conduct definition
178, 184–6
hegemonic stability theory 151–4, 156
HEOD *see* 1,2,3,4,10,10-hexachloro-
6,7-epoxy-1,4,4a,5,6,7,8,8a-
octahydro-1,4,5,8-dimethamon-
aphthalene
hepatotoxic, definition 11
herbicide, definition 11
Herbicide Assessment Commission 53
herbicides, residues 75
1,2,3,4,10,10-hexachloro-6,7-epoxy-
1,4,4a,5,6,7,8,8a-octahydro-
1,4,5,8-dimethamonaphthalene
(HEOD) 73
history, pest control 3–4
human poisoning 37–66
accidental 39–48
aldicarb 89
Bhopal disaster 45–8
domestically-used pesticides 43–5
drinking water contamination 93
epistemic consensus 161
food contamination 88–92
industrial accidents 45–8
Iraq 89
long-term exposure effects 40–2
malpractice 89
military use of pesticides 48–51
occupational 39–40
political aspects 52–66

Seveso disaster 47–8
suicide 38, 39, 40
wood preservatives 44–5

IARC *see* International Agency for
    Research on Cancer
IATA *see* International Air Transport
    Association
ICSU *see* International Council of
    Scientific Unions
IFCS *see* Intergovernmental Forum on
    Chemical Safety
ILO *see* International Labour
    Organization
importation 32, 110, 113–23
INCs *see* Intergovernmental
    Negotiating Committees
India 19, 39, 45–8
Indonesia 139, 140–1
industrial accidents 45–8
information exchange, FAO Code of
    Conduct 189–91
INFOTERRA *see* International
    Referral System for Sources of
    Environmental Information
insect sex pheromones 129–30
insecticides *see* pesticides
inspections/monitoring, FAO Code of
    Conduct 194–5
Integrated Pest Management (IPM)
    124–42
  FAO Code of Conduct definition
    179
  FAO/UNEP definition 131
  GCPF activities 24
  global facility 138, 141
  optimum yields 132
  political aspects 135–42
  popularization 1
  problems associated with 133–5
intentional exposure *see* suicide
Intergovernmental Forum on
    Chemical Safety (IFCS) 58
Intergovernmental Negotiating
    Committees (INCs) 117, 118
International Agency for Research on
    Cancer (IARC) 54
International Air Transport Association
    (IATA) 155–6

International Code of Conduct on the
    Distribution and Use of Pesticides
    (FAO) 54, 59–65
  annex text 195–6
  Article 1 177
  Article 2 178–81
  Article 3 181–3
  Article 4 183–4
  Article 5 184–6
  Article 6 186–7
  Article 7 187
  Article 8 112, 187–9
  Article 9 112, 189–91
  Article 10 191–2
  Article 11 192–4
  Article 12 194–5
  human poisoning issues 54, 59–65
  Integrated Pest Management 125,
    136
  international trade 112–13, 114
  leadership issues 157
  preface to the text of the Code 175–6
  text of the Code 177–95
International Council of Scientific
    Unions (ICSU) 21
international harmonization 60–2, 64–5
International Institute of Tropical
    Agriculture (IITA) 127, 128, 129
International Labour Organization
    (ILO) 33, 65
International Organization of
    Consumer Unions (IOCU) 53, 95
International Programme on Chemical
    Safety (IPCS) 22, 57–8
International Referral System for
    Sources of Environmental
    Information (INFOTERRA) 86
International Register of Potentially
    Toxic Chemicals (IRPTC) 57, 59,
    111–13, 121, 123
international relations theory 7–8, 11,
    14
  see also regimes
international trade 109–23, 147–8,
    187–9
International Union for Conservation
    of Nature and Natural Resources
    (IUCN) *see* World Conservation
    Union

International Union of Pure and
    Applied Chemistry (IUPAC) 21–2
IOCU *see* International Organization of
    Consumer Unions
IPCS *see* International Programme on
    Chemical Safety
IPM *see* Integrated Pest Management
Iraq, bread poisoning catastrophe 89
Ireland, aldicarb 90
IRPTC *see* International Register of
    Potentially Toxic Chemicals
issue systems 8–9, 147–51
issue-specific power 154–6
issues, crisis-occurrence 162–3
Italy, Seveso disaster 47–8
IUCN *see* World Conservation Union
    (formerly: International Union for
    Conservation of Nature and
    Natural Resources)
IUPAC *see* International Union of Pure
    and Applied Chemistry
ivermectin 28

Jamal, Goran 43
Japan 18, 19, 30, 153
Jeyaratnam, J 38, 39
Joint Meeting on Pesticide Residues
    (JMPR) 99, 106, 107, 161
Jonsson, C 155
JPMR *see* Joint Meeting on Pesticide
    Residues

Keohane, R 14, 156–7
kestrels, HEOD contamination 73
Krasner, S 121, 153
Kratochvil, F 12

labelling 56, 179, 191–2
larvicide, definition 11
Latin America 18
leadership 156
leishmaniasis 29, 34
lice-born typhus 29–30
lindane 45
lipophilic, definition 11
List, M 122
liver damage, dioxin 49–50
long-term pesticide exposure effects
    40–2

McEwen, F 26
MACs *see* maximum admissible
    concentrations
malaria 26–8, 126
Malayan emergency 48
Malaysia, suicide 39
malpractice, human poisoning 89
management of pesticides, FAO Code
    of Conduct 181–3
Mansbach, R 140
manufacturer, FAO Code of Conduct
    definition 179
MAP *see* Mediterranean Action
    Plan
marketing, FAO Code of Conduct
    definition 179
maximum admissible concentrations
    (MACs) 96, 99
maximum residue limits (MRLs)
    corporate interests 104–5
    establishment 99–100
    European Community 101
    FAO Code of Conduct definition
        179
    GATT talks 103–4
    pressure groups 95
Mediterranean Action Plan (MAP) 78,
    81, 150, 158–9
methyl bromide 82–3, 87, 147
methylisocyanate (MIC) 45–6
MIC *see* methylisocyanate
military use of pesticides 48–51
Ministry of Agriculture, Fisheries and
    Forestry (MAFF) 72
Montreal Protocol on Substances that
    Deplete the Ozone Layer (1987)
    82–3
Morgenthau, H 7
mortality
    see also human poisoning
    aquatic organisms 70
    birds 73, 74
    industrial accidents 45–8
    pesticide poisoning 37–8
mosquitoes 26–31
MRLs *see* maximum residue limits
Muller, Paul 4
Muller, H 165–6
mutagenic, definition 11

National Food Alliance 104
nature, balance of 75
nematode, definition 11
nervous system, organophosphates 43
Netherlands 125, 135, 141
New Zealand war veterans 50
Nicaragua 19, 140
nicotine 135
non-fatal chemical controls 129–30
norms of behaviour
  compliance with 13–14
  global 144–5
  importation of pesticide-
    contaminated foods 88
  international trade control
    requirement 110
  issue systems 9
  'optimal' pesticide use 136
  regime development 14–16
  regime effects 168–9
  rules 11–12
  salience rankings 145–6
  seven norms of pesticide politics 2,
    9–10, 12–13, 15, 143–5, 169–70
  value systems 9–13, 146–54
North Atlantic Treaty Organization
  (NATO) 152
North Sea, pollution agreements 79, 81
NRDC *see* National Resources
  Defense Council

occupational exposure to pesticides
  39–40
Oceania 18
OECD *see* Organization for Economic
  Cooperation and Development
onchocerciasis ('river blindness') 28,
  34, 35
OP pesticides *see* organophosphate
  pesticides
Operation Ranch Hand 49, 50, 51, 53
Organization for Economic
  Cooperation and Development
  (OECD) 64, 113–14
organochlorines 11, 41–2, 72–3, 74
  see also dichlorodiphenyltrichloro-
    ethane (DDT)
organophosphate (OP) pesticides 4, 11,
  42, 55

Osherenko, G 140
Oslo and Paris Commission
  (OSPARCOM) 79
overuse of pesticides 124–42
ozone depletion 82–3, 159

packaging 179, 191–2
PAN *see* Pesticides Action Network
paraquat 5, 39
PCP *see* pentachlorophenol
PEGS *see* Pesticide Exposure Group of
  Sufferers
pentachlorophenol (PCP) 45
persistent, definition 11
persistent organic pollutants (POPs)
  83–4
pest resistant crops 134
pesticide, FAO Code of Conduct
  definitions 179
Pesticide Exposure Group of Sufferers
  (PEGS) 85
Pesticides Action Network (PAN)
  Integrated Pest Management 137
  pesticides regulation 53–4
  Prior Informed Consent 113–14,
    115, 119, 157–8
  residues 92, 95
Pesticides Safety Precautions Scheme
  (UK) 56
pheromones 129–30
Phillips, Kristan 43
philosophical aspects of pesticide
    politics
  cognitive theories 166–8
  international relations theory 2–3,
    7–8, 11, 13, 14
  'stakes' 147
  utilitarianism 164–6
PIC *see* Prior Informed Consent
Pimentel, D. 17, 149
plague control 30
plants
  pesticide residues 72
  pesticide-resistant strains 128–9
PLUARG *see* Pollution from Land Use
  Activities Reference Group
poison, FAO Code of Conduct
  definitions 179
poisoning *see* human poisoning

political aspects
see also norms of behaviour
crisis occurrence 162–3
crop yield increases 21, 21–4
DDT use 148
decisionmaking 148–9
environmental pollution 76–87
food contamination 93–108
history/rationale 5–9
human poisoning 52–66
Integrated Pest Management 135–42
issues involved 143–71
public health programmes 31–5
Pollution from Land Use Activities
    Reference Group (PLUARG) 79
POPs *see* persistent organic pollutants
pressure groups 53–4, 84–5, 95
Prior Informed Consent (PIC)
    agrochemicals 147
    Bull, David 157–8
    definition 113
    environmental pollution 78
    epistemic consensus 161–2
    FAO Code of Conduct 180, 189–91
    importation of pesticides 31–2
    international trade 113–23
    list 116
    pesticides subject to PIC procedure
        in 1998 118
    utilitarian rationale 166
prioritizing issues *see* norms of
    behaviour, salience rankings
product, FAO Code of Conduct
    definition 180
production, global 18–20
protective clothing, FAO Code of
    Conduct definition 180
public health programmes 30–5
public sector groups, FAO Code of
    Conduct definition 180
pyrethroid, definition 12

Reagan, President 105
regimes
    see also epistemic communities;
        international relations theory
    actor behaviour influence 168–9
    Codex Alimentarius Commission
        106–7

cognitive theories 166–8
conceptual analysis 7–8
crisis response 162–3
environmental protection
    agreements 78–81
free trade 25
hegemonic stability theory 151–3
Integrated Pest Management 140
issue systems comparison 2–3, 8
leadership 156–8
norm-based development 14–16
Prior Informed Consent 121–2
utilitarianism 164–6
Regional Economic Integration
    Organization (REIO) 82
registration of pesticides 60–2, 180
regulation
    global 81–7
    national 77–8
    regional intergovernmental 78–81
REIO *see* Regional Economic
    Integration Organization
repackaging, FAO Code of Conduct
    definition 180
residues
    see also maximum residue limits
    epistemic consensus 161
    European Community 101
    FAO Code of Conduct definition
        180
    food contamination 1
    political aspects 93–108
    toxicity testing 90–4
    United States 102, 105
resistance to pesticides
    DDT in public health programmes
        30–1
    Integrated Pest Management 125–6
    mosquitoes 27
    Nicaraguan cotton yields 19
    plant breeding programmes 128–9
    plant strains 134
    public health programmes 30–1, 35
responsible authority, FAO Code of
    Conduct definition 181
resurgence of pests 126
Reynolds, P 6
risk 41–2, 54, 181
Rittberger, V 122

river blindness *see* onchocerciasis
rivers, pollution 69–70, 79, 81, 147
rodenticide, definition 12
Rosenau, J 8, 10
Rotterdam Convention (1998) 76–7
Royal Society for the Protection of
    Birds (RSPB) 74, 85
rules 11–12, 168–9

sandflies, leishmaniasis 29
schistosomiasis (bilharziasis) 28, 34
Schrader, Dr Gerhard 4
scientific opinion, epistemic consensus
    160
SEATO *see* South East Asian Treaty
    Organization
Sellbate (synthetic sex hormone) 129
Senegal 52
seven norms of pesticide politics 2,
    9–10, 12–13, 15, 143–5, 169–70
severely restricted, FAO Code of
    Conduct definition 181
Seveso disaster 47–8, 49
sex pheromones, insects' 129–30
sheep dips 42
Simulium black fly 28
sleeping sickness *see* trypanosomiasis
sodium trichloroacetate (STCA) 48
soil 67–9, 72
South East Asian Treaty Organization
    (SEATO) 152
sparrowhawks 73
Sri Lanka 38, 40
STCA *see* sodium trichloroacetate
Stephenson, G. 26
storage, FAO Code of Conduct 191–2
suicide 38, 39, 40
*Survey of Exposure to Organophosphorus
    Pesticides in Agriculture* (WHO) 55
Sweden 102, 125, 135, 141
systemic pesticide, definition 12

TBTO *see* tributylin oxide
technical requirements, FAO Code of
    Conduct 186–7
teratogenic, definition 12
teratogenicity 48, 49, 50
Thailand 139
toxicity

FAO Code of Conduct definition
    181
humans *see* human poisoning
testing 90–4, 183–4
trade 109–23, 147–8, 187–9
trader, FAO Code of Conduct
    definition 181
tributylin oxide (TBTO) 45
Trichodermavinide 127
Trioxane 48
trypanosomiasis ('sleeping sickness')
    29, 30, 34, 74
tsetse flies 29, 74
typhus, lice-born 29–30

UNCED *see* United Nations,
    Conference on the Environment
    and Development
UNEP *see* United Nations, Environ-
    ment Programme
UNESCO *see* United Nations,
    Educational Scientific and
    Cultural Organization
Uniform Principles Directive (EC) 62,
    80–1
Union Carbide, Bhopal disaster 45–8
UNITAR *see* United Nations, Institute
    for Training and Research
United Kingdom
    hegemonic stability theory 152
    military use of pesticides 48, 51
    Ministry of Agriculture, Fisheries
        and Forestry (MAFF) 72
    pesticide-resistant plant strains
        128
    Pesticides Safety Precautions
        Scheme 56
    sparrowhawks/kestrels 73
    water pollution 69
United Nations (UN)
    see also Food and Agriculture
        Organization
    Conference on the Environment
        and Development (UNCED) 58
    Consolidated List 111–12
    Development Programme (UNDP)
        138
    Educational Scientific and Cultural
        Organization (UNESCO) 84

Environment Programme (UNEP)
32–3
atmospheric pollution 71
environmental pollution 71, 80,
83–6
human poisoning 59
Integrated Pest Management 131,
137–8
international trade control 111
methylisocyanate 45
Prior Informed Consent 115, 117,
119, 123, 158
Global Environmental Monitoring
System (GEMS) 85–6
human poisoning 54–5
Institute for Training and Research
(UNITAR) 123
United States
American Association for the
Advancement of Science (AAAS)
53
bans on pesticides 109
carcinogens in food 91
crop yields/pesticide use 18
Environmental Protection Agency
(EPA) 52, 105
Federal Environmental Pesticide
Control Act (FEPCA) 77
Federal Insecticide, Fungicide and
Rodenticide Act of 1947 (FIFRA)
52
food contamination 93–4
hegemony 153
importation of contaminated food
110
International Air Transport
Association (IATA) 155–6
military use of pesticides 49–51
policies on pesticide use 149–51
use pattern, FAO Code of Conduct
definition 181
utilitarianism 164–6

values, norms of behaviour 6, 9–13,
146–54
Vasquez, J 140
vector-borne diseases 26–36, 33, 35
vegetables, cosmetic use of pesticides
92

Vietnam 49–51, 53

war *see* military use
water contamination 69–70, 93, 147
Weir, David 46, 47
WHO *see* World Health Organisation
WHOPES *see* World Health Organis-
ation, Pesticide Evaluation
Scheme
wildlife 71–4
Williams, Robin 10
wood preservatives 44–5
The World Bank 59
World Conservation Union (formerly:
International Union for
Conservation of Nature and
Natural Resources (IUCN)) 53, 84
World Health Organization (WHO)
see also Codex Alimentarius
Commission
Classification by Hazard Scheme
44–5, 55–7, 60
Conference on Food Standards
(1962) 97
DDT use 36
environmental pollution 85–6
Expert Committee on Insecticides
55
Expert Committee on
Leishmaniasis 29
Expert Committee on the Safe Use
of Pesticides 55
Expert Committee on Vector
Biology and Control 32–4
human poisoning 37–9, 54–7
Intergovernmental Forum on
Chemical Safety (IFCS) 58
International Programme on
Chemical Safety (IPCS) 57–8
International Union of Pure and
Applied Chemistry 22
malaria eradication programme
(1955) 26–7
Pesticide Evaluation Scheme
(WHOPES) 33
public health programmes 33–5
*Survey of Exposure to
Organophosphorus Pesticides in
Agriculture* 55

world production of pesticides 18–20
World Trade Organization (WTO) 25,
    103–4, 120
Worldwide Fund for Nature (WWF) 84
WTO *see* World Trade Organization

WWF *see* Worldwide Fund for
    Nature

yields *see* crop yields
Young, O 140, 156–7